T0075188

Trust, Security and Privacy for Big Data

Editors

Mamoun Alazab
Charles Darwin University
Casuarina Campus, Ellengowan Drive
Darwin, Australia

Maanak Gupta
Tennessee Technological University
Cookeville, USA

CRC Press
Taylor & Francis Group
Boca Raton   London   New York

CRC Press is an imprint of the
Taylor & Francis Group, an **informa** business

A SCIENCE PUBLISHERS BOOK

First edition published 2022
by CRC Press
6000 Broken Sound Parkway NW, Suite 300, Boca Raton, FL 33487-2742

and by CRC Press
2 Park Square, Milton Park, Abingdon, Oxon, OX14 4RN

Library of Congress Cataloging-in-Publication Data (applied for)

ISBN: 978-1-032-04750-8 (hbk)
ISBN: 978-1-032-04752-2 (pbk)
ISBN: 978-1-003-19453-8 (ebk)

DOI: 10.1201/9781003194538

Typeset in Times New Roman
by Radiant Productions

Preface

Data has revolutionized the digital ecosystem. The readily available large datasets foster AI and machine learning automated solutions. The data generated from diverse and varied sources including Internet of Things, social platforms, health-care, system logs, bio-informatics, etc., contribute and define the ethos of Big Data which is volume, velocity and variety. Data lake formed by the amalgamation of data from these sources requires powerful, scalable and resilient, storage and processing platforms to reveal the true value hidden inside this data mine. Data formats and its collection from various sources not only introduce unprecedented challenges to different domains including IoT, manufacturing, smart cars, power grids, etc., but also highlight the security and privacy issues in this age of Big Data.

Security and privacy in Big Data is facing many challenges, such as generative adversary networks, efficient encryption and decryption algorithms, encrypted information retrieval, attribute-based encryption, attacks on availability, and reliability. Providing security and privacy for Big Data storage, transmission, and processing have been attracting much attention in all Big Data related areas. Complex Big Data systems are progressively becoming attack targets by existing and emerging threat agents. Advanced persistent threat is increasingly tailored to exploit vulnerabilities and weaknesses. On the other hand, organisations struggle to manage the sheer volume of vulnerabilities discovered on their networks, when important volume of data is collected from and generated by different devices and sources. Hence, it is important for intelligent Big-Data analytical techniques to keep pace to mitigate cyber-attacks.

The purpose of this book is to offer a timely, and comprehensive information for researchers and industry partners in communications and networking domains to review the latest results in security and privacy related work of Big Data. The array of topics covered in this book include but not limited to Big Data framework for privacy in digital immortals, federated learning in Big Data, distributed and light weight Big Data pipelines for IoT, predictive Big Data analytics based decision support system, among others.

The book is expected to serve computer science and cybersecurity community including researchers, academicians, students, and practitioners who have wider interest in Big Data trust privacy and security aspects. It provides a comprehensive document and most recent development in terms of security of datasets from varied sources including IoT, cyber physical domains, Big Data architectures, studies for trustworthy computing, and approaches for distributed systems and Big Data security solutions, etc. Thanks to the holistic planning and thoughtful organization of the book, the readers are expected to gain in-depth knowledge of the state of the art solutions in terms of trust security and privacy of Big Data systems and technologies.

We hope you enjoy reading the book!

Sep 2021   Mamoun Alazab
                                                                        Maanak Gupta

Acknowledgement

We are grateful to many individuals and organisations for assisting with the preparation of this book. We would like to acknowledge the support from: Charles Darwin University, Northern Territory Government of Australia, and Tennessee Technological University, USA. We appreciate the support made by our respective employers who allowed us time in which to edit the chapters and attend to the many tasks that had to be undertaken to finalise the publication. We would like to acknowledge the support by the Ministry of Education of the Republic of Korea and the National Research Foundation of Korea (NRF-2021S1A5A2A03064391). We would also like to acknowledge the support from National Science Foundation grant # 2025682. We are grateful to all the authors for their insights and excellent contributions to this book. We greatly appreciate the professional assistance of the editorial staff of CRC Press. Finally, we would like to thank our families for their support and patience during the months we spent developing this book.

Mamoun Alazab
Maanak Gupta

Contents

1
DigImoPriv
A Big Data Framework for Preserving Privacy of Digital Immortals

Kumar Vikram and *Muhammad Rizwan Asghar**

ABSTRACT

As digital and Internet technologies shape our daily lives, we continue to store important information on the Internet. This information, also known as a digital asset, can be in the form of emails, pictures, videos, music files or online documents. Recently, researchers and technology designers have focused on building systems relating to digital assets being made available about someone following their death, known as digital legacy. Most of the work on digital legacy involves providing services, such as remembering the bereaved or providing the deceased's information to the loved ones. However, little research has gone into preserving the privacy of the deceased also known as afterlife privacy or digital immortal privacy. In this chapter, we have presented a digital legacy framework for big data, called DigImoPriv, which is based on the principles of policy-based access control mechanisms that can enable a fine-grained access mechanism to the digital asset. These policies defined in DigImoPriv will be the basis to preserve the digital immortal privacy of the digital asset owner. This work will enable future opportunities that will empower digital users to share their digital assets, preserve digital immortal privacy and ultimately be remembered as positive and happy citizens.

1. Introduction

Over the last decade, the Internet and digital technologies have fundamentally changed the way we interact, communicate, and store information. These technology tools and services, such as emails, data files, photos, videos, social network sites, and blogs are embedded in many aspects of our daily lives – at work, in our personal life, entertainment and civic behaviour. Consequently, we continue to generate and store substantial amounts of data throughout our lifetime. Recently, many researchers and technology designers have considered issues related to this information being made

School of Computer Science, The University of Auckland, New Zealand.
* Corresponding author: r.asghar@auckland.ac.nz

available about someone following their death – also known as digital legacy [1, 2]. The information that is stored as an online form becomes a digital asset [1, 2], which can be, for instance, photos, videos, music, emails, and blogs. These digital assets can originate from or be stored on: (a) online services including websites, social media, emails, and cloud services; and (b) digital devices, such as hard disks, mobile phones, and laptops [3].

While researchers and technology designers for digital legacy systems have focused on providing services (e.g., remembering the bereaved to sharing information with loved ones), little research has gone into preserving the privacy of the deceased person [4, 5], *a.k.a.* afterlife privacy or, more recently, digital immortal privacy [6]. Currently, there are no standard laws governing digital immortal privacy. In the absence of these digital immortal privacy laws, regulation of both the privacy and the digital asset rights of the deceased will fall under the service terms of the digital intermediary platforms where the digital assets are stored, such as social networks, cloud services, blogs, and emails [4, 7]. In such a situation, it is most likely that any future disputes or disagreements on digital immortal privacy will be handled by intermediary digital platforms and the beneficiaries of the deceased, provided they have the rights granted [4, 7]. The rights of the digital platforms are usually determined by their own unilaterally dictated terms of service, and rights granted to the beneficiaries are determined by succession laws [4, 7]. In both cases, neither side of this conflict has the best interests in preserving privacy of the deceased [4, 7].

In our literature review on digital legacy systems and digital immortal privacy, there is no work on designing a framework or solutions that offer users granular access to the digital asset and preserve digital immortal privacy. Such a system would provide enhanced user experience and greater flexibility to the digital asset owner in order to share digital assets with their loved ones. While digital assets can be broad – photos, emails, music files, data files, blogs, there is some work done on email digital assets in this area by Google [8]. Google has implemented the Inactive account manager for its users to share their data (organised into folders) with nominated persons in an event there is no activity for a specific time period [8]. However, this is still coarse-grained, where entire folders will be shared and thus may not have the appropriate privacy protection for the deceased. Preserving digital immortal privacy and providing a fine-grained access control mechanism is a challenge as most digital assets are heterogeneous and have unstructured data [1, 8–11].

To address the need for enhanced user experience and greater flexibility with granular access to the digital asset and to preserve digital immortal privacy in digital legacy systems, we have designed a digital legacy framework for big data – DigImoPriv–that will provide the digital asset owner defined policies with a fine-grained access mechanism. These defined policies delivered through the access control mechanism will protect the Personally Identifiable Information (PII) in the digital asset against unauthorised access, thus preserving digital immortal privacy. There are two types of users defined in the digital legacy framework, the owner of the digital asset and the bereaved. The bereaved is the contact who has been given access to digital assets by the owner. The authentication and appropriate access to the folders are determined by a policy-based access control mechanism. DigImoPriv will have an intelligent data classifier to annotate the contents of the digital asset based on data labels into categories, such as private, confidential, unrestricted, or even events/sentiments, such as happy and sad moments. These components in DigImoPriv will work together with the support of a synchronous system – a timer that would periodically check the owner's living status by checking the user's online activity. In the event of no activity, the system will send invitations to the nominated persons or contacts to access the digital asset. The novelty of this solution is in the design of DigImoPriv, which brings the three components working together, i.e., a policy-based access control mechanism to provide the fine-grained access control, the logic required to categorise the PII contents of the digital asset that will preserve digital immortal privacy and the synchronous system to monitor the digital asset owner's activity. In this chapter, our research problem is to find an approach to protect digital immortal privacy and provide a fine-grained access control mechanism to the digital asset, as data within the digital assets are heterogeneous and unstructured. The main contributions of this work are:

- We define use case scenarios where digital immortal privacy was important to the digital asset owner.

- We propose high-level system requirements that address the issues in digital immortal privacy and enables a fine-grained access control mechanism to the digital asset.

- We provide a thorough literature review in the areas of digital legacy systems, digital immortal privacy, PII, and access control mechanisms.

- We present DigImoPriv that addresses digital immortal privacy to the digital asset owner and enables a fine-grained access control mechanism to the digital asset.

- We instantiate DigImoPriv by considering emails as digital assets and discuss solution details.

- We present future research opportunities in digital immortal privacy and fine-grained access control in digital legacy systems.

This chapter is organised as follows. Section 2 defines four scenarios where the digital asset owner's digital immortal privacy was violated. Following the scenarios section, we enumerate the high-level requirements. Section 3 reviews various research approaches in digital legacy systems, PII and different access control mechanisms. Section 4 presents the proposed idea, design of the digital legacy framework, define the high-level system model, different entities and the general overview. Section 5 explains the detailed design of the digital legacy framework using email digital asset as an example. Section 6 concludes this work and provides research directions for future work.

2. Scenarios and Requirements

In this section, we present scenarios where there is a need to protect and preserve the user's reputation, dignity, integrity, secrets, or memory after their death.

2.1 Use Case Scenarios

Army Officer Died in Combat on an International Mission

A young army officer died in combat in an overseas assignment. His widow, who was the beneficiary, petitioned to have access to the army officer's email account. However, the email service provider disagreed and refused to transfer the account passwords and its contents and decided to stand by its service agreements. Further, they argued as per their service terms, on the account of the email owner's death, they would terminate the account and delete all the contents. The widow petitions the court, after which, the email service provider agreed to transfer the contents of the account, which she managed to download. After going through the contents, the widow found evidence of emails where her husband had a homosexual affair with a fellow serviceman adding to her grief and agony. In some of the emails, the army officer explicitly conveyed that his wife was never to know about this private information [12].

Well-Known Writer Died Leaving his Unfinished Work in the Cloud Storage

A well-known writer died after a long illness. During his illness, he conveyed to his lawyer that he did not want to publish any unfinished work after his death. The reasons for the request were that the unpublished work could of be sub-standard or might reveal secrets for which he might not yet have obtained permissions to disclose. Before his death, he destroyed all the physical manuscripts but forgot about his unfinished work on the online digital storage. Meanwhile, his only son, James, found out about the work on the online storage and persuaded the service provider to share the files left by his father. The service provider did not have any published rules on afterlife access and shared the files with James after presenting the death certificate and proof of his relationship. Later, James sold the unfinished work to an international publisher for a large sum [13].

Teenage Girl Died from a Drug Overdose

A teenage girl died from a drug overdose in a party. Her Facebook page became a shrine to her memory, with friends sharing pictures and notes in the comments. Her parents, who were not social media users, noticed the profile posts relating to alcoholism and drugs, adding to their pain and distress. As a bereaved family member, they requested Facebook to delete the page and provide them with access to the Friends-locked posts that they were not able to see. In the posts, they found many photos of their daughter's indulgence in drugs and alcohol. These photos had already been shared with her friends through the social media feed [14].

A Middle-Age Technology Geek Died in a Car Accident

A middle-age technology geek from a developed country died in a car accident[1]. He used to work for a large multinational company as a software developer. During his

---

[1]Adapted from: https://www.cbc.ca/news/canada/british-columbia/services-advisor-app-refugees-1.3339989.

free time, he used to live another life in the digital world, mostly spending time in the dark web helping Syrian, Yemeni, and Venezuelan refugees escape their country due to war and political oppression. He had stored all his refugee contacts and email conversations in a non-encrypted format. After his death, his parents got access to his emails and knew about his digital life. They talked to a local newspaper and shared this information not realising that they had put the refugees lives at risk [15].

A Young Man Died on a Camping Trip

A young man from Colorado, the United States died on a camping trip. He used to invest in cryptocurrencies since 2012[2]. All of his private keys were stored in his personal laptop. His family was unaware of his private keys and online wallets. On going through his laptop, his parents got the keys and posted a question on Reddit asking for more information on the keys and wallet. By the time, they received the reply, the contents of the online wallet got stolen and the young man lost the anonymity of the wallet address [16].

These are some of the scenarios that are concerned with the rights and privacy of death. Due to the growth in creation and sharing of digital assets, there is a requirement to preserve and respect the user's reputation, dignity, integrity, secrets or memory even after death [4, 7]. This research problem becomes more challenging as the data in the digital assets become voluminous, unstructured, shareable, hard to destroy, and difficult to categorise within the current legal norms of property or rights [3, 8, 17].

2.2 System Requirements

In the aforementioned scenarios, there is a requirement for the digital asset owner to share her online information with her family and friends and, most importantly, to preserve her privacy, reputation, secrets or memory even after death. In what follows, we list the main requirements below:

- A platform where users can share their digital assets with their loved ones with a granular level of access.

- Categorisation of the online data, content, emails based on PII, such as confidential, private, unrestricted, and sentiments including happy or sad moments.

- Provide some feedback to the digital asset owner about the online content on what can be shared, destroyed, archived in the event of death.

- In the event of death, nominate people who can have access to the categorised data in a way that the privacy, reputation, dignity, secrets of the data owner are not lost.

- Safeguarding the data from unauthorised access.

- Create and update policies for the nominees to have the right level of access to the digital asset.

---

[2] Adapted from: https://fortune.com/2017/09/26/cryptocurrency-bitcoin-death/.

- Create and update contacts or nominees with whom the digital asset can be shared.

- A method to delete all the personal or private information that should not be shared after death.

- An authentication and authorisation mechanism to determine the user and its privileges within the system and access to the digital asset.

- A framework for digital immortals where the created policies will be applied to the digital asset owner's nominees, say a spouse, friends, or family members.

- A framework for digital immortals that will continue to safeguard and preserve the created policies and digital assets.

In the remainder of this chapter, we examine and explore possible design solutions that can satisfy these requirements. In the following section, we present the literature review in the areas of digital legacy system, digital immortal privacy, PII, and access control methodologies.

3. Literature Review

In this section, we review the related work done in the field of digital legacy systems, digital immortal privacy laws, and explore the current access control mechanisms. Later in this section, we highlight the gaps relating to the current research with respect to the scenarios and requirements explained in Section 2.

3.1 Digital Legacy Systems

In this section, we explore the work done in the field of digital legacy systems, elaborate on some of the existing systems and tools available to the users today.

Webster's dictionary defines legacy as "anything handed down from past, as ancestor or predecessor". As per this definition, we can broadly classify legacy into three categories including biological, material, and values [18]. This categorisation of a legacy involves the creation and dissemination of identity across generations and time [18]. However, an individual's legacy is usually a subset of these three categories and is influenced by the relationship between the deceased and those who survive [18]. Generally, people would like to be remembered positively and will choose to pass on these artefacts as well as information to reinforce this positive and happy identity [3, 18]. These artefacts can also be classified as a combination of tangibles – such as houses, books, vehicles, jewellery, and intangibles, such as life experiences and values. Traditionally, people have drawn up their wills to state their desires and needs regarding their legacy [3, 18, 19].

In the digital realm, as information is becoming more important in our daily lives, there is a need to explore newer ways for designing systems that must manage digital assets adhering to the inheritance practices [3, 5, 20]. The problems associated with digital assets are usually around classification, storing and sharing of digital artefacts [2,5,19–22]. At a high-level, there are three main actors in the digital legacy system: (a) Users who want to plan for their digital assets; (b) the bereaved, contacts of the digital asset owner; and (c) Intermediaries, such as the digital platform or legal firms or curators [7].

Research Approaches in Digital Legacy

In this section, we will explore the research done in digital systems with a perspective from digital legacy users those who want to plan for their digital assets and users who are bereaved.

For digital asset owners who want to plan for their digital assets, Prates et al. [8] classify the digital legacy systems based on the functionality or the scope of services these systems provide. These range from: (a) remembering the bereaved; (b) allowing users to plan what is to be done with their own digital legacy; (c) how to choose the different information within the digital legacy of a loved one to be shared; or (d) even allowing users to create messages to be delivered after their death [8,20,22,23]. Gulotta et al. [3,21] explore the ideas of how digital artefacts and information are integrated into existing practices relating to death, family, and inheritance. They go further to validate how people perceive and consider digital artefacts in the context of their personal legacy, against the backdrop of other material practices and physical heirlooms. Based on group discussions and interviews from participants, they propose three opportunities for designing the legacy systems: (a) based around family, how their digital information would be valuable to future generation; (b) file management through selective archiving, a subset of archives that can be passed to future generation; and (c) comfort with long-lasting digital legacies, the archiving and safekeeping of digital data, focused on experiences that fall outside of daily activities that could be embarrassing or revealing [3,5,21].

From a bereaved's perspective, Massimi et al. [17] and Vale-Taylor [24] present research on sensibilities involved with the end of life and the bereaved. They demonstrate that a sensitive orientation towards the needs of the bereaved is more important than problem-solving assumptions about grief [5,17,20]. Through focus group discussions involving bereaved people, they derive a set of empirically grounded information that forms the issues with the Human-Computer Interaction (HCI) community. These are classified into three categories: (a) interpersonal communication, to maintain good relationships with condolers (such as returning phone calls, writing thank-you letters, or receiving guests into the home). These relationships can become strained due to a gap of misunderstandings surrounding the loss; (b) new ways of being in the world, working with bereaved people requires an acknowledgement and understanding the difficulty of coping with grief, and the design of technologies for the bereaved must accommodate the ongoing, long-term needs during grief; and (c) materiality, to manage the physical objects with respect to the psychological and social practices [17,20].

In short, digital legacy systems can have two types of users: (a) users who plan for their digital assets; and (b) users who are bereaved. In the following section, we will explore some of the commercially available online systems and tools for managing digital legacy.

Existing Systems and Tools

These are some of the commercially available digital legacy systems and tools that are available to support users who want to plan for their death and users who are bereaved.

- **Legacy.com:** This organisation's website claims to be the world's largest commercial provider of online memorials. The website hosts obituaries and memorials for almost a third of all the deaths in the United States [25]. It also hosts obituaries for more than half of the 100 top newspapers in the United States [25]. The site is one of the top trafficked websites in the United States and is visited by more than 30 million unique users every month [25].

- **Mywishes.co.uk:** An online platform that provides users to plan both physical and digital assets in the event of death. It also provides services, such a digital will, which can be legally and non-legally binding. The digital will can then be shared, with the beneficiaries, healthcare professionals, and funeral directors. The website is part of DeadSocial group [26].

- **Google Inactive Account Manager:** Google announced the creation of the "Inactive Account Manager", which allows ownership and control of inactive accounts be transferred to a beneficiary. It enables beneficiary users to access accounts belonging to their loved ones who are deceased. After proving the relationship, Google works with the beneficiaries to transfer the contents of the dead [27].

- **DeadSocial:** It is an online integrator platform that provides the tools and support resources to help support society deal with the issues relating to death, remembering the deceased and grievance. They deliver these services by building partnerships with third party service providers in the area of healthcare, technology, hospice, and funeral homes [28].

- **Seniornet:** A Kiwi organisation that teaches computers and digital legacy to seniors. This is delivered through workshops, online courses, and teachings [29].

- **Safebeyond.com:** The organisation claims to be the worlds most advanced ongoing legacy management service. The platform hosts online and mobile app solutions for user's life story and digital content [30]. It provides sharing capabilities for the delivery of personalised messages and digital assets in the future. The users have the option to decide when, where and with whom the messages and other digital assets will be shared [30].

- **Forevermissed:** This is an online memorial website, where people can create online memorials to collect and share memories of the people they have lost [31].

- **Facebook memorial:** Facebook introduced "memorial pages" in late 2009 in response to the users affected by Virginia Tech shooting of 2007. Facebook converts a profile page into a tribute page after receiving the proof of death. The tribute page is a webpage with basic personal details and for the bereaved users to leave messages [32]. In early 2015, Facebook provided its users an option to delete their account permanently in the event of death or nominate a family member or a friend as a "legacy contact". The legacy contact will have the rights to manage the page after the user's death. As of mid 2019, all three options were active [32].

Table 1 summarises the aforementioned commercially available digital legacy systems based on functionality, the target users, and geographical coverage. It also shows that most online tools are for the users who are bereaved. For the digital asset owners, there is no service that supports the requirements listed down in Section 2. In the next section, we explore the work done in digital immortal privacy laws.

3.2 Digital Immortal Privacy

With respect to digital immortal privacy laws, Buitelaar [7] explores the ethical and moral discussions related to identity after death, i.e., exploring the possibility of legal consequences of a biological death for transferring the concept of informational self-determination, grounded in human dignity from the living world, to the digital immortal phase of a digital identity. Currently, there are no laws that can protect the privacy of an individual after death [7, 33]. This is because death is the end of one's biological life, which also means the non-existence of the living individual. The living individual had an interest in preserving the information regarding personal identity and character traits in order to excel and realise their existence in this world with human dignity [7, 33]. As the individual is unable to exercise this sovereign right after death, the privacy laws of today hold that the privacy rights are terminated with death. He then proposes that digital immortal privacy should not only be a legal obligation but also an ethical and moral obligation. He also explores the idea of an ontological approach characterised by strands of information as a basis for recognising a right to privacy for digital immortal identity [34]. He suggests that social networking sites could be the guardians of these aspects of the information/digital double during the individual's living phase.

Edwards et al. [4] discuss that preserving digital immortal privacy is not dependent upon one single entity of a legal organisation, but rather through the support of a range of legal instruments and institutions. This could vary based on origin and purpose across multiple legal systems. The range of legal instruments that can be supported within a set of legal institutions along with digital immortal privacy can include laws relating to defamation, breach of confidence, intellectual property, publicity, succession, and data protection [4]. Currently, the regulation property rights of the individual to the digital assets is determined by the service terms and contractual rules of the digital intermediary forms, such as social networks, where assets are stored and shared. They argue that any disagreements that affect digital immortal privacy, the arguments will be between the rights granted to intermediary platforms and the rights of the beneficiaries. The rights of the digital intermediaries are set by their own terms of service and rights of the beneficiary is determined by the succession laws or legal will. They go further to suggest ways to enforce digital immortal privacy: one through legislation and the other through contract. They acknowledge that legislation would take more time and that the current contract structure managed by the intermediary platforms lack norms to protect digital immortal privacy.

Table 1: Online tools for digital legacy.

Online Systems and Tools	Functionality	Target Users	Other Info
Legacy.com	Online memorial	For users who are bereaved	Focused on the US Market
mywishes.co.uk	Digital will (binding and non-binding)	For users to plan death	Focused on the UK market
Google Inactive Account Manager	Email access	For users to allow access to Google emails after death	Global
Deadsocial	Integrator platform	Both users to plan their death and for the bereaved	Integrator platform that includes services from charities, healthcare organisations, funeral hospices
Seniornet	Education about technology/digital legacy	For users to plan death	NZ based organisation
Safebeyond.com	Digital time capsule	Both users to plan their death and for the bereaved	US based, but claim that services delivered to worldwide
Forevermissed	Online memorial	For the users of the bereaved	Worldwide
Facebook Memorial	Online memorial	For the users of the bereaved	Worldwide

In the work by Buitelaar [7] and Edwards et al. [4], we found that there are no privacy laws protecting the death and any enforcement lies within contract structure of the intermediary platforms, such as third party service providers, say Google and Yahoo. These platforms lack a generic framework and do not protect digital immortal privacy. In the next section, we explore the research done on PII and discuss how PII and privacy are related.

3.3 Personally Identifiable Information (PII)

Privacy of personal data is related to identifying Personally Identifiable Information or PII. Data that can be used to identify any specific individual is called PII [35]. Krishnamurthy et al. [9] describe PII as that data that could be used to differentiate one person from another. It can also be used for de-identifying anonymous data [9]. PII data can further be classified as sensitive or non-sensitive [9, 36]. Non-sensitive PII is that information that requires less care and can be stored or transmitted in an unencrypted form without any harm to the individual. The information can be gathered from publicly available records, such as council records, phone books, corporate directories, and websites [9]. However, sensitive PII is that information when revealed, can result in harm to the individual's privacy. There are laws governing the protection of sensitive PII, such as the EU General Data Protection Regulation (GDPR). Hence, most organisations that gather, store, and transmit sensitive PII will have the data in an encrypted format. An example of sensitive PII can be biometric information, medical information, financial information, passport or social security numbers. In the current environment, the protection of PII is increasingly demanded by both customers and data protection regulation governing bodies. The regulations, such as GDPR, provide protection to the individual by monitoring and then prohibiting any collection and processing of PII by the data controller based in origin, transfer and purpose [9, 35]. Thus, there is a need to safeguard and control the PII through detection, labelling and tracking solutions [9]. With the exponential growth of data, it is a challenge to do that in ad hoc. Bier et al. [10] propose a solution for usage control and provenance tracking. They pose the following questions: (a) how does one know that the information received or created contains PII?; and (b) how to tie privacy policies to PII. They argue that this information is processed manually. Any automation is difficult as the data is unstructured and heterogeneous [10].

Emails systems are one of the earliest online systems that enable users to create, store, and transmit information [37]. It is also the most widely used online application in today's world. In the next section, we explore the research done on PII with respect to emails.

PII and Emails

PII within emails are usually heterogeneous and hence difficult to label and identify [10, 11, 37–39]. We will explore three research-based approaches to privacy protection in email systems.

Bier et al. [10] present a model that can recognise emails containing PII and annotate them with policies. The fundamental idea they propose is based on applying a spam filter technology to the classification of PII for incoming emails. They design a framework for PII detection, usage control and provenance tracking. The framework protects sensitive data through attaching and enforcing policies [39]. A prototype has been developed to show feasibility of the idea with an email agent. Finally, an extensive evaluation based on test data shows that the framework is promising for the detection of PII in emails.

Geng et al. [11] put forward two methodologies to ensure privacy compliance for emails. The first one is by monitoring the email content before the emails are sent out. Emails could be blocked for any violations that have been detected according to policies and operational context. The advantage of this approach is that privacy violations can be prevented before an email is sent out [11]. The disadvantage is that it may not be flexible enough. In real scenarios, there may be exceptions and emergencies, which require immediate access to private information. The prevention approach may be a hindrance in these scenarios. In the second approach, which is also known as the audit approach, software tools are used to find traces of the privacy leaks on an as-needed basis, or to report privacy violations on a regular basis [11]. The advantage is that it provides greater user flexibility. The disadvantage of this method is that it may work after the violation is detected by which time, the damage has been done [11].

Armour et al. [38] recommend an email compliance engine to detect privacy violations. The engine would consist of two components: (1) an entity extraction module that can identify private information, such as names, phone numbers, social insurance numbers, student numbers, and addresses; (2) privacy verification module that determines whether the email should be blocked according to the type of private information detected, the recipients of the email, and the electronic policies or rules stored in a database [38]. This method is targeted to prevent any private information leaks. They experiment with four types of PII elements, email addresses, telephone numbers, addresses, and money [38]. They also include an association rule mining to predict private information according to other PII identified. Finally, they have a classification model to predict the PII according to the content of the emails.

In all the aforementioned approaches, the access control mechanism is used as a fundamental component to preserve confidential information and unauthorised access. The main challenge is to implement a fine-grained access control mechanism that can have superior user experience and at the same time preserve digital immortal privacy.

Access Control Mechanisms

In this section, we explore the most common access control mechanisms. The goal of access control is to minimise the risk of unauthorised access to physical and logical systems. The common access control mechanisms are briefly explained as follows.

3.4 Mandatory Access Control (MAC)

In a Mandatory Access Control (MAC) mechanism, the access of a subject accessing an object is constrained according to the operating system classification, authentication and configuration. The security policies that define if a subject can access an object within the operating system is enforced by a system administrator and is managed centrally in one secure network. The users will not have any ability to override the security policy [40].

Discretionary Access Control (DAC)

Discretionary Access Control (DAC) is a mechanism where the object owner determines operations that can be performed [40]. In this mechanism, the object owner regulates the access to the object and can delegate the information access to other users and hence is named as discretionary [40]. In DAC, user identification, such as username and password, is used to establish controls and access privileges [40].

Role-Based Access Control (RBAC)

Role-Based Access Control (RBAC) is the one in which a person's role within the organisation is used to determine the access privileges to an object [40]. It has policy-neutral access control, as the privileges are determined by the duties of the employee role and can only access the information relevant to that role and preventing access that is not needed. The role permissions are an easy way to assign user assignments. Therefore, it enables employees of senior roles to restrict access to sensitive information to employees of junior roles [40].

Policy or Attribute-Based Access Control (PBAC)

In a Policy-Based Access Control (PBAC) model, polices made up of attributes work together to determine the access rights to an object [40]. The attributes can be a single or a combination of parameters, such as user, resources, environment, and object attributes. The use of user attributes is the most common in the PBAC access control as it defines the access control rules and access requests based on the user logging into the system. In the current information age, where there are multiple systems working in tandem within an organisation, PBAC is considered the next generation authorisation mechanism that can be made context-aware and risk-intelligent as the model enables many attributes from different information systems to resolve any authorisation and provide the flexibility to scale. The building blocks can be defined through structural language, such as eXtensible Access Control Mark-up Language (XACML) [40].

In this section, we have discussed and explored the various approaches related to digital legacy systems, existing online tools and application, reviewed digital immortal privacy laws and later PII in emails. We also investigated the most famous access control mechanisms. From the literature review, we have noticed that there is very little research done in the area of preserving digital immortal privacy and there is a lack of granular access to the digital asset. We found that there is some work done in the area of detection of PII in emails. In Section 5, as an example, we will leverage some of the technology developments in the detection of PII in emails and apply the same to the digital legacy framework that will be discussed in the next section. In the next section, we will design a high-level framework that will provide the digital asset owner a fine-grained access control mechanism using which they can enable granular access to the digital asset and continue to preserve digital immortal privacy.

4. DigImoPriv: Proposed Idea

In Section 2, we discussed four scenarios where the victim's digital immortal privacy was violated. We also enumerated the system requirements needed to preserve digital immortal privacy with granular access to the digital asset. Based on these require-ments, we design a new digital legacy framework for big data, called DigImoPriv. The framework can have two types of users: (a) the owner of the digital asset; or (b) the nominee/bereaved. It is modelled to sit between the digital user and the on-line digital asset. The framework has three main components: (a) an access control mechanism to authenticate and authorise in order to provide the necessary access rights to the user. We propose a policy-based access control mechanism because it enables the digital asset owner to provide a fine-grained access control mechanism and hence a superior user experience and greater flexibility to the digital asset. These policies will restrict unauthorised access to the PII data and hence will be the basis to preserve digital immortal privacy; (b) an intelligent data annotation system that can label PII data and categorise the digital asset into categories, such as private, confi-dential, unrestricted, or even based on sentiments, such as happy or sad moments; and (c) a synchronisation system that will have two main functions, a periodic alert function to check on the owner's activity/inactivity and a periodic synchronise func-tion that initiates an update of the online digital asset with the data store, so that DigImoPriv has the latest version of the data from the online digital asset.

In this section, we will discuss the different entities of the system model followed by the threat model and finally how the entities will interact.

4.1 System Model

The different entities of the system model are:

- **User:** It represents an authorised entity that is part of the system. The user here can represent two roles. One is the owner of the digital asset who wants to preserve their digital immortal privacy. The other is the bereaved user who is the digital asset owner's nominee to access the digital asset. The information of the nominees will be stored in a contact list.

- **Policy Store:** A policy-based access control mechanism to authorise the user and provide the necessary access rights. The policies defined by the owner form the basis of preserving her privacy. This entity is responsible for im-plementing and enforcing the policies on the data from the digital asset. The policy store would have all the components required to minimise or eliminate the risk of unauthorised access to the data store. It would have a platform to define policies based on the contextual relationship between the data and the owner in such a way that if the data is shared with the nominees, the privacy of the owner is maintained after death.

- **Contacts Store:** A database of all the contacts that would have access to the data store after the digital owner's death. The contacts database will have an interface for the digital asset owner to input, update, or delete the contacts. It will also have a field against the contact to input a relationship to the owner for example friend, family, or colleague.

- **Data Annotation System:** It is responsible for labelling the data in the data store as private, non-confidential, or unrestricted. It is designed to incorporate an artificial intelligence system to label the data based on the contextual reference to the owner, such as happy or sad moments.

- **Data Store:** The data store entity will store all the annotated data. It would be a replication of the online system data that forms the digital asset of the owner with additional data labels. It should be updated periodically through the control of synchronisation system.

- **Synchronisation System:** This entity will have two main functions. The first one is to make sure that the data store is updated at regular intervals, say daily, weekly, or fortnightly. The second function is to check on the digital asset owner's activity (alive or dead). This can be done by periodically sending an alert message to the owner for which a response is required. If the response is not received after multiple alerts, then the framework concludes that the digital asset owner has passed away and the system will be made available to the contacts based on the policy set by the owner.

- **Online System:** This entity is the target digital asset that the owner would like to share with her contacts. It can be an email system, feeds in social networks, pictures/photos on cloud, or even files on the cloud storage.

4.2 Threat Model

The framework DigImoPriv illustrated in Figure 1 is modelled based on the assumption that the online system will have the relevant Application Programming Interfaces (APIs) that will allow DigImoPriv to access the data in real-time to replicate the same within the data store. These APIs might be prone to Man-in-the-Middle (MitM), replay, or Denial of Service (DoS) attacks. Additionally, the data within the data store and the contacts store will be stored in an encrypted format to be protected from any unauthorised access or attack on the system.

It is assumed that the synchronisation system is operating in the background to schedule regular updates to replicate the data within the data store. If the connection to the online system goes down during the update, then the system will initiate another update once the connection is maintained. This system also sends regular alerts to the digital asset owner to check their online activity. Only in the event when the system does not receive a reply from the digital asset owner, DigImoPriv will conclude that the owner has passed away, and the system will send an update to the people in the contact list and make DigImoPriv available as per the policies set by the owner.

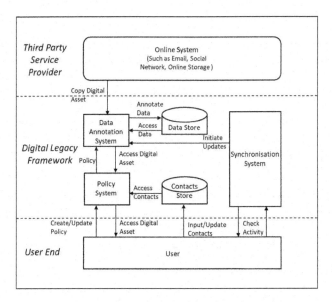

Figure 1: DigImoPriv: Our proposed digital legacy framework for big data.

4.3   General Overview

In this section, we discuss how the different entities of DigImoPriv will interact with each other. As we already mentioned in this section, DigImoPriv will have three main components: (a) a policy-based access control mechanism to authorise the user and provide the necessary access. The policies form the basis of restricting unauthorised access to the digital asset and thus preserving the digital immortal privacy of the digital asset owner; (b) an intelligent data annotation system that labels or categorises the data in the digital asset based on labels, such as private, confidential, and unrestricted; and (c) the timer or a synchronous system that periodically checks the digital asset owner's activity and updates the data store. The different entities of these components are:

- **A Policy-Based Access Control Mechanism:** The entities that facilitate this mechanism are the policy store, the contact,s store and the data annotation system. The policy store checks and authorises the user based on the information in the contact store and provides the necessary access by enabling the appropriate view from the data annotation system. For example, if the user is the owner, then the access control mechanism provides full access to the system. If the user is a friend, then the access control mechanism, depending on the policy set by the owner, may prohibit any access to the data that is labelled as private or confidential.

- **Data Annotation System:** The entities that form this system are data annotation entity and data store. The data annotation entity is designed to incorporate an Artificial Intelligence (AI) logic that labels the data within the data store, such as private, confidential, and unrestricted. The data store is the replication of the digital asset. This system will interact with the policy store and provide some feedback to the control mechanism the type of the data, i.e., private, confidential, and unrestricted.

- **Synchronous System:** This system interacts with the data annotation system periodically to update with the latest version of the data from the online system. It also interacts with the digital asset owner to periodically check their activity. If inactivity is confirmed even after multiple alerts, it alerts the framework that the owner is dead and opens the digital asset to the nominees.

Based on the interactions of the various components, the operation of DigImoPriv can be viewed from two perspectives. First, when the user is the owner and second when the user is the bereaved or nominee (post-death of the digital owner).

When the User is the Digital Asset Owner

These are the expected operations of the various entities within the framework when the user of the system is the digital asset owner. In this scenario, the digital asset owner should be able to configure the system, i.e., create, update, delete policies, contacts, and set alerts.

- **Contact Store Entity:** The user can create, update, and delete the contacts that will have access to her digital asset in the event of the owner's death. The user will also be able to set roles to his contacts. The roles can be relationship status with respect to the user, i.e., primary contact, spouse, children, parents, or friends.

- **Data Annotation System:** The user can create data labels that form input to the AI engine to classify or annotate the data. The data labels can be confidential, private, or contextual information, such as happy or sad moments.

- **Data Store:** This data store will be the exact replica of the digital asset that the user would like to share. The user can choose to delete or create any data in the data store. Once the data is deleted or created from the data store, the same is applied to the online system as well.

- **Policy Store Entity:** The user can create, update and delete policies for each contact in the contact store based her relationship with the contact, i.e., the role. This entity will work together with the data annotation system. For example, the user can create policies, that say:

  - Happy moments and non-confidential data can be shared or viewed by everyone on the contact list.

  - Confidential data should be shared only with the primary contact or the spouse.

  - Sad and private data should not be shared with anyone and should be deleted permanently after death.

- **Synchronous System:** This entity will operate in the background to monitor and initiate periodic updates between the online system and the data store of the interface. However, the user should also be able to initiate a voluntary operation to initiate an update to the data annotation system. The other operation of this entity is to send periodic alerts to check on the owner's activity. The owner should be able to configure the frequency of the alerts and the number of reminders.

When the User is the Bereaved

In this scenario, DigImoPriv has determined inactivity from the owner of the digital asset. The user in this case can be referenced as the bereaved. The bereaved user must in one of the contacts in the contact data store.

- **Synchronous System:** Once the system confirms that there is no response from the digital asset owner, the system will send an alert to the primary contact intimating that there has been no response from the owner. Upon the confirmation from the primary contact (the confirmation can be through the submission of a death certificate), the system will now send invitation mails with the appropriate access to all the contacts within the contact store.

- **Contact Store Entity:** In this scenario, the user should not be able to access, change or view any contact (except the logged-in user details) in the contact store.

- **Data Annotation Entity:** In this scenario, the user should not be able to access or change any labels in the data annotation entity.

- **Policy Store Entity:** The entity should authenticate the user based on information in the contact store and apply the appropriate policy. The user should be authorised to view only that data that is applicable as per the policy.

- **Data store:** In this scenario, the user should not be able to access or change any data in the data store.

4.4   Mapping to Use Case Scenarios

In this section, we will apply the system model to the use case scenarios discussed in Section 2. The objective is to establish that the digital legacy framework discussed in the system model can preserve digital immortal privacy for the victims discussed in the scenarios. Table 2 gives the details of the use case scenarios when applied to the framework.

5. Solution Details

In the previous section, we discussed the high-level framework that supports the requirements discussed in Section 2. In this section, we will explain the technical details of DigImoPriv illustrated in Figure 2.

Table 2: Mapping to the Use Case Scenarios.

Scenario	Digital Asset	Policy	Outcome
Army officer died in a combat on an international mission	Emails	• Label all private conversation emails as confidential • Delete or restrict the view of all confidential emails • Share only happy moment emails with spouse	• By applying this policy, the system will delete or restrict all confidential emails permanently and this preserving digital immortal privacy of the Army Officer
Well-known publisher died leaving his unfinished work in the cloud storage	Files	• Label the files of unfinished work • Delete or restrict the view of the files marked unfinished	• By applying this policy, the system would delete or restrict all the files marked as unfinished work and would prohibit anyone from publishing the author's unfinished work
Teenage girl died from a drug overdose	Photos, possibly feeds	• Label the photos into categories, such as happy, unhappy, and private • Delete or untag all unhappy and private photos	• In this case, the system will restrict the photos tagged as unhappy or private from the parents thus preserving teenager of her digital immortal privacy and her parents from misery
A middle age technology geek died in a car accident	Emails	• Label all refugee emails to private • Delete or restrict the view of all the emails marked as private	• This scenario is similar to the Army Officer case wherein all private emails would be deleted or restrict from viewing • In this case, the privacy of the geek and the lives of refugees would be preserved
A young man died in a camping trip	Files	• Label all files containing online private keys to private and confidential	• The system will allow his immediate family to access the private keys and provide information on the purpose of the keys. This would stop the immediate family from posting the question in Reddit and thus preserving the anonymity of the wallet address.

In all the five scenarios, by applying the necessary policy, DigImoPriv would continue to preserve digital immortal privacy of the digital asset owner and at the same time enable granular access to his or her contacts to the other parts of digital asset.

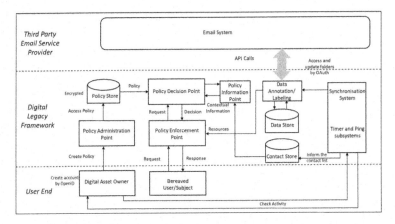

Figure 2: The detailed architecture of DigImoPriv.

Earlier in this chapter, we pointed out that the digital asset can be of different forms, such as emails, photos, data files, social media feeds and messages. In this section, we have focused on the email digital asset given some initial work has been done by Google. Actually, Google has implemented the Inactive Account Manager [8] for its users to share its folders with nominated persons in an event there is no activity for a certain time period. However, this is coarse-grained, where entire folders are shared and thus may not have the right privacy protection for the deceased. In DigImoPriv, we show that by applying the digital legacy framework to the email digital asset, we enable a fine-grained access control mechanism and preserve digital immortal privacy. As discussed in Section 2, we leverage some of the technologies in labelling of data in email systems to overcome the challenge unstructured and heterogeneous data. In this section, we will first discuss the technical solution for identity management followed by labelling of emails. After that, we discuss the policy access control, system in action, and discuss some security measures.

5.1 Identity Management

In this section, we discuss the solution approach for user identity management and authorisation of regular access to the resources managed by the third party service provider. For the email digital asset, we have considered Gmail services. As the owner of the digital asset, the solution should incorporate an easy process for the application to register with the identity providers. Hence, we suggest using OpenID Connect that allows dynamic registration. By registering the application with the OpenID providers, we procure a client ID and token. The solution approach is illustrated in Figure 3(a). Here, we use OpenID Connect as the authenticate layer on top of the OAuth protocol [41, 42], which is the authorisation layer.

Figure 3(a) shows the architecture of OpenID and OAuth, while Figure 3(b) illustrates the detailed steps involved in authentication and authorisation of the client application to use the email resource. We point out that we use this approach only for the scenario when the digital asset owner is using the system, i.e., the user activity

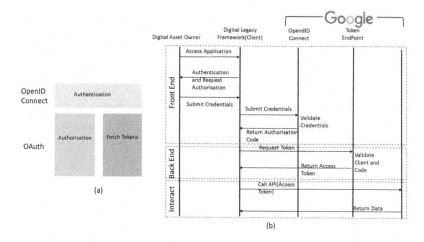

Figure 3: Identity management with OpenID connect and OAuth.

will involve the access of the email digital resource for labelling of the PII. Post the death of the digital asset owner, we only enable the OpenID Connect for authentication of the bereaved users. The authorisation of the bereaved users is done by the policy store. The benefits for using OpenID Connect [41, 42] are: (a) it provides a dynamic registration and discovery of client applications to automatically register; (b) easy to consume tokens; and (c) enables user consent, enable authorisation and easy to configure.

5.2 Labelling of PII

In this section, we propose a solution to identify and label emails that have Personal PII. The basis of this approach is that by identifying, labelling, and protecting and finally categorising emails with PII, we will protect privacy of the digital asset owner and eventually digital immortal privacy. The solution leverages the work done by Bier et al. [10], Geng et al. [11] and Joachins [43]. The idea is similar to a spam filter technology in the classification of PII. The main challenge we are addressing here is that PII data is mostly heterogeneous and differs from scenario to scenario.

Let us consider a scenario where the emails are in binary text and with a scope of five types of PII elements, email addresses of specific contacts, telephone numbers, bank accounts, money and addresses. Similar to a spam filter that classifies emails into ham and spam, we leverage the solution to classify the emails into various classes, such as emails with all five PII, emails with 3 or less PII, with no PII, emails with money and bank account PII. Naive Bayes classifier, for instance, is a common algorithm used to classify binary text in a spam filter. The algorithm works on the principle of conditional probabilities and estimates a probability for each class based on previously classified data. Some other classification systems are neural networks, classification rules, and support vector machines [11, 43].

Once we have grouped the emails into different classes, we can label each class. For example, the class with all five PII can be labelled as private and confidential.

Table 3: Email classes and PII labels, where *PII = email addresses, telephone number, bank account, money, physical address.*

Classes or Categories	Label
Any Emails with bank account and money	Private and Confidential
Emails with PII two or a smaller number of PII	Non-Confidential
Emails with spouse email addresses	Close Family
Emails with all three or more PII	Confidential
Emails with friend email addresses	Friend

Table 3 gives an example of the type of labels that can be tagged to classes. It shows how emails can be categorised into various classes based on PII and tagged with appropriate labels, such as private, confidential, and non-confidential.

5.3 Policy-Based Access Control (PBAC)

The objective of identifying and labelling emails with PII is to preserve digital immortal privacy. In this section, we will discuss a simple Policy-Based Access Control (PBAC) to authorise the bereaved users on the contact list based on the policy set by the digital asset owner.

In a PBAC model, there are different entities in the technical architecture including a Policy Enforcement Point (PEP), a Policy Decision Point (PDP), and a Policy Information Point (PIP). The PEP is integrated into the data annotation entity where the policies must be enforced. Each time, when a bereaved user performs a "view email" event, the PEP contacts the PDP and asks if the event is allowed or not. The PDP decides if the request based on the policies deployed by the digital asset owner. As in the case of data-centered policies, the PDP obtains from the PIP the required contextual information that is applicable to the event. In this case, the PIP might authenticate the user based on OpenID. The PDP allows the event to happen depending on the information from the PIP. Later, the PEP enforces the appropriate policy and thus allowing access to the class of emails as requested by the subject. The process is as follows. First, the policy of the email digital asset is deployed at the PDP. Second, classes and labels of the email digital assets holding the detected PII are provided at the Data annotation container. Additional meta information (authentication of the bereaved user in the contact store, IP address, time) is provided by the PIP. Third, the PEP enforces the policy by connecting the appropriate class or labels of the email digital asset and the data subject, i.e., a bereaved user.

5.4 System in Action

In this section, we discuss how the system operates in different scenarios, e.g., when the user is the digital asset owner and when the user is bereaved. The functions or activities on how the system operates in these two situations are different. In the scenario, when the user is the digital asset owner, the primary activities include: (a) creating and updating policies on their digital asset; and (b) creating and updating contacts in the contact list. In the scenario, when the user is bereaved, the system must authenticate the user and apply the associated policies, i.e., the class of emails a bereaved user can access. For simplicity, we have assumed that the system allows only the view activity for bereaved user, i.e., to view the digital asset. The system prohibits any other activity, such as downloading, copying or deleting. It should also be noted that the system assumes that the timeline of the two scenarios does not overlap. That is, it is assumed that the system is initially used by digital asset owner to create policies and contacts and only after the digital owner user's death, the system is used by the bereaved user. Hence, there can never be a situation, where bereaved user can use the system when the digital asset owner is alive.

Let us now look at an example of how DigImoPriv operates. Alice is the digital asset owner who plans to share after her death her emails with Bob, Eve, Mallory, and Trent. Her objective is to preserve her digital immortal privacy and provide granular access to the email digital asset based on her relationship with the contacts.

When the User is the Digital Asset Owner

Alice as the digital asset owner logs into the Digital Asset Framework, the identity management layer authenticates Alice using OpenID [41, 42]. Once authenticated, Gmail services get the consent of Alice if the digital legacy framework can access the emails.

Figure 4 presents the login page and the consent page that Alice will see. Once the consent is provided by Alice, she creates contacts as per Table 4.

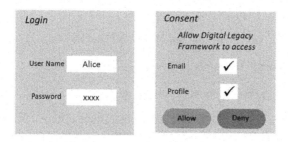

Figure 4: Login and consent screens.

Table 4: Contacts in the contacts store.

Contact Name	Contact Email	Relationship
Bob	bob@email.com	Spouse
Eve	eve@mail.com	Family
Mallory	mallory@mail.com	Friend
Trent	trent@mail.com	Lawyer

After the contacts have been created in Table 4[3], and the PII labels discussed in Table 3, Alice will now create the following policies that will be stored in the policy store.

---

[3]The email IDs are used only for explaining the context and are hypothetical. Any similarity to living or a dead person is only coincidental.

- Private and confidential emails can be viewed only with spouse and Lawyer (P1).

- Non-confidential emails can be viewed by anyone (P2).

- Close family emails can be viewed by only Spouse (P3).

- Confidential emails can be viewed by Family (P4).

- Friend emails can be viewed only by Friend (P5).

The synchronous entity of the digital legacy framework will now continuously check the activity of Alice by sending reply request emails. If Alice does not reply to the emails even after periodic requests, DigImoPriv assumes that Alice has passed away. In such an event, an email notification goes to the people in the contacts list intimating that Alice has died and has invited the people in the contacts list to view her emails.

When the User is the Bereaved

Once the contacts are informed to view Alice's emails, the system authenticates them using OpenID Connect. Once the user is authenticated, the PDP loads the appropriate policy and PEP enforces the policy by providing access to the user with the appropriate label/class of emails set by Alice. For example:

- Bob is Spouse. The applicable policies are P1, P2 and P3.

- Eve is Family. The applicable policies are P2 and P4.

- Mallory is Friend. The applicable polices are P2 and P5.

- Trent is Lawyer. The applicable policies are P1 and P2.

By these policies, we can notice that each contact has a different view of the email digital asset. Mallory who is the friend, will not have the same access as Bob who is the spouse to the same digital asset, thus protecting Alice's digital immortal privacy. DigImoPriv has provided Alice with a platform to enable fine-grained access control to her digital asset and preserve digital immortal privacy. In the next section, we discuss the security measures needed to be taken for the digital legacy framework.

5.5 Security Measures

In this section, we look at some of the system threats in the framework and discuss the appropriate measures that need to be taken. Since framework leverages OpenID Connect, it is prone to MitM and phishing attacks. It is important that the users and the resource owners are made aware of the authenticity of the login pages. One way is to enable 2-factor authentication. The system might also be vulnerable to the replay attacks due to OAuth, however, it is recommended that timestamp and nonce are used during authorisation. At the same time to protect the confidentiality of the data that is exchanged, it is recommended to protect the resources by employing

Transport Layer Security (TLS). To ensure the integrity of the requests between the framework and third party service providers, it is recommended to use Hash-Based Message Authentication (HMAC) or digital signature. In DigImoPriv, the contact store, policy store and data store should be encrypted to protect it from unauthorised access.

6. Conclusions and Future Work

Recently, we have seen an exponential growth in the use of online systems for communication, interaction, and storing of information. This online information forms a digital asset for the user who owns it. Currently, there has been a lot of work done around the information being made available about someone. In this chapter, we have presented DigImoPriv– a digital legacy framework for big data that provides better user experience and greater flexibility to the digital asset owner without the fear of losing digital immortal privacy. DigImoPriv also offers a fine-grained access control mechanism.

While the framework proposed in this chapter is designed to include all types of digital assets, such as files, videos and pictures, the solution example is explained only for the plaintext emails. As more online information is becoming heterogeneous and unstructured, there is a future potential opportunity, such as the inclusion of data mining or AI capabilities to classify the unstructured data based on human emotions, such as happy and sad. Some of the aspects that could be investigated and incorporated into the framework are: (a) a more conclusive way to confirm the digital owner's death, such as validating a death certificate or certificate from funeral home; (b) enhanced user experience by including more operations for the nominees on the digital asset, such as download and print; (c) incorporate multiple types of digital assets, such as online storage, emails, videos and chats into one single framework; (d) enable multiple users from different domains, such as users from Yahoo, Gmail and Outlook into a single framework; (e) incorporate policy rules as a smart contract; (f) conduct a user study to show the feasibility and further consolidate the framework.

Investigating privacy-aware access control policies is a key direction for further research. Such policies should enable individuals to express their privacy preferences over their digital assets. To achieve this, it is necessary to formalise new privacy notions for heterogeneous data.

The essence of human existence is that we would like to be remembered positively and hence we would like to share or pass on information to reinforce this positive and happy identity. We believe this work will build foundations for designing robust systems for digital asset owners who would be interesting in sharing their online assets and continue to be remembered as positive and happy individuals.

References

[1] S. Paul-Choudhury. Digital legacy: The fate of your online soul. *New Scientist*, 210(2809): 41–43, 2011.

[2] C. Öhman and L. Floridi. The political economy of death in the age of information: A critical approach to the digital afterlife industry. *Minds and Machines*, 27(4): 639–662, 2017.

[3] R. Gulotta, W. Odom, J. Forlizzi, and H. Faste. Digital artifacts as legacy: Exploring the lifespan and value of digital data. *In Proceedings of the SIGCHI Conference on Human Factors in Computing Systems*. ACM, 2013, pp. 1813–1822.

[4] L. Edwards, and E. Harbina. Protecting post-mortem privacy: Reconsidering the privacy interests of the deceased in a digital world. *Cardozo Arts & Ent. LJ*, 32: 83, 2013.

[5] W. Odom, R. Harper, A. Sellen, D. Kirk, and R. Banks. Passing on & putting to rest: Understanding bereavement in the context of interactive technologies. *In Proceedings of the SIGCHI Conference on Human Factors in Computing Systems*. ACM, 2010, pp. 1831–1840.

[6] M. Savin-Baden. Postdigital after life? *Postdigital Science and Education*, 1(2): 303–306, Oct 2019. [Online]. Available: https://doi.org/10.1007/s42438-019-00056-9.

[7] J. Buitelaar. Post-mortem privacy and informational self-determination. *Ethics and Information Technology*, 19(2): 129–142, 2017.

[8] R.O. Prates, M.B. Rosson, and C.S. de Souza. Making decisions about digital legacy with Google's inactive account manager. *In IFIP Conference on Human-Computer Interaction*. Springer, 2015, pp. 201–209.

[9] B. Krishnamurthy, and C.E. Wills. Characterizing privacy in online social networks. *In Proceedings of the First Workshop on Online Social Networks*. ACM, 2008, pp. 37–42.

[10] C. Bier, and J. Prior. Detection and labeling of personal identifiable information in e-mails. *In IFIP International Information Security Conference*. Springer, 2014, pp. 351–358.

[11] L. Geng, L. Korba, X. Wang, Y. Wang, H. Liu, and Y. You. Using data mining methods to predict personally identifiable information in emails. *In International Conference on Advanced Data Mining and Applications*. Springer, 2008, pp. 272–281.

[12] Drawn from the facts of the U.S. case of in re ellsworth, no. 2005-296, 651-de (mich. prob.ct. 2005).

[13] Drawn from, the inside story of Nabokov's last work, guardian (Nov. 17, 2009). http://www.guardian.co.uk/books/2009/nov/17/insidestorynabokov-last-work.

[14] Jefferson Puff, Brazil Judge Orders Facebook Memorial Page Removed, BBC News (Apr. 24, 2013). http://www.bbc.co.uk/news/world-latinamerica-22286569.

[15] Drawn from stories at. https://www.cbc.ca/news/canada/britishcolumbia/services-advisor-app-refugees-1.3339989.

[16] Drawn from stories at. https://fortune.com/2017/09/26/cryptocurrencybitcoin-death/.

[17] M. Massimi, and R.M. Baecker. Dealing with death in design: Developing systems for the bereaved. *In Proceedings of the SIGCHI Conference on Human Factors in Computing Systems*. ACM, 2011, pp. 1001–1010.

[18] E.G. Hunter, and G.D. Rowles. Leaving a legacy: Toward a typology. *Journal of Aging Studies*, 19(3): 327–347, 2005.

[19] E. Harbinja. Post-mortem privacy 2.0: Theory, law, and technology. *International Review of Law, Computers & Technology*, 31(1): 26–42, 2017.

[20] T. Walter, R. Hourizi, W. Moncur, and S. Pitsillides. Does the internet change how we die and mourn? Overview and analysis. *OMEGA-Journal of Death and Dying*, 64(4): 275–302, 2012.

[21] R. Gulotta, W. Odom, H. Faste, and J. Forlizzi. Legacy in the age of the internet: Reflections on how interactive systems shape how we are remembered. *In Proceedings of the 2014 Conference on Designing Interactive Systems*. ACM, 2014, pp. 975–984.

[22] W. Odom, R. Banks, and D. Kirk. Reciprocity, deep storage, and letting go: Opportunities for designing interactions with inherited digital materials. *Interactions*, 17(5): 31–34, 2010.

[23] L. Edwards and E. Harbinja. What happens to my facebook profile when i die? Legal issues around transmission of digital assets on death. *In Digital Legacy and Interaction*. Springer, 2013, pp. 115–144.

[24] P. Vale-Taylor. We will remember them: A mixed-method study to explore which post-funeral remembrance activities are most significant and important to bereaved people living with loss, and why those particular activities are chosen. *Palliative Medicine*, 23(6): 537–544, 2009.
[25] http://www.legacy.com.
[26] http://www.mywishes.co.uk.
[27] https://support.google.com/accounts/answer/3036546?hl=en.
[28] http://deadsocial.org/about.
[29] http://www.seniornet-glenfield.org.nz/site/.
[30] http://www.Safebeyond.com.
[31] https://www.forevermissed.com.
[32] https://www.facebook.com/help/1506822589577997.
[33] J. Berg. Grave secrets: Legal and ethical analysis of postmortem confidentiality. *Conn. L. Rev.*, 34: 81, 2001.
[34] L. Floridi. The ontological interpretation of informational privacy. *Ethics and Information Technology*, 7(4): 185–200, 2005.
[35] P.M. Schwartz, and D.J. Solove. Reconciling personal information in the united states and european union. *Calif. L. Rev.*, 102: 877, 2014.
[36] R. Gross, and A. Acquisti. Information revelation and privacy in online social networks. *In Proceedings of the 2005 ACM workshop on Privacy in the Electronic Society*. ACM, 2005, pp. 71–80.
[37] E. Harbinja. Emails and death: Legal issues surrounding post-mortem transmission of emails. *Death Studies*, 43(7): 435–445, 2019.
[38] Q. Armour, W. Elazmeh, N. El-Kadri, N. Japkowicz, and S. Matwin. Privacy compliance enforcement in email. *In Conference of the Canadian Society for Computational Studies of Intelligence*. Springer, 2005, pp. 194–204.
[39] S. Whittaker, and C. Sidner. Email overload: Exploring personal information management of email. *Culture of the Internet*, pp. 277–295, 1997.
[40] P. Samarati, and S.C. de Vimercati. Access control: Policies, models, and mechanisms. *In International School on Foundations of Security Analysis and Design*. Springer, 2000, pp. 137–196.
[41] N. Sakimura, J. Bradley, M. Jones, B. de Medeiros, and C. Mortimore. OpenID Connect core 1.0 incorporating errata set 1. *The OpenID Foundation, Specification*, 2014.
[42] D.N. Sakimura, J. Bradley, M. Jones, B. de Medeiros, C. Mortimore, and E. Jay. OpenID Connect implicit client implementer's guide 1.0-draft 12, 2013.
[43] T. Joachims. Text categorization with support vector machines: Learning with many relevant features. *In European Conference on Machine Learning*. Springer, 1998, pp. 137–142.

2

Federated Learning Role in Big Data, Iot Services and Applications Security, Privacy and Trust in Iot

A Survey

Supriya Yarradoddi[1] and *Thippa Reddy Gadekallu*[2,*]

ABSTRACT

The Internet of things or IOT is a large number of inter connected or interrelated devices that share data through the internet without manual intervention. The data collected in IOT is very large and Big Data plays an important role in analyzing this data through various AI mechanisms or algorithms like Machine learning, deep learning and federated learning. Big data analytics play a vital role in IOT which helps in decision making. With Internet of Things (IOT) emerging as the next phase of the internet evolution, it is important for us to discuss various applications, and research challenges that are associated with these applications. While using the benefits of IOT, new problems with IOT have also been emerging. To understand these application and their challenges this survey will explain the applications of IOT, various challenges faced in the application of IOT. We also address the issue of security, privacy and trust of IOT. In order to address this issue, Federated Learning (FL) technology is combined with IOT by the researchers'. In this paper we give a complete overview of combining FL with IOT. The survey starts with explaining the applications of IOT, fundamentals of Machine Learning and Distributed Learning concepts in IOT. The motivation behind integrating Fl and IOT is explained. We also give the overview of the FL in IOT applications. Finally we concentrate on the challenges, some possible solutions and directions for future research.

[1,2] School of Information Technology and Engineering, Vellore Institute of Technology, India.
* Corresponding author: thippareddy.g@vit.ac.in

Table 1: ACRONYMS.

IOT	Internet of things
M2M	Machine to Machine
AI	Artificial Intelligence
X DL	Deep Learning
ML	Machine Learning
FL	Federated Learning
FML	Federated Machine Learning
FDL	Federated Deep Learning
DRL	Deep Reinforcement Learning
DML	Distributed Machine Learning
MMVFL	Multi Class Multi Participant Federated Learning
DP	Differential Privacy
EC	Edge Computing
DLN	Deep Learning Network
TPU	Tensor processing unit
IORT	Internet of Robotic Things

1. Introduction

Internet of Things, IOT is a revolution which has changed the lives of people and made it smarter and more advanced than before. IOT has been constantly emerging as finest phenomena in this century. It has made things easier in our day to day life and focuses mainly on machine to machine communication (M2M). Internet of things (IOT) is a network of physical devices which are associated with each other and are connected to internet to send and receive data from each other. Multiple devices can be connected on one platform and they can be monitored from one particular location. The data collected from various devices in IOT can be processed and used in many different fields like the healthcare industry, automobile industry, in building smart cities, home appliances, etc., IOT has a substantial influence on our daily lives and it has various applications everywhere we go. Each device which is connected to the internet in IOT is somehow embedded with many other concepts such as sensors, software or certain electronic devices. Figure 1 explains the basics of IOT.

The size of data in Internet of Things is a major concern. As the number of devices is increasing day by day the amount of data collected from these devices has also been increasing. This is where both Big Data and IOT go hand in hand. Big data handles this large amount of data with its various technologies. It plays an important role in handling the data collected from IOT in a proper manner and helps in a better decision making. IOT BIG DATA comes across major hurdles like large data volumes, problems in data collection, new security threats, and issues with data reliability, and concerns with the privacy of data. Amongst all these issues, privacy and security tend to be major hurdles when we design or develop IOT devices and referring to such concerns is said to be given a high priority.

Figure 1: Internet of things.

Whenever a new technology is being released or developed it is mandatory to keep an eye on the privacy and security issues. The developers of the new technology should think about the new security protocols that assure the end-to-end transmission of sensitive data [1]. IOT networks are more prone to the security threats as its usage is being increased day by day. In order to ensure the confidentiality, authentication, integrity and access control in IOT networks, deployment of security and privacy protocols are greatly needed. The majority of IOT devices and applications do not handle privacy and security issues. The major security issues are leakage of information and loss of services. The collection of the large amounts of sensitive information like the location, financial data or health related information will create a privacy risk. The user's privacy is also important as lot of personal information is being shared with others. In such a case, an efficient mechanism is needed to secure the devices connected to the internet against intruders and attackers [2].

IOT technology deals with large amounts of data. The best way to handle large amounts of data is big data using AI techniques like machine learning algorithms and Deep learning techniques [3].

However, these algorithms have few drawbacks. The Machine Learning (ML) model is not acceptable for large scale IOT networks. Google came up with a new concept called the federated learning (FL) for on-device learning and privacy preservation. The FL model has enabled the IOT device to train its model with the help of the locally collected data. The local data need not be transmitted to the central server like in the machine learning concept. FL has been adopted in many IOT applications like healthcare, smart cities, smart agriculture, etc. However, FL also has its own pros and cons like privacy, security, data management, etc., [4]. A number of research works have been dedicated over the last few years to enable the FL and IOT applications. For example, Ji Chu Jiang [5] investigated a solution for IOT security problems using the federated learning frameworks and proved that the frameworks can increase security and the performance. ThienDuc Nguyen [6], investigated a self-learning anomaly detection system for IOT. This system applies federated learning for intrusion detection.

In spite of the rapid development of FL and emergence of many IOT applications, there is no perfect study which provides an overview of FL, IOT and applications of FL to IOT areas. In this work we focus on explaining the fundamentals of FL, IOT and state-of-the-art research works on FL for IOT applications and the security and privacy issues in IOT.

A. State of the Art and Contributions

There have been many papers which focus on FL and IOT and these two topics have been studied separately. With respect to IOT a survey is presented in [7] which explains the various applications of IOT in domains like smart cities, healthcare, smart agriculture and water management, retail and logistics, smart living and the smart environment. The survey also discusses the research challenges like privacy and security, processing, analysis and management of data, monitoring and sensing, M2M communication and communication protocols and the block chain of things and interoperability. Also there are similar survey papers on IOT like [8]. This paper explains the applications of IOT which make a city into a smart city using various devices, making agriculture smart. IOT plays a key role in securities and emergencies, domestic and home automation, the medical field and industrial control. This paper also proposes an IOT based E-advertising system which can be displayed in large shopping complexes. There are other research papers [9] which we will discuss which are about the 3 layer and 4 layer architecture of IOT, various elements of IOT like unique identification for smart devices, sensing devices, communication, data storage and analytics and visualization. The Key features of IOT, advantage and disadvantages of IOT are also explained in this paper. Paper [10] deals with the applications, elements of IOT, architecture of IOT, IOT key features, IOT

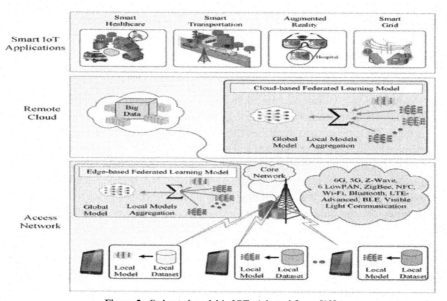

Figure 2: Federated model in IOT--Adapted from: [12].

technologies, enabling technologies, IOT framework, IOT security. A recent survey on IOT security and privacy is presented in [11]. This explains a shared approach that helps in developing a solution for challenges in IOT. This survey also discusses the authentication problems, information security issues and middleware attacks and privacy concerns related to the IOT.

Reference [23] Gives a detailed study of the Internet of Things like the history of IOT, applications of IOT, and IOT adoption. In [2] we discuss the applications of IOT in industries, personal medical devices, and in the Home. Security requirements like resilience to attacks, data authentication access control and client privacy are also explained. Threats like end to end data life cycle protection, secure thing planning, visible/usable security and privacy are a great hindrance in IOT network.

With regards to Big Data and the security challenges, several surveys have been presented on federated learning like [40–42].

This [40] paper discusses the various challenges in big data analytics and focuses on major challenges like data storage and analysis, knowledge discovery and computational complexities, scalability and visualization of data and information security. The study also specifies about the open research issues in big data analytics like IOT for big data analytics, cloud computing for big data analytics, bio-inspired computing for big data analytics and quantum computing for big data analytics. Various tools for big data processing are Apache Mahout, Apache spark, Dryad, Storm, Apache Drill, Jasper soft and splunk. Also a recent paper [41] has discussed big data and business analytics. It studies various developments in big data technology, big data analytics platforms like hadoop ecosystem, the hadoop distributed file system, and some common big data analytic tools, functional layers of big data architecture and its success factor and challenges in this field. This paper [42] discusses the eleven Vs of Big data like Volume, velocity, variety, validity, volatility, value, variability, visualization, valence, veracity and vulnerability. Security and privacy challenges of big data are also studied in this paper. Various security and privacy challenges of big data are data acquisition, data analytics and data storage. Few big data security strategies are discussed here.

With regards to FL, several surveys have been presented on federated learning like [13–17, 4, 45–49].

This paper [13] discusses the drawbacks of the traditional machine learning approaches and the advantages of FL algorithms over the machine learning algorithms. This paper also describes the challenges faced by the FL architecture in implementing the various applications. Also, we elaborate on the various architectures present in the FL. The architectures described in this paper will be about the vertical FL architecture, horizontal FL architecture. Federated transfer learning is also described in this paper. The horizontal Federated architecture is where the features are similar but the data is different. Google proposed this architecture to handle android phones. In the case of vertical federated architecture the data IDs are similar but the features are different. This is also feature driven architecture. The horizontal federated architecture is better known than the vertical federated architecture. The other architecture proposed here is the Federated transfer learning which has got a lot of attention in the last few years. This architecture enables the minimal accuracy loss. Also this paper discusses other frameworks like MMVFL (Multi class Multi participant Vertical federated Learning). PerFit is another framework discussed in this paper which deals with the challenges of FL and IOT like the heterogeneity of devices, statistical heterogeneity and heterogeneity of models. We discuss various frameworks that are applicable in various applications of IOT and federated learning. Reference [14] will discuss various architectures present and it also deals with the differences between the federated Learning and the distributed machine learning and the edge computing. It also discusses the Federated database systems. Reference [15] will deal with the one of the important challenges of the Federated learning which is communication cost. To handle the uplift in communication costs two approaches called the sketched updates and structured updates are explained thoroughly in this paper. Reference [16] describes the classifiers that implement machine learning, distributed learning and federated learning. It clearly explains the difference between these three classifiers with their styles of working. We can analyze the issue of the private data training by evaluating 3 different approaches called the basic, distributed and federated learning approaches. Reference [17] completely works on the concept of Federated Learning. It explains a few research questions on Federated Learning. From the start this paper explains why federated learning is adopted, applications of federated learning, challenges of federated learning, addressing the challenges of federated learning [45]. Studies advance and open problems in federated learning.

In [46] Discussions about the next generation big data federation access control. It explains the Hadoop federation, Access control in HDFS, Federation access control reference model, implementation and validation, access audit log management and analysis.

Few Surveys made on the integration of FL and IOT are [4, 18, 19, 6, 20]. Figure 2 explains the FL and IOT combination.

This paper [4] completely explains the feature of IOT, IIOT and the various machine algorithms and the Deep Learning algorithms involved in solving various issues with the IIOT. This paper is completely about the combination of FL and Industrial IOT. This paper [18] explains the application of federated learning in one of the IOT applications called the smart city. It discusses about the various challenges faced in building smart cities and also the various solutions provided by federated learning. Reference [19] describes the various challenges and solutions in preserving the data privacy which is one of the major drawbacks in AI. The above paper [6] explains completely about a DIOT which is a self-learning anomaly detection system for IOT. Reference [20] explains the comparison between distributed learning and the federated learning approaches for dealing with the IOT. The complete paper is the comparison and analysis of the 2 approaches to solve the challenges of IOT.

- We explain the fundamentals of distributed learning, FL, IOT architecture and characteristics and also motivations for integrating FL with IOT.

- We also review the state-of-the arts on FL-IOT, also we include the FL increasing the security and privacy in IOT.

- We also explain about the challenges related to the FL-IOT, and also discuss about the open research issues that are to be addressed.

B. Paper Organization

This paper is organized in the following manner:

Applications of IOT are discussed in Section 2.

In Section 3, we discuss the fundamentals of IOT and federated learning and also the, motivations of the integration of FL and IOT.

In Section 4, we review FL for security in IOT.

In the next Section (5) we discuss the implementation of FL in IOT applications. In Section 6 we completely explain about the challenges and future directions of the FL and IOT integration.

Finally in Section 7 we present the conclusion to the paper.

2. IOT Applications

In this section we mainly discuss the applications of IOT in various fields. The applications of IOT are enormous and different. They are practically into all areas of the everyday life of human beings, industries, society as a whole. Figure 3 gives the example of a few applications of IOT. The major focus of the applications of IOT are said to be in healthcare, the environment, manufacturing, energy, smart cities, commercial, industrial and infrastructural fields. Enabling the communication between different objects makes this IOT a very expensive, variable and unlimited application [21].

1. **IOT in Healthcare:** Healthcare has unique opportunities for the implementation of IOT. This IOT has the capacity to change the healthcare process and how it reaches the end user. The advent of the Internet of Health mainly focuses on the health of the people, monitoring their condition, diagnostics, medical administration, fitness, etc. The IOT healthcare applications mainly improve the access of care to the people who are in remote locations or who have no capacity

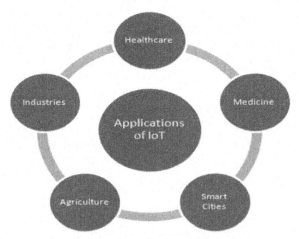

Figure 3: Applications of IOT.

to visit the hospital frequently. The IOT healthcare applications need to take care of the data access and sharing of health information against the concerns in security and privacy concerns. All the information is not accepted to be shared with the physician [22].

2. **Wearable:** Wearable is said to be one of the oldest industries to have deployed the IOT at its service. Fit Bits, heart rate monitors and smart watches are everywhere these days.

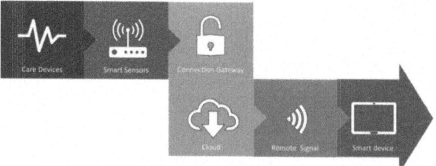

Figure 4: Working of IOT enabled devices.

3. **Smart Cities:** There many elements that make a smart city like smart society, smart buildings, smart lighting, smart mobility, smart water management, smart energy. The constant way to be "smart" is using information and communications.

The various components required to make a smart city will be sensors, actuators and electronic systems to software, data, internet and edge computing. IOT helps in making a smart city by making it independent, secure and trusted. The wide range of networks around the city will provide the real-time information on the movement of the citizens, pollution, traffic and the weather conditions. Based on this real time information continuous improvements in the city can be made. The local authorities can manage the city operations which help in cost reduction, economic growth and social and environmental sustainability. The communication, collaboration and exchange of the data between IOT devices will lead to the realization of a smart city. All the participants should be willing to share their information, security and privacy challenges need to be overcome for this to be successful [5].

4. **Agriculture and Animal tracking:** IOT has the efficiency to strengthen and improve the agriculture sector. It has different technologies which help to examine the soil moisture, also it enables us to control and preserve the quantity of the vitamins found in agricultural products. IOT also helps in controlling the climate conditions in order to improve the quality of the vegetable and fruits. Studying weather conditions will help to improve the quality and quantity of the agricultural products.

When it comes to animal farming and tracking, IOT helps in tracking the animals grazing in open pastures and control the growing conditions in offspring to enhance its survival and health.

5. **IOT in industry:** IOT in industry is where the smart components are embedded into the ordinary objects so that they can be counted as IOT devices. In this sector, IOT is used for many purposes like detecting the gas levels and leakages, toxic gases will be checked, oxygen levels are checked. Also IOT helps in the repair and maintenance of the systems and will check if any device is malfunctioning. All these can be achieved through the installation of sensors inside the machinery to monitor their functionality.

3. IOT and Federated Learning

A. Fundamentals of Distributed Learning

We are in a new era of the communication technology and the Internet of Things (IOT) ecosystems take the lead for the interaction between humans, nature and the physical objects. The large amount of data is processed and converted into some useful actions which make our lives easier and simpler. Traditional approaches limit the development of the intelligent systems because they have a very limited amount of data available. These days, a large amount of the training data is available and the analyzers are also necessary to evaluate that data. The bottleneck in such case is that the limitation of the ML algorithms which cannot use all of the big data in the available time [23].

Since the amount of data has been increasing the, computing power of the computing machinery should also increase which has led to the distribution of machine learning across multiple machines and further which ends up with a distributed system from the centralized system.

To address the above discussed problems we need to discuss Distributed Machine Learning. Distribution of the training data in DML is done in two approaches. The training data is first divided into horizontal fragments and each fragment is stored as node. The second approach is vertical fragmentation. The machine learning algorithms are executed on each node in the distributed network [24].

DML has large number of applications and also it has its own limitations. It has limitations in security, privacy and platform dependency. Here comes the concept of Federated Learning. The following section will discuss federated learning and how it deals with the security issues in Machine learning and distributed machine learning [25].

B. Fundamentals of Federated Learning

Federated learning is new breed of artificial intelligence that completely works on the decentralized data and the learning is done directly on-device. Federated learning provides privacy to the user by decentralizing data from the centralized server. Two reasons why the federated learning came into the limelight is because of insufficient data to reside on the central server and to enable privacy to the user data in machine learning [26]. Federated learning is a training model which allows devices to learn collectively from the shared model. The shared model is trained initially using data proxy data on the server. The models are then downloaded by each device. The devices then train the data that is available locally. Any specific changes made to the model are sent as an update to the cloud. For the updates to be sent faster these models are compressed using random rotations. The models are then averaged to get a combined model. This process is repeated until a high quality model is fetched. Federated learning ensures privacy, less power consumption, smarter models.

Federated learning focuses on training the datasets on the local devices like mobile phones whereas the DML will focus on the parallelization of the computing power. The DML deals with the identical datasets and FL deals with the heterogeneous datasets.

C. Characteristics of IOT

Connectivity: IOT devices are connected globally and have a good communication infrastructure and they can be accessed from anywhere and at any time. IOT service providers provide a type of service or application which decides if the connection of IOT devices is connected locally or globally. They are connected locally in the case of car technology or they are globally connected if they are connected in smart homes [27].

Things: IOT devices can be connected to any device. The device can be from sensors to any other kind of home appliances to tagged livestock.

Data: Data or the information is considered to be very important in any communication.

Communication: Another important feature of the IOT is the communication without the central server involvement. Devices are connected to each other and stay communicated either at short distances or at long distances.

Intelligent systems: The most intriguing features of the IOT is its intelligence through which decisions are to be made timely and are to be informed. The data collected from various devices which are connected to IOT devices are to be processed and the perfect decisions are to be made on the basis of the processed data.

Action: Action is considered to be the consequence of the timely decisions made by the intelligent systems that are connected to the IOT devices.

Table 2: Characteristics of IOT.

CONNECTIVITY	•M2M •NETWORK •INTERNET
THINGS	•SENSORS •DEVICES
DATA	•INFORMATION
COMMUNICATION	•DATA FLOWS
INTELLIGENCE	•SMART/ANALYTICS
ACTION	•DECISION/AUTOMATION
ECOSYSTEM	•COMMUNITY/CONTEXT/IoE

Ecosystem: IOT itself is considered to be an ecosystem. It is a network of devices that transfer the data. The IOT ecosystem is connected to the Big Data, sensors, connectivity, etc.

D. Motivations for Integrating Federated Learning and IOT

The drastic growth in IOT is obstructed by various issues like the security, privacy of the data, cost of communication, scalability. The major motivations for integrating FL and IOT are the following:

- **Security and privacy of data**
  The emergence of IOT has given a scope for the growth in the intelligent systems around the world. Deep Learning has made a revolution in the way the data is being collected from the data resources. Deep learning has been a success in dealing with large amounts of data collected from data resources. At the same time data privacy is also considered to be a major issue for the users. Data leakage cases have been reported in recent times. Federated learning has brought a change in the way the users can deal with large data while in the meanwhile securing the data in a good manner [28]. Since the data is being trained on the local user device and is not sent to the cloud, the data is safe and only the proxy data is shared to the cloud.

- **Lesser cost of communication and computation**
  In the case of distributed learning since the training computation is dispersed among different devices which are connected with internet, communication is considered to be a main problem. Federated learning presents a model called the model averaging. Also federated Learning models can work on wireless communication networks which are a big boost up for communication and computation costs.

- **Network performance is improved**
  The Ml/Dl model is worked out on the data that is generated from IOT applications stored in an edge device and only the summary of the results is sent to the central server when we use FL. The congestion in the network is reduced and the performance of the network is improved significantly.

- **Scalability**
  Since FL works on the edge devices, their learning will only work on the small amounts of data. The central server algorithms only works on the summarized data and not on the large amounts of data. This enables the scalability and training is done only on the data that is generated from the edges devices.

4. Federated Learning for Security in IOT

Federated learning techniques enable machine learning without accessing raw data directly which is sensitive and personal and there by preserves the data without it being leaked and being secured. In this particular section we will be discussing the machine learning distributed learning algorithms used for security in IOT.

A. Machine Learning for Security in IOT

Many start-ups are designing IOT software, IOT devices with one thing in mind to release innovative IOT products as quickly as possible. Due to this many IOT products are not designed with security in mind. Much malicious software will exploit the IOT devices and services. Due to this reason their security is considered to be important.

In IOT, sensors generate large amounts of data. The dominant method to deal with such Big Data is machine learning. Machine learning algorithms play an important role in the security of IOT devices.

There are different machine learning algorithms like supervised learning, unsupervised learning, semi supervised learning and reinforcement learning algorithms used for security in IOT.

Almost all the IOT applications are dependent on the data exchange. The data is being exchanged across different platforms. The data which is collected from the IOT systems is sent through some decision support systems to which sequence there will be some meaningful action. When some user requires data, authentication of the user is required and this is the basic security needed which is based on the ML based access control mechanism.

There are a few limitations that are associated with the ML in IOT. ML has some memory and computational complexity problems when working in IOT. Also ML algorithms do not efficiently support scalability. ML algorithms also cannot work on heterogeneous data. Merging of ML algorithm with some of the existing solutions can enhance the complexity of an algorithm.

FL learns the global model by providing security to the data. But sharing updates in training process will some times lead to the leakage of data. FL implements some methods to ensure privacy in ML models.

Differential Privacy: DP defines the information about the data that is available for the analysis of a third party. Information can be grouped as general information and personal private data.

Table 3: Data processing tasks in ML algorithms.

Support Vector Machine	• Regression/classification
Random Forest	• Regression/classification
Linear Regression	• Regression
Naïve Bayes	• Classification
K-Means	• Clustering
K-Nearest Neighbour	• classification
Classification and regression tree	• Regression/classification

DP framework provides privacy for the personal data with some of its features [29].

Homomorphic encryption: In this kind of encryption the computation is done in such a way that the hacker cannot find the original information.

Secure multiparty computation: Multiple parties combine and compute without loss of any data to third parties [30].

B. Deep Learning in IOT

In recent times the combination of DL models with IOT devices has become very popular which provides real time analytics with limited resources. DL computations are too costly and that is why we decentralize the DL model. Deep Learning is implemented through federated Learning in IOT. FDL (Federated Deep Learning) model [31] is implemented in IOT. The Federated Deep Learning Model will follow some aspects of Edge Computing (EC) like decreasing the computational complexities, improving the privacy and security. FDL provides an architecture that increases the value of applying DL (Deep Learning) to the edge and end devices.

FDL MODEL: The FDL model follows the Federated transfer learning where the Deep Learning network (DLN) is copied to fit the user specific goals. Later, once the DLN is trained, FDL will follow the Horizontal Federated Learning model.

FDL Communication and Networking: FDL is built for a company's private use. It combines two types of communications like an Intra Communication Channel and Inter Communication Channel. In the Intra Communication Channel each tier will communicate with other tiers. In the Inter Communication Channel each layer communicates with other layers. Inter Communication Channel is done in three different ways namely edge inter communication, cloud inter communication and IOT inter communication [32].

FDL Privacy and security: FDL builds models that do not reveal information. The security mechanism sometimes may delay responses and the privacy is a very computationally intensive task.

FDL Optimization techniques: The computational capabilities are limited and the memory is limited within the IOT. So hardware optimization is necessary. FPGA and Google's Tensor processing unit (TPU) are two DL devices that perform the optimization.

C. Block Chain in IOT using FL

The machine learning algorithms are conducted on the centralized data center. However, data may be sensitive and the data owners might be unwilling to share their data, thus collecting data is a tough job that obstructs the process of Machine learning. To avoid a problem like data deficiency, decentralized machine learning called Federated Learning is proposed. In FL data is distributed among different users. FL communicates the combined updates to the global model. Security issues might arise while sending the updates to the global model. To overcome these security issues a block chain concept is introduced.

Researchers in [33] investigated some security concerns in block, node and model. These are designed using blockchain in FL. Blockchain implements consensus for each and every block which is time consuming. So it is important to reduce the cost. Nodes security in blockchain is implemented using the chain of nodes. Whenever there is an update in the parameters or the model is modified nodes are created. Each node is validated if it is a danger or not. The model constructed on the centralized server can be hacked by an unauthorized person. So the model should be preserved both locally and globally [34].

The Blockchain in FL will work in such a way that devices train the model with local data. All the local updates are sent to the edge node where they are combined. Edge nodes in turn send the aggregated updates to the fog nodes. All the updates are converted to block which is validated using a smart contract. The verified block is combined with one chain which is tamper proof and secured. All the local updates are sent to the centralized server to train the global model. Table 4 specifies the differences between FML and FDL.

Table 4: Differences between Machine Learning and Deep Learning.

Features	Federated Machine Learning	Federated Deep Learning
Communication	Channel Based Communication	Hierarchical Communication
Privacy	Less Privacy	More Privacy
Devices connected to cloud	Devices are directly connected to cloud	Edges devices act as buffer between IOT and cloud
Model access	Private Model access	Public model access
Data control	Centralized data control	Decentralized data control
Optimization	required	Not required

5. Applications

A. Federated Learning in Applications of IOT

Federated learning is one of the categories of distributed machine learning which can train large amounts of decentralized data. It also preserves the confidentiality of the data. Federated learning has shown great improvement in protecting data privacy and also reduces the traffic in the network.

(1) Smart City Sensing

Smart city sensing is an emerging paradigm to facilitate the transition into a smart city. IOT helps in the acquisition of large amounts of data which can be used to train the AI models that are beneficial to the smart services in a society. Centralized machine learning models entail some security and privacy concerns. To overcome these challenges Federated learning serves as a solution which can address the security and privacy concerns. A few federated learning applications that contribute to smart city sensing are federated visual security sensing, Federated autonomous vehicles and federated aided diagnosis. Federated visual security sensing: Traditionally the security in a city relies on the security cameras, monitoring rooms and security personnel. This method is labor-intensive and inefficient because the data collected from various sources is not used together to detect the possible threats. An AI-based model can be used to improve the community safety and community management efficiency. Federated learning can be established to train multi-community data for security models while preserving their privacy [5].

The major challenges and issues in incorporating federated learning in smart sensing are energy consumption, adversial attack and data distribution.

FL implementation in smart cities sensing will consume much more of the user's battery. Several solutions for this problems have been proposed like energy consumption threshold, optimize learning performance. In various research papers the energy consumption is optimized using different techniques based on the communication time and selection of computational parameters and also adaptive methods are also implemented. Also the adaption of mobile crowd sensing methodologies will help in solving this problem. There are different kinds of attacks like poisoning attacks, inference attacks, insider attacks, outsider attacks. Different solutions like Generative Adversarial networks and participant level DP can help protect the users.

(2) Self-Driving Cars

IOT is the major reason behind the fast growing self-driving car industry. Each self-driving car is embedded with hundreds of sensors and all these sensors together generate a large amount of data per second. The data which is collected is used by machine learning algorithms to enable major functions like avoiding any obstacles and any other crucial changes. The self-driving cars need an immediate response in complicated situations. Also the data security is very necessary in the case of these self-driving cars to secure the sensitive information of the users. Federated Machine learning trains the AI models very efficiently and securely.

A large amount of data is generated from various sensors like RADAR and LIDAR, proximity and temperature sensors in self-driving cars. Machine learning algorithms have been developed to learn from sensor measurements as they have low computational complexities. The ML in vehicular networks works on the centralized algorithms like a neural network that trains a massive dataset which is collected from the vehicles. This NN model provides the mapping between the input which is the vehicle sensor data and the output which are the labels of the sensor data. In this case the transmission of data is said to be too costly. Federated learning has been recently introduced which will not involve the transmission of the whole dataset. FL is considered to be a promising model to train the dataset without losing privacy. Using FL in vehicular networks faces many challenges like data diversity, labeling, efficient model training, transmission overhead, delay, security and privacy, scheduling and resource management.

(3) Unmanned Aerial Vehicles in smart agriculture

UAVs are used in different fields like the delivery of the cargo, traffic monitoring and in many civilian and commercial domains. These UAVs have a combination of wireless connectivity with integrated intelligence that gives support to the

Figure 5: Applications of FL in IOT.

IOT applications. AI tasks in these UAV networks will sometimes lead to the communication and also a network delay because there will be constant communications going on between the cloud centers in remote places. Federated Machine learning reduces these delays in the network by training the AI models across the UAVs [35]. There are different types of UAVs like multi rotor UAVs, Fixed wing UAVs, single Rotor UAVs, Hybrid vertical Take-off and Landing. Multi rotor UAV is used for aerial surveillance, photography, fixed wing UAVs are ideal for long distance operations, and single rotor UAVs are very similar to helicopters. UAVs have many challenges for example, a short remote range, achieving higher-data rates for dynamic storage of data, Interference, UAV technology Acceptance.

(4) Healthcare

Machine learning proved to be of a very high potential in increasing the quality of the health care industry; it has developed many fields in health care such as in generating diagnostic tools and estimating disease risk. The healthcare data is considered to be very sensitive. The federated machine learning has proved to be efficient mechanism or the strategy to improve the healthcare unit by preserving the data. The locally stored information is encrypted before being transferred. Federated Learning holds great promises on healthcare data analytics for both the provider and the consumer. It also protects the patients privacy [39].

(5) Robotics

The combination of the robotics and the IOT is IoRT. These IoRT has vast applications in manufacturing industries, agriculture and in industrial IOT. They need to collect information from the surroundings and react immediately to the required changes. Federated machine learning understands the computational capabilities and achieves the intelligence [38].

(6) Supply Chain Finance

Supply chain finance combined with machine learning and IOT will enable the flow of the information throughout the supply chain. It reduces the gas between the buyers and the suppliers. The data from the industries in the supply chain systems is to be sent to the different business entities. The major interests of the business entities which are highly sensitive are more prone to the security issues in distributed systems. Federated machine learning gives new methods to prevent data leakage and also reduces the risks of performance and credit for the supply chain finance [36].

6. Challenges and Solutions

The research challenges in IOT are divided into different categories like design, scientific or engineering, and management. Security or privacy challenges arise in both the design and operational stages. The key issues faced in IOT as discussed in [43] are:

- Privacy and data protection;
- Global misinformation systems;
- Big data problems;
- Public attitudes, opinions and behavior;
- Tightly coupled systems;
- Quality of service issues;
- New forms of risk; and
- Linking the IOT to work on responsible innovation.

The following are the key research directions in the area of IOT:

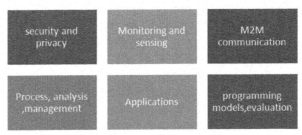

Figure 6: Overview of IOT research areas.

Though Federated learning provides much potential for the IOT, it also faces a number of challenges like imbalanced data, limited battery power and heterogeneous computational capabilities.

Federated Learning Challenges in Smart City Sensing

Smart city sensing is classified as dedicated and non-dedicated sensing where dedicated sensing is the traditional way of gathering the data from the sensors which are fixed in a specific range. Non-dedicated sensing is mobile crowd sensing which uses the sensors present in the smart devices of the users. Mobile crowd sensing is more prevalent because of some of the advantages like flexible coverage areas and low cost overheads. There are other issues like data trustworthiness, user incentives, data quality management, node deployment, energy consumption, user privacy protection. Data trustworthiness deals with the truthfulness of the crowd-sensed data. The data authentication is made by some cryptographic technologies such as digital signatures, message authentication code and biometrics. In order for users to participate in crowd sensing and data gathering the user needs to pay for some incentives. The data gathered from the crowd sensing should be checked for inaccuracy and unreliability using data quality management. While sensing the data in a crowd a large amount of energy is consumed which can be solved by wireless communication methods. Preserving the users personal data is very important [5].

Federated learning also faces different challenges like statistical challenges, communication efficiency, client selection and scheduling, security concerns, privacy challenges, service pricing. We mainly discuss the security concerns and privacy challenges. Federated learning is more targeted to attacks which are classified into targeted attacks and untargeted attacks. Untargeted attacks cause some failure in the training process whereas targeted attacks have clear objectives. Byzantine attack is an untargeted attack which seeks to degrade the performance at the training level and there are various approaches to tackle them like security analysis, statistics and auto encoders. Targeted attacks seek to change the behavior of training model for a particular data instance. The two approaches to encounter these attacks are security analysis and statistics [44].

Communication Challenge

Federated learning goes through large number of iterations for communication as the need for the update parameters is necessary. The local models are update through so many iterations, so the communication overload in federated learning is more. The high rate of communication creates network congestion and due to which the network becomes very slow. This communication challenge is tackled with a scheme based on AirComp which follows the wireless technologies.

Data Skewing and Data Imbalance

Data skewing is also another major problem faced with the federated learning in IOT. Data skewing is due to reasons like data imbalance, missing classes, missing features and missing values.

Data imbalance can happen when one or more entities have less data, i.e., class A has thousands of data and its partner has far less data. Federated learning is very poor in handling this because of data imbalance [38].

Missing classes can happen when one or both the entities have training data but that class is not present in others entity data.

Missing features and missing values are also one of the causes of the data skewing which is one of the biggest challenges in the federated learning in IOT.

There are also other problems along with the above mentioned challenges like systems heterogeneity, privacy, etc.

Device and Model Heterogeneity

There are large numbers of different hardware involved in IOT applications. These different types of hardware lead to device heterogeneity resulting in high communication cost. Sometimes the IOT devices take a longer time for responding.

Solution: In the federated learning each of the local models have to be gathered or aggregated to form a global model. Each local model is different and the local models may not be shared due to privacy issues.

Interoperability

IOT systems are comprised of multiple systems like machines, sensor, robots, wearable, actuators which need to be integrated as a whole system which is a challenging system.

Solution: The developers need to concentrate more on the resource sharing techniques, synchronizing techniques, data sharing techniques.

Data Leakage
The data that is generated by the smart devices is very sensitive and very confidential. Data leakage as shown in [50–54] is one of the most important obstacles in the distributed networks. Researchers have to majorly focus on the data loss issues.

Solution: Combining the FL and blockchain can improve the data management conditions. The blockchain environment will preserve the data leakages and prevents the data breaches.

Data Privacy
The problems regarding the data privacy of the user is the major concern for the complete adoption of the IOT. A lot of work is being done to ensure that IOT is defining the privacy issues like increasing the surveillance and tracking.

Solution: Several models have been proposed to preserve the privacy of data. They help in preserving the privacy of the user data.

Data Management
Data management is one of the more important aspects of the Internet of Things. In the Internet of Things the objects are connected and every object exchanges the data with all types of information. The volume of the data generated and the processes which are involved in handling those data is considered to be very crucial.

7. Conclusion

FL and IOT integration is surveyed and various approaches and techniques related to FL and IOT integration are introduced. We also highlighted the characteristics of IOT in terms of FL and distributive learning. We discussed the motivations behind integrating FL and IOT. We also summarized the details about the ML, DL and blockchain models for privacy preservation in IOT. Applications of FL in IOT and challenges and solutions are summarized in the above work. We have also specified the future works in the path of FL and IOT.

In future, researchers can try to develop algorithms which impose the privacy constraints on the data that will be shared to the global servers. Also the algorithms to reduce the communication cost on the edge device without exploiting the sensitive information of the user can be developed.

References

[1]   F. Jindal, R. Jamar, and P. Churi. Future and challenges of internet of things. *Int. J. Comput. Sci. Inf. Technol.*, 10.2: 13–25, 2018.
[2]   Abdur Razzaq, Mirza, Habib, Sajid, Ali, Muhammad, and Ullah, Saleem. Security issues in the Internet of Things (IoT): A comprehensive study. *International Journal of Advanced Computer Science and Applications*, 8.6: 383, 2017.
[3]   D. Andročec, and N. Vrček. Machine learning for the internet of things security: a systematic. *13th International Conference on Software Technologies.* https://doi. org/10.5220/0006841205970604, 2018.

[4] M. Parimala, P. Swarna, Q.-V. Pham, K. Dev, P. Reddy, T. Gadekallu, and H.-T. Thien. Fusion of Federated Learning and Industrial Internet of Things: A Survey, 2021.

[5] J.C. Jiang, B. Kantarci, S. Oktug, and T. Soyata. Federated learning in smart city sensing: challenges and opportunities. *Sensors*, 20(21): 6230, 2020.

[6] T.D. Nguyen, S. Marchal, M. Miettinen, H. Fereidooni, N. Asokan, and A.R. Sadeghi. DÏoT: A federated self-learning anomaly detection system for IoT. *In 2019 IEEE 39th International Conference on Distributed Computing Systems (ICDCS)* July, 2019, pp. 756–767. IEEE.

[7] Z.H. Ali, H.A. Ali, and M.M. Badawy. Internet of Things (IoT): Definitions, challenges and recent research directions. *International Journal of Computer Applications*, 128(1): 37–47, 2015.

[8] V. Sharma, and R. Tiwari. A review paper on "IOT" & It's Smart Applications. *International Journal of Science, Engineering and Technology Research (IJSETR)*, 5(2): 472–776, 2016.

[9] A. Tiwary, M. Mahato, A. Chidar, M.K. Chandrol, M. Shrivastava, and M. Tripathi. Internet of Things (IoT): Research, architectures and applications. *International Journal on Future Revolution in Computer Science & Communication Engineering*, 4(3): 23–27, 2018.

[10] T.S. Bharati. Internet of Things (IOT): A critical Review. *International Journal of Scientific & Technology*, 2019.

[11] L.A. Tawalbeh, F. Muheidat, M. Tawalbeh and M. Quwaider. IoT Privacy and security: Challenges and solutions. *Applied Sciences*, 10(12): 4102, 2020.

[12] L.U. Khan, S.R. Pandey, N.H. Tran, W. Saad, Z. Han, M.N. Nguyen and C.S. Hong. Federated learning for edge networks: Resource optimization and incentive mechanism. *IEEE Communications Magazine*, 58(10): 88–93, 2020.

[13] M. Aledhari, R. Razzak, R. Parizi, F. Saeed. Federated learning: a survey on enabling technologies, protocols, and applications. *IEEE Access*, 8: 1–1, 2020. 10.1109/ACCESS.2020.3013541.

[14] Q. Yang, Y. Liu, T. Chen, and Y. Tong. Federated machine learning: Concept and applications. *ACM Transactions on Intelligent Systems and Technology (TIST)*, 10(2): 1–19, 2019.

[15] J. Konečný, H.B. McMahan, F.X. Yu, P. Richtárik, A.T. Suresh, and D. Bacon. Federated learning: Strategies for improving communication efficiency, 2016. *arXiv preprint arXiv:1610.05492*.

[16] K. Chandiramani, D. Garg, and N. Maheswari. Performance analysis of distributed and federated learning models on private data. *Procedia Computer Science*, 165: 349–355, 2019.

[17] S.K. Lo, Q. Lu, C. Wang, H. Paik, and L. Zhu. A systematic literature review on federated machine learning: from a software engineering perspective, 2020. *arXiv preprint arXiv:2007.11354*.

[18] J.C. Jiang, B. Kantarci, S. Oktug, and T. Soyata. Federated learning in smart city sensing: challenges and opportunities. *Sensors*, 20(21): 6230, 2020.

[19] Z. Li, V. Sharma, and S.P. Mohanty. Preserving data privacy via federated learning: Challenges and solutions. *IEEE Consumer Electronics Magazine*, 9(3): 8–16, 2020.

[20] Q. Wu, K. He, and X. Chen. Personalized federated learning for intelligent IoT applications: A cloud-edge based framework. *IEEE Open Journal of the Computer Society*, 1: 35–44, 2020.

[21] R. Hassan, F. Qamar, M.K. Hasan, A.H.M. Aman, and A.S. Ahmed. Internet of things and its applications: A comprehensive survey. *Symmetry*, 12(10): 1674, 2020.

[22] A.H. Hussein. Internet of Things (IOT): Research challenges and future applications. *International Journal of Advanced Computer Science and Applications*, 10(6): 77–82, 2019.

[23] D. Peteiro-Barral, and B. Guijarro-Berdiñas. A survey of methods for distributed machine learning. *Progress in Artificial Intelligence*, 2(1): 1–11, 2013.

[24] J. Verbraeken, M. Wolting, J. Katzy, J. Kloppenburg, T. Verbelen, and J.S. Rellermeyer. A survey on distributed machine learning. *ACM Computing Surveys (CSUR)*, 53(2): 1–33, 2020.

[25] S. Victor, and S. Hart. Distributed learning: a flexible learning and development model. *In E-Learn: World Conference on E-Learning in Corporate, Government, Healthcare, and Higher Education* November, pp. 281–290. Association for the Advancement of Computing in Education (AACE), 2016.

[26] F. Sattler, S. Wiedemann, K.R. Müller, and W. Samek. Robust and communication-efficient federated learning from non-iid data. *IEEE Transactions on Neural Networks and Learning Systems*, 31(9): 3400–3413, 2019.

[27] F. Hussain, R. Hussain, S.A. Hassan, and E. Hossain. Machine learning in IoT security: Current solutions and future challenges. *IEEE Communications Surveys & Tutorials*, 22(3): 1686–1721, 2020.

[28] Zhan, Y., P. Li, Z. Qu, D. Zeng, and S. Guo. A learning-based incentive mechanism for federated learning. *IEEE Internet of Things Journal*, 7(7): 6360–6368, 2020.

[29] P.C.M. Arachchige, P. Bertok, I. Khalil, D. Liu,S. Camtepe, and M. Atiquzzaman. A trustworthy privacy preserving framework for machine learning in industrial iot systems. *IEEE Transactions on Industrial Informatics*, 16(9): 6092–6102, 2020.

[30] G. Raja, Y. Manaswini, G.D. Vivekanandan, H. Sampath, K. Dev, and A.K. Bashir. AI-powered blockchain-a decentralized secure multiparty computation protocol for IoV. *In IEEE INFOCOM 2020-IEEE Conference on Computer Communications Workshops (INFOCOM WKSHPS)* (pp. 865–870). July, 2020, IEEE.

[31] S. Elnagar, and M.A. Thomas. Federated Deep Learning: A Conceptual Model and Applied Framework for Industry 4.0, 2020.

[32] D. Vasan, M. Alazab, S. Wassan, H. Naeem, B. Safaei, and Q. Zheng. IMCFN: Image-based malware classification using fine-tuned convolutional neural network architecture. *Computer Networks*, 171: 107138, 2020.

[33] C. Rupa, G. Srivastava, T.R. Gadekallu, P.K.R. Maddikunta, and S. Bhattacharya. A blockchain based cloud integrated IoT architecture using a hybrid design. *In International Conference on Collaborative Computing: Networking, Applications and Worksharing* (pp. 550–559). Springer, Cham, October, 2020.

[34] N. Deepa, Q.V. Pham, D.C. Nguyen, S. Bhattacharya, T.R. Gadekallu, P.K.R. Maddikunta, F. Fang, and P.N. Pathirana. A survey on blockchain for big data: Approaches, opportunities, and future directions. 2020, *arXiv preprint arXiv:2009.00858*.

[35] P.K.R. Maddikunta, S. Hakak, M. Alazab, S. Bhattacharya, T.R. Gadekallu, W.Z. Khan, and P.V. Pham. Unmanned aerial vehicles in smart agriculture: applications, requirements, and challenges. *IEEE Sensors Journal*, 2021.

[36] K. Yang, Y. Shi, Y. Zhou, Z. Yang, L. Fu, and W. Chen. Federated machine learning for intelligent IoT via reconfigurable intelligent surface. *IEEE Network*, 34(5): 16–22, 2020.

[37] P.V. Pham, S. Mirjalili, N. Kumar, M. Alazab, W.J. Hwang. Whale optimization algorithm with applications to resource allocation in wireless networks. *IEEE Transactions on Vehicular Technology*, 69(4): 4285–4297, 2020.

[38] R. Kumar, P. Kumar, R. Tripathi, G.P. Gupta, T.R. Gadekallu, and G. Srivastava. SP2F: A secured privacy-preserving framework for smart agricultural Unmanned Aerial Vehicles. *Computer Networks*, 187: 107819, 2021.

[39] J. Xu, B.S. Glicksberg, C. Su, P. Walker, J. Bian, and F. Wang. Federated learning for healthcare informatics. *J. Healthc. Inform. Res.*, 5: 1–19, 2021. https://doi.org/10.1007/s41666-020-00082-4.

[40] D.P. Acharjya and A.P. Kauser. A survey on big data analytics: Challenges, open research issues and tools. *International Journal of Advanced Computer Science and Applications(IJACSA)*, 7(2), 2016. http://dx.doi.org/10.14569/IJACSA.2016.070267.

[41] I.A. Ajah, H.F. Nweke. Big data and business analytics: Trends, platforms, success factors and applications. *Big Data Cogn. Comput.*, 3: 32, 2019. https://doi.org/10.3390/bdcc3020032.

[42] S. Venkatraman, and R. Venkatraman. Big data security challenges and strategies[J]. *AIMS Mathematics*, 4(3): 860–879, 2019. doi: 10.3934/math.2019.3.860.

[43] P. Ryan and R. Watson. Research challenges for the internet of things: What role can or play? *Systems*, 5: 24, 2017. 10.3390/systems5010024.

[44] O. Wahab, A. Mourad, H. Otrok, T. Taleb. Federated machine learning: survey, multi-level classification, desirable criteria and future directions in communication and networking systems. *IEEE Communications Surveys & Tutorials*, 2021, 10.1109/COMST.2021.3058573.

[45] P. Kairouz, H.B. McMahan, B. Avent, A. Bellet, M. Bennis, A. Nitin Bhagoji, K. Bonawitz, Z. Charles, G. Cormode, R. Cummings, R.G.L. D'Oliveira, H. Eichner, S.E. Rouayheb, D. Evans, J. Gardner, Z. Garrett, A. Gascón, B. Ghazi, P.B. Gibbons, M. Gruteser, Z. Harchaoui, C. He, L. He, Z. Huo, B. Hutchinson, J. Hsu, M. Jaggi, T. Javidi, G. Joshi, M. Khodak, J. Konečný, A. Korolova, F. Koushanfar, S. Koyejo, T. Lepoint, Y. Liu, P. Mittal, M. Mohri, R. Nock, A. Özgür, R. Pagh, M. Raykova, H. Qi, D. Ramage, R. Raskar, D. Song, W. Song, S.U. Stich, Z. Sun, A.T. Suresh, F. Tramèr, P. Vepakomma, J. Wang, L. Xiong, Z. Xu, Q. Yang, F.X. Yu, H. Yu, and S. Zhao. Advances and open problems in federated learning. *ArXiv* abs/1912.04977 (2019): n. pag.

[46] F.M. Awaysheh, M. Alazab, M. Gupta, T.F. Pena, and J.C. Cabaleiro. Next-generation big data federation access control: a reference model. *Future Gener. Comput. Syst.*, 108: 726–741, 2020.

[47] M. Gupta, F. Patwa, and R. Sandhu. POSTER: access control model for the hadoop ecosystem. *In Proceedings of the 22nd ACM on Symposium on Access Control Models and Technologies*, pp. 125–127, 2017.

[48] M. Gupta, J. Benson, F. Patwa, and R. Sandhu. Secure V2V and V2I communication in intelligent transportation using cloudlets. IEEE Transactions on Services Computing, 2020.

[49] M. Gupta, and R. Sandhu. Authorization framework for secure cloud assisted connected cars and vehicular internet of things. *In Proceedings of the 23nd ACM on Symposium on Access Control Models and Technologies*, pp. 193–204, 2018.

[50] M. Gupta, F. Patwa, and R. Sandhu. Object-tagged RBAC model for the Hadoop ecosystem. *In IFIP Annual Conference on Data and Applications Security and Privacy*, pp. 63–81. Springer, Cham, 2017.

[51] M. Gupta, F. Patwa, J. Benson, and R. Sandhu. Multi-layer authorization framework for a representative Hadoop ecosystem deployment. *In Proceedings of the 22nd ACM on Symposium on Access Control Models and Technologies*, pp. 183–190, 2017.

[52] M. Gupta, J. Benson, F. Patwa, and R. Sandhu. Dynamic groups and attribute-based access control for next-generation smart cars. *In Proceedings of the Ninth ACM Conference on Data and Application Security and Privacy*, pp. 61–72, 2019.

[53] M. Gupta, M. Abdelsalam, S. Khorsandroo, and S. Mittal. Security and privacy in smart farming: Challenges and opportunities. IEEE Access, 8: 34564–34584, 2020.

[54] D. Gupta, S. Bhatt, M. Gupta, O. Kayode, and A.S. Tosun. Access control model for google cloud iot. *In 2020 IEEE 6th Intl Conference on Big Data Security on Cloud (BigDataSecurity), IEEE Intl Conference on High Performance and Smart Computing, (HPSC) and IEEE Intl Conference on Intelligent Data and Security (IDS)*, pp. 198–208. IEEE, 2020.

3

From the Cloud to the Edge
Towards a Distributed and Light Weight Secure Big Data Pipelines for IoT Applications

Feras M Awaysheh

ABSTRACT

Part of the broader development of Internet-of-Things (IoT) architecture for intelligent environments is the developing of sophisticated Edge communications that support the modern requirements of IoT-to-Cloud connectivity. Big Data (BD) and Cloud computing represent a practical and cost-effective solution for supporting IoT operations and advanced analytics. Such a vision involves developing data pipelines, facilitating BD flow from the network's edge (e.g., sensors, actors, etc.) to the cloud data warehouse. However, security is always a concern among practitioners and developers alike. There are vital factors relating to performance impacts and security vulnerabilities that may emerge during the increased deployment of such a system. Highly secure integration of BD pipelines is a cornerstone in our ability to exploit modern IoT-to-Cloud applications. Given the high impact of BD pipelines security measurements on the system performance, it was not a subject of intensive analysis in the literature.

In this study, we analyze the building blocks that support data pipelines as a commodity service for IoT-to-Cloud applications to address the previous research gap. A structured multi-layer security pattern method supporting Edge/Cloud architectures is presented. Data confidentiality was investigated in the complete data pipeline life cycle, i.e., allocation, transmission, and storage. Our study carried the examination of access control, wire encryption, and at-rest data encryption techniques impact on the overall performance. The analysis guides potential large-scale data analytics to model their infrastructure in a secure context using an integrated scheme, technologies, and frameworks. It also highlights a timely demand for lightweight security

Data Systems Group, University of Tartu, Tartu, Estonia.
Email: feras.awaysheh@ut.ee

approaches that supports the widespread of BD pipelines. Our findings point out the critical need for future research in Edge Intelligence and Artificial Intelligence IoT (AIoT) for sustainable Edge integration in the Cloud. Finally, this study is bridging a knowledge gap between the existing BD pipeline security approaches and problems related to security impact on large-scale edge data processing performance, emphasizing the necessity of lightweight security techniques toward achieving this vision.

1. Introduction

Recently, technological advancements have led to a unique communication paradigm that connects different smart objects, at anytime and anyplace together, by embedding a microcontroller chip to the Internet-of-Things (sensors, mobile, smartwatch, etc.) [1]. This progression gives them the ability to sense specific parameters from the surrounding environment. Accordingly, communication channels (i.e., data pipelines) are established through the internet to transmit the collected data and interact with it [2]. The number of these devices and smart objects is expected to increase daily [3, 4]. This tremendous boost implies that IoT-based systems will be involved in all aspects of our lives. However, this brings more challenges to the deployment and management of such deployment architectures [5]. First, unlike cloud computing, the deployment landscape is no longer flat. Instead, we can view the deployment landscape as a hierarchy (see Figure 1). At the top level, cloud servers are hosted with virtually unlimited capabilities. Fog servers are hosted on intermediate levels. They can be of geographical proximity to the data and hosted on multiple layers on their own. At the bottom layer, edge devices are the closest to the data sources.

The proliferation of IoT devices leads to the generation of a considerable heterogeneous amount of data. The allocated data must materialize in storage (e.g., the cloud), remotely accessible for processing [6]. Consequently, these data can serve business intelligence and applications within various domains [7]. These domains include, but are not limited to, healthcare, education, smart cities, and transportation systems, among many other fields [8]. However, data should be located and

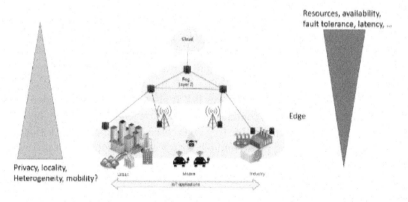

Figure 1: Deployment hierarchy for IoT Applications.

transmitted securely through the whole life-cycle to guarantee such deployment architecture's high data privacy.

In this chapter, the realization of secure data pipelines and the Edge-to-Cloud data transmission security challenges are investigated. A secure data pipeline for modern IoT applications is introduced. We propose a secure architectural pattern for supporting the implementation of the IoT data pipeline as a commodity service for data scientists in three tires. Namely, IoT tire (nodes at the edge of the network), IoT-to-Cloud communication channels, and centralized cloud storage. Such security measurement performance on data processing is experimentally analyzed, emphasizing the light-weight security models' importance. Furthermore, we provide various insights into the latest ongoing developments and open challenges in this domain. The question we are addressing regarding the data flow in IoT-to-Cloud communication is as follows: *how to set up a modern, efficient, and reusable security architecture for IoT applications and frameworks in Edge-to-Cloud deployment models?*

This work contributes to the adoption of a secure data pipeline as a scalable data transmission environment for IoT applications by:

- Propose a modern and secure IoT-to-Cloud architecture of the state of the art frameworks from the BD and cloud computing realm.

- Provide an experimental evaluation and an in-depth analysis of the performance impact of the proposed architecture's security measurements.

- Draft the best practices and performance improvements for the sustainability of security cloud-IoT integration.

The remainder of this chapter is organized as follows. Section 2 introduces our proposed data pipeline and the security pattern analysis. The experimental analysis of our results takes place in Section 3. Section 4 discusses the study findings, future trends, and open challenges in the IoT era. Finally, we conclude in Section 5.

2. Security Pattern Analysis

In general, an architecture pattern is a standard design of a highly cohesive but loosely-coupled components (frameworks, subsystem, etc.) that addresses a common issue. It forms a technical foundation for a practical solution of different implementations within a given context of the same paradigm (i.e., the same environment variables). For instance, an IoT architecture pattern may be utilized by health care, connected vehicles, smart cities, and other IoT applications of a typical challenge (e.g., security) and reference architectures [9]. It also serves as a knowledge capture of the optimal solution, which contains solution knowledge (e.g., mapping current technologies) and domain knowledge (e.g., use cases and scenarios). Also, it covers the transfer of the modelling phase into the design and development of that optimal solution.

This research employs the architecture patterns concept to manifest the imposed security challenges of converging IoT and big data analytics over cloud computing. It next intensively evaluate and analyze these challenges and their impact on

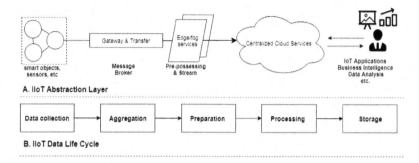

A. IIoT Abstraction Layer

B. IIoT Data Life Cycle

Figure 2: High-level design of the IoT-to-cloud data communication. Functionalities as a rectangle and data flows with arrows.

the system performance. These experiments introduce the broad-scope of security measurements to facilitate the development process by proposing the best practices. Figure 2 is a structural description of our architectural pattern promoting the main layers and elements, including their environment for a general and reusable solution of the IoT Cloud-based paradigm. The proposed architectural pattern is a conceptual implementation that delineates the essential aspects of a IoT architecture, e.g., data streaming feedback [10]. This model aims at guiding different solutions using the same pattern and share the related characteristics for the efficiency of secure data pipelines deployment for IoT applications.

The abstracted design of the IoT-to-cloud data pipeline in Figure 2A, outlines a data communication architecture with the primary architectural components, where data flows from left to right of the tiered spectrum. In general, a typical data hierarchy deployment within IoT has at least four access layers. Namely, (i) device layer (mash networked) comprises embedded systems, sensors and actuators at the edge of the network. (ii) The network layer comprises data transfer and aggregation from the mash network to the upper layers. (iii) The service layer contains the required software middleware sitting between processing/communication hardware and IoT applications providing a rich set of functions needed by many IoT applications. It also provides some pre-processing features as data cleaning, tagging, and carrying data to the cloud. Finally, (iv) the application layer where different IoT applications occur to deliver specific services to the end-users. Figure 2B represents, from the Data life cycle development, the abstracted communication layers of IoT-to-Cloud data pipeline. The proposed architecture involves data collection (a.k.a, data allocation) from different smart objects, Data aggregation in a summarized form to decrease the number of transmissions among objects, data preparation including data cleaning and labelling, data processing at the decentralized edge or centralized cloud, and data storage (data on halt) stage.

The proposed security pattern in Figure 3 is a multi-tier IoT-to-Cloud deployment model. Its components are tailored explicitly with high-security design requirements in mind. This model is classified into five domains (i.e., tiers). However, it simplifies the three security domains of security zones. Namely, the network edge, consisting of intelligent and less intelligent things. The transmission media represents the

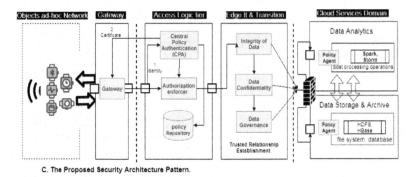

C. The Proposed Security Architecture Pattern.

Figure 3: A multi tier security pattern in IoT-to-Cloud deployment model.

network and transfer protocols. And the centralized cloud backend processing and storage capacities. Data pipelines usually serve geographically separated regions, where each area has multiple isolated locations, known as availability zones. The availability zones are structured through a set of correlated domains abstracted from the IoT scenario but independent of any particular technology or implementation. These zones are categorized into several security levels of abstraction, realizing a hierarchical structure domain.

A network segmented with a different security domain meant to keep separation (using encryption and access control) of functionalities. This separation in the access logic tire improves the isolation of edge operations and maintains integrity, confidentiality, and governance. Besides, helping with advanced audibility capabilities. The edge and transition tier function includes providing secure paths to transmit data between multiple security domains (sub-networks) and edge IT. In general, IoT applications and architectures yield advanced operations closer to the data source by harnessing machine intelligence's empowered abilities. This scenario relies on using different AI systems to support IoT and Edge-to-Cloud activities. Such a scenario is expected to have a direct reflection on the industrial IoT and its applications. These applications include but are not limited to healthcare, vehicular, and mobile IoT deployment models. Next to that is the centralized cloud tier of computation and storage capacities. The function of this tier includes hosting IoT applications that are critical in providing end-to-end services. Security services in the internal cloud communication must ensure the IoT application security against any threat.

Tier-One. Gateway access deals with the basic set of external entities (physical smart devices like sensors) identification and network access. These devices can communicate with each other and other devices using various communication technologies, e.g., Bluetooth or WiFi.

Tier-Two. Access logic discussion (assign authorization): The entitytID is passed to the policy authentication, exposes policies and validates to contact internal services, and issue a session. If successful, it responds with a certificate and establishes a session. This certificate contains the entityID and a copy of the session key, which is then used to communicate with the authorized cluster components.

Tier-Three. A trust relationship is the core of the security establishment. This layer requires a robust model that unifies the security mechanism of different dimensions, i.e., the security trio of integrity, confidentiality, and governance. A high-level data access layer may be connected to that trio, in which access calls require an authorized session. This session is connected to a particular policy agent that provides access control with a means for detecting unauthorized operations. The data and call traffic may remain behind a firewall in the fifth-tier. This way allows the edge to connect to several buses as a transceiver that provides an additional security layer.

Tier-Four. Low-level data access specifies each entity's roles within this tier (associated with the previous stage). This phase includes granting access (e.g., submitting jobs or querying status) with fine-grain control, i.e., which database, columns, queues, etc., over the specific data blocks within the shared data repository. Edge IT systems' location is close to the sensors and actuators in the building of an IoT architecture, end-to-end wire encryption is crucial.

Tier-Five. High-level data access gives the final level of granularity by designating the authorized entity (could be a private list of the previous tier) to contact the cloud services and cloud storage. This tier establishes the session to enable private services or classified data.

In the component diagram in Figure 3, the gateway is normalizing the authentication process by abstracting the ticket (access certification) exchange of different components. This capability results in a universal authentication platform that scales the access control process in a multi-tier architecture. Both Ranger and Knox daemons may represent access control. The gateway contacts the central policy authentication to validate the session and set up their access level. A different access level may attach to different data pipelines.

Meanwhile, the metadata manages their data in tier-4, which requires a high-level data access session. Without the access certificates, each entity would need to authenticate and authorize with other entities on its own. In contrast, by employing the SITS components, it only needs to combine a central authority that issues an access certificate (based on admin policies) that applies to every entity within variant access tiers.

3. Experimental Analysis

This section introduces the experiment results to validate the study claims on the necessity of modern security solutions for the Edge architecture supporting IoT applications. For that, we demonstrate the impact of native architecture (no security) against access control, wire encryption, and at rest encryption.

3.1 Experimental Setup

The proposed architecture in this work compromises the layers. First, an IoT environment with dynamic resource allocation (i.e., number of participated nodes vary in a time unite) as Edge architecture. Second, a network carries to simulate a data transfer from the Edge to the cloud using IoT data protocols, e.g., MQTT. A centralized cloud as back end storage for the data. For the implementation, we create a simulated IoT environment using Docker containers where the number of active containers changes randomly every two minutes. The containers run a python script

Figure 4: Data confidentiality techniques used in this study.

which publishes MQTT messages using Mosquitto message broker that implements the MQTT protocol versions 5.0 to send loop traffic to the cloud. Third, the cloud environment was deployed over AWS IaaS by configuring the WebHDFS file system. To validate the study claims, we test three security layers that represent the critical threat in each of the previous layers. In particular, we compare the results of native operations (with no security measurements) against operations with access control, wire encryption with Transport Layer Security (TLS), at-rest encryption with Transparent Data Encryption (TDE) as showen in Figure 4.

3.2 Experimental Results

This section reflects on this study's experiments' main findings concerning traditional security measurements on BD performance over the data confidential three layers of security.

3.2.1 Access Control Impact

Privacy and security on IoT-to-Cloud architectures remain significant concerns among practitioners in both industry and academia [11, 12]. Selectively controlling access to the data, and edge resource using the restriction of authentications and authorizations is critical in the architecture security [13]. Aiming to analyze the impact of adding an access control layer to the performance, we perform read/write calls from an edge node into a WebHDFS in the cloud. Figures 5 and 6 discuss our findings with the WebHDFS results using Apache Knox as a reverse proxy authentication for distributed access control. Our experiment (Tables 1 and 2) showed the performance degradation using traditional access control methods on IoT-to-Cloud data flow. This complexity resulted in a performance bottleneck, and light approaches are required. Decentralized identity for Edge computing using blockchain technology seems promising. In such architecture, the blockchain ledger containing six optional components is used to keep the privacy. Figure 7 shows an example of distributed identification policy in a blockchain access control system. The proposed distributed blockchain-based access control includes the ID, public keys list, and authentication for delegating the operation. Also, it includes a list of service for communicating based on the ID. Besides, a timestamp log record of creating and update the system with proof of digital signature for non-repudiation.

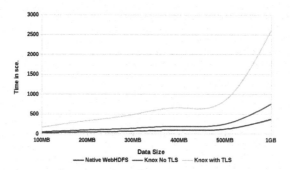

Figure 5: Access control impact on Read operation.

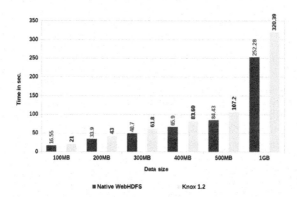

Figure 6: Access control impact on Write operation.

Table 1: Access control impact on Read operation.

	100MB	200MB	300MB	400MB	500MB	1GB	Transfer Speed
Native WebHDFS	23.64	47.45	69.63	94.23	120.62	371	25 MB/s
With Apache Knox	25.07	49.63	72.05	98.1	127.85	392	26 MB/s

Table 2: Access control impact on Write performance.

	100MB	200MB	300MB	400MB	500MB	1GB	Transfer Speed
Native WebHDFS	16.55	33.9	48.7	65.9	84.43	252.28	42 MB/s
Apache Knox 1.2	21	43	61.8	83.69	107.2	320.39	-

Next, we give more insights on the WebHDFS access control primitives, supporting the Cloud storage of the proposed IoT-to-Cloud deployment architecture.

HDFS has supported a permission model that controls distinct user classes with
a restricted list of control roles in the ecosystem services. This way, security is sufficient with different levels of authorization access for each user-class that allow/deny
the service call based on the predefined access levels. HDFS, therefore, enforces permissions during user connection to DNs (e.g., access file system) by the user class

```
{
  "@context": "https://w3id.org/did/v1",
  "id": "did:io:123456789abcdefghij",
  "publicKey": [{
    "id": "did:io:123456789abcdefghij#keys-1",
    "type": "RsaVerificationKey2018",
    "controller": "did:io:123456789abcdefghij",
    "publicKeyPem": "-----BEGIN PUBLIC KEY...END PUBLIC KEY-----\r\n"
  }],
  "authentication": [{
    "type": "RsaSignatureAuthentication2018",
    "publicKey": "did:io:123456789abcdefghij#keys-1"
  }],
  "service": [{
    "id": "did:io:123456789abcdefghij;exam_svc",
    "type": "ExampleService",
    "serviceEndpoint": "https://example.com/endpoint/1576358"
  }],
  "created": "2019-02-08T15:23:42Z",
  "proof": {
    "type": "LinkedDataSignature2015",
    "created": "2019-02-08T15:12:30Z",
    "creator": "did:io:8uQhQMGzWxR8vw5P3UWH1ja#keys-1",
    "signatureValue": "QNB13Y7Q9...1tzjn4w=="
  }
}
```

Figure 7: An example of distributed identification policy in a blockchain access control system.

and then assign roles to secure files and directories. Additionally, HDFS operations rely on checking the user permission of all components of a path, which requires traversal access. Each user service call that reaches HDFS has a two-part identity the user name and groups list.

To allow a service-call, it demands that the owner has the required permissions, which granted by file/job ownership, group membership or other authorities (e.g., ACL). For instance, a file owner (creator by default) service-call will grant an inclusive authorization level of access (read, write, execute) if his UserID matches the owner permissions. Else if the user is not the owner but a member of the groups' list, HDFS checks the authorities of that group as a non-owner class with a limited level of access (could be read-only). If a permissions check fails, the client operation fails as well.

As mentioned earlier, authorization control applies at the whole path components. Hadoop checks permissions hierarchically in HDFS files-level. Further, the path components can describe as (i) Parent: the parent directory of the requested path. (ii) Ancestor: the last existing element of the inquired path. (iii) Final: the final component of the requested path [14]. Meanwhile, directories paths are defined as sub-tree (directory and child sub-directories) path recursively. Changing the data owner requires administration authorization level access. This process can also set to a superuser upon a policy. However, a user may change the group and, still, be the owner of the data, if he is a member of the specified group.

Next, we Define the different user-classes and their roles in a Hadoop cluster:

- User: Regular system client with limited access level, only submit jobs and query results of his data access over a predefined availability zone (NN). The user may belong to one or more groups.

- Superuser/owner: The user who creates the file (upload data) in the cluster and user with an authorization level of access to these files. The superuser may act on behalf of another user by impersonating (based on Kerberos credentials) their ID [15]. In general, many scenarios can be applied in this category. First, Hadoop cluster with a simple authentication policy (without secure mode), in this case, any user logs as a superuser (no IAM required) with a complete access level of authorization. Second, the user registers with the Kerberos authentication protocol in a secure mode. Data owners (the user who submitted the job) hold superuser privileges over their tasks within the cluster (e.g., he may cancel the job). However, the system admins may implement ACL at the authorization level to mitigate the security risks using the POSIX ACL model over both the files and directory using a single API gateway-access for all ecosystem components [14]. Even though, superuser does not control the underlying infrastructure but has limited control (based on the SLA policy) of select networking components (e.g., virtual networks) and configurations.

- `Administrator`: The one who sets the policy for other users of the system. With administrative privileges, the admin has absolute power over the use of the services and components. The Hadoop administrator daily tasks include correctly setting the configuration files, implementing secure ACL and SLA policies, and managing the underlying resources. These underlying capabilities include hardware, network, and runtime environment with arbitrary software that includes operating systems (OS), virtual machines (VM) and containers. Delegations allow the administrator to give another user the ability to perform actions on their behalf.

- `Daemon`: The processes that started under Hadoop and run in the background to be functional. The main Hadoop Yarn and HDFS daemons are Resource-Manager (RM), NodeManager (NM), NameNode (NN), and DataNode (DN). Besides, there can be secondary NameNode, standby NameNode, Job HistoryServer, etc.

Each Hadoop command (operation) can belong to one role of the authorization levels listed in Table 3. For instance, when a user runs `hadoop job -list` it authorizes the connection requests at the READ authorization level. Meanwhile, an attempt with an unauthorized access level, e.g., `hadoop job -kill jobid` that does not belong to job owner (nor he is an admin) will be denied. A complete list of HDFS methods that may categorized based on our classification can be found in [16]. Besides, the relation between different levels of access and user-class in the Apache BD cluster is illustrated in Table 4. It worth it to mention that those roles are not alternatives for the general Hadoop file permission values (read, write, execute). The Role-based access control is well discussed in the leatreature [17, 18]. On the contrary, those roles represent a categorization of the HDFS operations by aggregating them based on their role. This categorization aims at setting each operation/command to proper access level state. In an operational HDFS environment, any command may categorize to:

- **READ**: permission is required to read or list the contents of DN, querying information, and check job status and results.

Table 3: Examples of authorization level classification.

Role	Example

READ	`HDFS fs -ls <args>|`
	`HDFS fs -cat/-get <file>|`
	`HDFS dfs -count [-q] <paths>|`

WRITE	`HDFS fs -put <dir>|`
	`dfs -copyFromLocal <localsrc>|`
	`intra-node disk balancing|`

EDIT	`hadoop namenode -format|`
	`Chmod/Chmown <file>, setPermission <path>|`
	`delete <Path>, removeDefaultAcl.|`

CONFIG	`Start/stop-dfs.sh|`
	`hdfs dfs -setReplication [-R] [-w]|`
	`setAcl, <numReplicas> <path>|`

INTERNAL	Heart beat, ApplicationMaster to NodeManager, NM to container. Data pipelining with Hive, HBase, etc.
UNDERLY	administrative commands edit etc/hosts, directory foo machines on/off, etc.

- **WRITE**: permission is required to add data or append it to DN, submitting jobs to NN, and updating information in HDFS.

- **EDIT**: permission is required to access data blocks, delete data, cancel a job, formate the NN, and perform data balance.

- **CONFIGURATION (CONFIG)**: permission is required to access runtime variables, paths, add/remove Hadoop features, change the scheduler (e.g., Fair), etc.

- **INTERNAL COMMUNICATION (INTERNAL)**: permission is required to access daemon to daemon communication, as for task updates and cluster resource status, etc.

- **UNDERLYING Capabilities**: permission is required to access infrastructure variables, add nodes, OS, VM, Network, Hardware.

We characterize the conceptual classes of Hadoop Yarn cluster users and the HDFS operation roles in a federation architecture. From these specifications, we try to characterize each service-call with constraints into five main classes to refer as authorization level classification. This categorization deliberates, indeed, as the foundation for future secure API design and standardization work.

An exciting trend might be using Blockchain-based encryption based on ciphertext policy attributes access control. Procedures for access control can be written as smart contracts and implemented on the blockchain.

3.2.2 Wire Encryption Impact

Harnessing different security layers will improve the architecture security. The question that one should ask is; how will that impact the performance? It is reported

Table 4: The relation between levels of access and user-class.

	Read	Write	Edit	Configuration	Internal	Underlying
User	√	√				
Superuser/Owner	√	√	√			
Administrator	√	√	√	√		√
Daemon	√	√			√	

that wire encryption returns with cost on the communication throughput [19] [20]. Herein, we rap the edge communication through frontend nodes flow in the pipeline with Transport-Layer Security (TLS) protocol [21]—even that it is believed that SSL/TLS protocols consume a lot of CPU time and network bandwidth. However, in this scenario, less than 1% of the CPU load, less than 10 KB of memory per connection and less than 2% of network overhead. TLS implementations streaming on commodity resources are adequate to handle intensive traffic load without requiring dedicated cryptographic hardware. However, our experiment in Figure 8 demonstrates that lightweight wire encryption mechanisms are still required in an IoT-to-Cloud data pipeline. TLS harms the modern data streaming software implementations running on commodity resources that providing a fast TLS implementation is recommended.

TLS includes two principal components, (i) handshake protocol and (ii) record protocol. The handshake establishes shared keying material and authenticates the communicating parties using cryptographic algorithms and parameters. The record protocol carries the handshake messages and application-layer data to be transmitted and divides traffic up into a series of records, each of which is independently protected with the handshake protocol's parameters. To measure the performance impact, we set up an echo server that responds to the client requests on edge with the same data sent to the server. It is expected to improve the performance with three folds over the JDK. GCM, which is used by the only cypher suite required by the HTTP/2 RFC implementation. Also, we deployed over Conscrypt in Table 5 that shows standard deviations are quite large. Both `wrk` with a `lua` script were used to benchmark the contents. Overall, we implement several workloads size ranging from 1, 10, 100 kilobyte to 1 megabyte. However, no load balancer was used even that TLS provide fast encrypted traffic between machines with a prohibitive time cost.

Seeking more reliable performance, proposed solutions include Unix domain sockets for interprocess communication for end-to-end secure communication. Another trend is utilizing the combination of IoT blockchain technology and software-defined networking (SDN) for scalable security [22]. SSL/TLS can be expensive when working with non-optimized implementations, especially with data streaming pipelines. However, even that increased it's complexity, based on our results that measure performance to confirm that TLS is causing the slowdown. It is valid to state that data-driven improvement using SDN and blockchain technologies is a starting point for secure IoT applications in the network's edge [23]. For instance, using the SDN capabilities to route the network traffic and the blockchain features to store the encryption keys. Adding to that, tracking the IoT devices' history, e.g., log files and metadata in the decentralized blockchain ledgers. The blockchain has to be accessible by both the key management and trust modules in such proposed

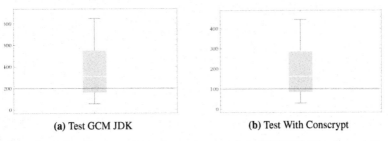

(a) Test GCM JDK   (b) Test With Conscrypt

Figure 8: TLS performance improvement against default JDK TLS implementation.

Table 5: TLS performance improvement against the default JDK TLS implementation.

	100MB	200MB	300MB	400MB	500MB	1GB	SPI	Improvement %
TLS	114.84	235.1	349.67	470.31	604.64	1855	569.6	-
Disabling GCM	54.13	108.66	159.45	215.78	276.17	849.59	257.1	~43%
With Conscrypt	28.36	56.94	83.55	113	144.74	445.2	135.1	~83%

architecture. Besides, the SDN controller has to be connected with the blockchain. Algorithm 1 presents an end-to-end secure wire-based communication that identifies the phase where the communication is encrypted in the IoT layer.

The presented TLS communication can describe the added cost in the network. However, at a particular timestamp, these functions are expected to follow a particular operation. These operations help apply approximation to predict a particular time latency in the network and ensure that the cloud's data pipeline is secure. The proposed method uses mechanisms expressed in the IoT-to-Cloud data pipeline to maintain privacy among the edge resource. Algorithm 1 aids in realizing the model on the initial architecture and validates the conditions expressed by the Edge controllers.

Algorithm 1: Secure end-to-end communication with wire encryption.

Input: $M_T S$: Max Transfer Speed and DP: Data Points
Output: Safe end-to-end communication with lower time control limit

Init(), Generating Function (GF) With TLS: Max time $M_i^+ t$, Min time $M_i^- t$ $R= \frac{(\frac{M_T S}{5})}{DP}$
while $Incoming(R)==True$ **do**
    ⌊ compute time ratio for the TLS process at specified time;

if $R > threshold$ **then**
    | $M_i^+ = \max[\,0, x_i\,(\,T + K\,) + C_{i-1}^+\,]$
    | ;

else
    | $M_i^- = \max[\,0, (\,T - K\,) - x_i + C_{i-1}^-\,]$
    | reload and reset, no shifting required.
    ⌊ **end**

Average TLS length for a loop
$$S_t = \sum_{i=1}^{t} z_i = \sum_{i=1}^{t} \frac{\bar{X}_i - \mu_0}{\sigma_{\bar{x}_i}}$$

3.2.3 At Rest Encryption Impact

Any comprehensive discussion on the security impact on performance has to concede all the aspects that may affect the system. This paper analyses the data pipeline security in the data life cycle from the allocation to storage through transmission and process. Hence, we decided that measuring the data at rest (in the cloud storage) is mandatory for drafting valuable conclusions on a complete end-to-end data pipeline security. In this regard, Transparent Data Encryption (TDE) is a well-recognized encryption practice at file level for protecting data at rest in databases, and distributed file systems [24]. Many IT firms have employed TDE, e.g., Microsoft, IBM and Oracle, to encrypt database files. Hence, many distributed file systems implement their capabilities for end-to-end backend storage encryption as for Hadoop HDFS [25].

In our WebHDFS, we set a TDE configuration over directories giving the client the ability to encrypt and decrypt the files across the cluster. The key concept and components of TDE can be summarized as follows [26]:

- Centralized access authority, for issuing the encryption service that controls the client access to the encrypted data. Also, it represents the first stage of the data confidentiality method.

- Key Management Server that validates permissions to the service in the encrypted zone. It affords the master key to encrypt or decrypt the data. All encryption and decryption processes of data are managed in this layer. Apache Ranger may utilize as a third-party key management server.

- encrypted zone represents the file path for the encrypted directory or a database. When establishing a new encryption zone, a single encryption key is associated with each of these zones. Moreover, the content files within these zones hold a private data encryption key. These keys are never handled directly by the centralized access authority, as they only see a stream of encrypted chunks.

  1. Create Key: After creating the targeted encrypted zone, the admin creates a key for each particular zone.
  2. Create Policy: The admin launch policy against each encrypted zone key, which spawn service inclusion (who can read/write to the encrypted zone) and add clients/applications to that policy.

Nevertheless, it has been reported that TDE has an estimated performance impact of around 3–5% [27] and can increase in intensive I/O tasks. That performance can usually be tackled by storing the data in memory, but such an act will be very costly. Another limitation in TDE is that it does not provide fine-grain security (as the whole file system has to be encrypted or not). Besides, held data in memory is not encrypted. Our experimental results in Table 6 demonstrates the impact on a read operation from WebHDFS aginst native (non-secure) one. The performance degradation is observed. Even though an intensive analysis of TDE is out of this study scoop, we only aim to discuss it on a high level of abstraction.

Table 6: Transparent data encryption impact on read operation.

	100MB	200MB	300MB	400MB	500MB	1GB
Native WebHDFS	23.64	47.45	69.63	94.23	120.62	371
With TDE	30.49	62.15	92.6	132.86	156.78	534.24

4. Extended Summary

In this Big Data era, we are witnessing a continuous increase in IoT processing systems in general and precisely IoT to Cloud streaming systems. This trend has attracted much interest from academia and the industry for several purposes and applications. This interest, however, is expected to continue growing significantly with the rising momentum of generated data at the edge of the networks with crucial needs of secure data pipelines. In this research, an extensive experiment on the performance impact of security measures has been conducted. Our results have shown some unusual characteristics of performance degradation that leads to open research challenges and trends. A motivation scenario realizes in capitalizing on the research results in developing cutting edge security techniques. Such a trend aims at guiding different solutions using the same pattern and share the related characteristics for the efficiency of secure data pipelines deployment.

This study also concludes that the future IoT secure vision can not be achieved without addressing the operational latency response time in data pipelines caused by security impact over performance. Novel security architectures employ blockchain technology and resourceful network management that separates the network components into control and data spheres as in the SDN. In this regards, decentralized blockchain-based access control with smart contracts and proxy re-encryption algorithms are proposed as future work. The smart contracts can serve as a results validator based on the majority of encrypted workloads in the data pipeline, e.g., in osmatic computing.

We aim to create full-fledged research and technical agenda that will advance state of the art in IoT application management. We foresee the data pipelines as a realization for future IoT deployment and development. As such, we classify the results of future trends in this area in the following means:

4.1 Data Management

There is an urgent need to enhance the data management supporting edge allocated data. At any particular point of the architecture, the data has to follow the Findable, Accessible, Interoperable and Reusable (FAIR) principle both for machines and users [28]. This principle is challenged even further with the vast nature of connected devices in an IoT network, e.g., sensors and actuators. Such a deployment model is posing exceptional security and scalability challenges to support efficient and secure runtime over large-scale data allocated at the edge of the network [29]. The data heterogeneity, lack of trust, the vast attack surface, and complexity of multi0layer security approaches are contemporary security challenges, to name some, in such a scenario. Hence, any future solution must address these shortcomings, besides exploring state-of-the-art solutions for supporting data management in the edge. For instance, deploy Blockchain-based computational integrity for maintaining the IoT node to perform accurate computation or not with an immutable ledger [22]. Also, in such deployment architecture, Malware's are affecting many solutions [30, 31, 32], which has to be considered.

4.2 Communication Management

Ensuring the network and communication availability to handle emergency tasks that require excessive handling of services, setup of rescue operations and even deploying on-demand communication facilitated by edge computing is critical in IoT application prosperity. With the pressure of connecting billions of intelligent devices and having mobile terminals as a part of the IoT, the intensity of communication services and assuring operations' safety is high. This facilitation is covered as a part of communication management. The provisioning demands high quality, better control, quality of operations, security, and privacy, which withholds all the information that may help an intruder pick its target based on handling specific service requests. These networks often require many reconfigurations and several load-balancing solutions, which must ensure appropriate allocation of resources. Herein, resources refer to the handling servers, and the load is the service requests generated from the end-users (at the edge). However, with such decentralization, communication management requires better privacy as an advertisement of the handling servers may expose the network leading the way to several cyber-attacks. An eavesdropper can prohibit the network from handling the load and deny services with many unauthorized requests and denial messages. Such a situation can be tackled using privacy-aware models [20].

Another issue related to IoT challenges is the components heterogeneity and the design of communication channels, and other characteristics [26, 33]. Ensuring automation security among IoT nodes communication using end-to-end security is essential for many IoT application scenarios. The first step to achieving this is identifying and authenticating the edge nodes, followed by identification and access control approaches and wire encryption. A promising approach is smart contracts with blockchain implementation for authentication [34]. Moreover, lightweight Transport-Layer Security (TLS) Protocol for IoT with minimal latency over the communication [35, 36].

4.3 Resource Management

Resource management is the process of efficiently managing and allocating available machines in the infrastructure to deliver computation as needed, with optimal utilization. It can be classified into resource provisioning and application (or task) placement. The large-scale processing system resources can be employed as dedicated, non-dedicated, or hybrid architectures within clusters of homogeneous or heterogeneous computing nodes. Due to the distributed nature of the IoT, where vast numbers of devices interact autonomously through various standards and protocols, security is more complicated than in other, more monolithic computing environments.

IoT architectures network can be shared among different end nodes and operators. Therefore, reliable and secure scheduling is a fundamental aspect of improving the system trustability, which plays a decisive role in the widespread adoption of IoT architectures. Hence, the IoT practitioners must reimagine and repurpose traditional security approaches to suit this new paradigm. A leading example of such a trend is employing blockchain-based solutions using smart contracts [37]. Furthermore, applying Blockchain-based encryption based on ciphertext policy attributes access control—where procedures for access control can be written as smart contracts and implemented on the blockchain [38].

4.4 Edge Intelligence

Employing methods to extract knowledge and gain insights from many structural and unstructured data is the ultimate goal of Artificial Intelligence (AI) and Machine Learning (ML). Alongside the growth of the IoT, AI has emerged as the next technology phenomenon. For a long time, centralized deployment models were utilized to facilitate AI/ML methods' operations. However, a novel paradigm known as the Artificial Intelligence of Things (AIoT) comes into play. The possibility of improving the IoT architectures that generate enormous data using the AI/ML approaches, which consume these data to support intelligent management, is extensive. IoT applications and architectures yield advanced operations closer to the data source by harnessing machine intelligence's empowered abilities. This scenario depends on using different AI systems to support the IoT and Edge-to-Cloud scheduling activities.

   Edge intelligence refers to Large-scale connected software systems and devices for data operations, e.g., collection, processing, and analysis proximity to where data is captured based on artificial intelligence. Edge intelligence aims at enhancing data processing and protects the privacy and security of the data and users. Although it recently emerged, this research field has shown explosive growth over the past five years. A wide range of techniques have been recently proposed, yet the problem of how to efficiently orchestrate edge-cloud architectures remains an open challenge. The foundations of such a revolutionary model are, however, not completely understood. Among such proposals, federated machine learning stands up to overcome the previous challenges [39, 7]. Federated learning [40, 41] is a distributed and secure operating system that enables training on the edge of decentralized data residing on devices like mobile phones. Federated learning is one instance of the more general approach of "bringing the code to the data, instead of the data to the code" and addresses the fundamental problems of privacy, ownership, and locality of data. Accordingly, it answers many of the security (and privacy) of data at the edge deployment models in an IoT environment [42].

5. Acknowledgment

The work by Dr. Feras M. Awaysheh is funded by the European Regional Development Funds via the Mobilitas Plus programme (grant MOBTT75). Also, I would like to thank the announimuce reviewers for their valuable comments and suggestions.

References

[1] B. Varghese, and R. Buyya. Next generation cloud computing: New trends and research directions. *Future Generation Computer Systems*, 79: 849–861, 2018.

[2] D. Wu, L. Zhu, X. Xu, S. Sakr, D. Sun, and Q. Lu. Building pipelines for heterogeneous execution environments for big data processing. *IEEE Software*, 33(2): 60–67, 2016.

[3] N. Lu, N. Cheng, N. Zhang, X. Shen, and J.W. Mark. Connected vehicles: Solutions and challenges. *IEEE Internet of Things Journal*, 1(4): 289–299, 2014.

[4] J. Wang, C. Jiang, Z. Han, Y. Ren, and L. Hanzo. Internet of vehicles: Sensing-aided transportation information collection and diffusion. *IEEE Transactions on Vehicular Technology*, 67(5): 3813–3825, 2018.

[5] C.-H. Hong, and B. Varghese. Resource management in fog/edge computing: A survey on architectures, infrastructure, and algorithms. *ACM Computing Surveys (CSUR)*, 52(5): 1–37, 2019.

[6] M.H. ur Rehman, E. Ahmed, I. Yaqoob, I.A.T. Hashem, M. Imran, and S. Ahmad. Big data analytics in industrial IOT using a concentric computing model. *IEEE Communications Magazine*, 56(2): 37–43, 2018.

[7] T.L. Duc, R.G. Leiva, P. Casari, and P.-O. Östberg. Machine learning methods for reliable resource provisioning in edge-cloud computing: A survey. *ACM Computing Surveys (CSUR)*, 52(5): 1–39, 2019.

[8] J. Pan, and J. McElhannon. Future edge cloud and edge computing for internet of things applications. *IEEE Internet of Things Journal*, 5(1): 439–449, 2017.

[9] I. Homoliak, S. Venugopalan, D. Reijsbergen, Q. Hum, R. Schumi, and P. Szalachowski. The security reference architecture for blockchains: Toward a standardized model for studying vulnerabilities, threats, and defenses. *IEEE Communications Surveys & Tutorials*, 23(1): 341–390, 2020.

[10] V.R. Kebande, S. Alawadi, F.M. Awaysheh, and J.A. Persson. Active machine learning adversarial attack detection in the user feedback process. *IEEE Access*, 9: 36908–36923, 2021.

[11] F.M. Awaysheh, M. Alazab, M. Gupta, T.F. Pena, and J.C. Cabaleiro. Next generation big data federation access control: A reference model. *Future Generation Computer Systems*, 108: 726–741, 2020.

[12] M. Gupta, F. Patwa, and R. Sandhu. Poster: Access control model for the hadoop ecosystem. *In Proceedings of the 22nd ACM on Symposium on Access Control Models and Technologies*, pp. 125–127, 2017.

[13] M. Gupta, F.M. Awaysheh, J. Benson, M. Al Azab, F. Patwa, and R. Sandhu. An attribute-based access control for cloud-enabled industrial smart vehicles. *IEEE Transactions on Industrial Informatics*, 2020.

[14] Apache Hadoop. HDFS Permissions Guide, Hadoop 3.x. https://hadoop.apache.org/docs/r3.1.1/hadoop-project-dist/hadoophdfs/HdfsPermissionsGuide.html, 2019. Accessed: 2021-03-10.

[15] Apache Hadoop. Superuser Authorization for Hadoop 3.x cluster. https:https://hadoop.apache.org/docs/r3.1.1/hadoop-project-dist/hadoopcommon/Superusers.html, 2019. Accessed: 2021-03-10.

[16] Apache Hadoop. HDFS operations and their methods. https://hadoop.apache.org/docs/r3.0.0/api/org/apache/hadoop/fs/FileSystem.html, 2019. Accessed: 2021-03-10.

[17] M. Gupta, F. Patwa, and R. Sandhu. An attribute-based access control model for secure big data processing in hadoop ecosystem. *In Proceedings of the Third ACM Workshop on Attribute-Based Access Control*, pp. 13–24, 2018.

[18] M. Gupta, F. Patwa, and R. Sandhu. Object-tagged rbac model for the hadoop ecosystem. In *IFIP Annual Conference on Data and Applications Security and Privacy*, pp. 63–81, Springer, 2017.

[19] C. Shen, E. Nahum, H. Schulzrinne, and C. P. Wright. The impact of tls on sip server performance: Measurement and modeling. *IEEE/ACM Transactions on Networking*, 20(4): 1217–1230, 2012.

[20] P. Li, J. Su, and X. Wang. Itls: Lightweight transport-layer security protocol for iot with minimal latency and perfect forward secrecy. *IEEE Internet of Things Journal*, 7(8): 6828–6841, 2020.

[21] E. Rescorla, and T. Dierks. The transport layer security (tls) protocol version 1.3, 2018.

[22] S. Hameed, S.A. Shah, Q.S. Saeed, S. Siddiqui, I. Ali, A. Vedeshin, and D. Draheim. A scalable key and trust management solution for iot sensors using sdn and blockchain technology. *IEEE Sensors Journal*, 21(6): 8716–8733, 2021.

[23] K. Gai, Y. Wu, L. Zhu, Z. Zhang, and M. Qiu. Differential privacy-based blockchain for industrial internet-of-things. *IEEE Transactions on Industrial Informatics*, 16(6): 4156–4165, 2019.

[24] D. Deshmukh, Anwar Pasha, and D. Qureshi. Transparent data encryption–solution for security of database contents. *arXiv preprint arXiv:1303.0418*, 2013.

[25] Apache Hadoop. Transparent Data Encryption in HDFS. https://hadoop.apache.org/docs/current/hadoop-project-dist/hadoophdfs/TransparentEncryption.html, 2021. Accessed: 2021-03-11.

[26] F.M. Awaysheh, M.N. Aladwan, M. Alazab, S. Alawadi, J.C. Cabaleiro, and T.F. Pena. Security by design for big data frameworks over cloud computing. *IEEE Transactions on Engineering Management*, 2021.

[27] Microsoft. Transparent Data Encryption performance impact. https://docs.microsoft.com/en-us/dynamics365/business-central/devitpro/security/transparent-data-encryption:text=TDE2021. Accessed: 2021-03-11.

[28] M.D. Wilkinson, M. Dumontier, I.J. Aalbersberg, G. Appleton, M. Axton, A. Baak, N. Blomberg, J.-W. Boiten, L.B. da Silva Santos, P.E. Bourne, and J. Bouwman. The fair guiding principles for scientific data management and stewardship. *Scientific Data*, 3(1): 1–9, 2016.

[29] M. Tang, M. Alazab, and Y. Luo. Big data for cybersecurity: Vulnerability disclosure trends and dependencies. *IEEE Transactions on Big Data*, 5(3): 317–329, 2017.

[30] N. Etaher, G.R. Weir, and M. Alazab. From zeus to zitmo: Trends in banking malware. *In 2015 IEEE Trustcom/BigDataSE/ISPA*, 1: 1386–1391, IEEE, 2015.

[31] S. Venkatraman, and M. Alazab. Use of data visualisation for zero-day malware detection. *Security and Communication Networks*, 2018.

[32] D. Vasan, M. Alazab, S. Wassan, H. Naeem, B. Safaei, and Q. Zheng. Imcfn: Image-based malware classification using fine-tuned convolutional neural network architecture. *Computer Networks*, 171: 107138, 2020.

[33] M. Aladwan, F. Awaysheh, J. Cabaleiro, T. Pena, H. Alabool, and M. Alazab. Common security criteria for vehicular clouds and internet of vehicles evaluation and selection. *In 2019 18th IEEE International Conference on Trust, Security and Privacy in Computing and Communications/13th IEEE International Conference on Big Data Science and Engineering (Trust-Com/BigDataSE)*, pp. 814–820, IEEE, 2019.

[34] F.M. Awaysheh, J.C. Cabaleiro, T.F. Pena, and M. Alazab. Poster: A pluggable authentication module for big data federation architecture. *In Proceedings of the 24th ACM Symposium on Access Control Models and Technologies*, pp. 223–225, 2019.

[35] M. Mitev, M. Shekiba-Herfeh, A. Chorti, and M. Reed. Multi-factor physical layer security authentication in short block length communication. *arXiv preprint arXiv:2010.14457*, 2020.

[36] F. Awaysheh, J.C. Cabaleiro, T.F. Pena, and M. Alazab. Big data security frameworks meet the intelligent transportation systems trust challenges. *In 2019 18th IEEE International Conference on Trust, Security and Privacy in Computing and Communications/13th IEEE International Conference on Big Data Science and Engineering (TrustCom/BigDataSE)*, pp. 807–813, IEEE, 2019.

[37 A.A. Battah, M.M. Madine, H. Alzaabi, I. Yaqoob, K. Salah, and R. Jayaraman. Blockchain-based multi-party authorization for accessing ipfs encrypted data. *IEEE Access*, 8: 196813–196825, 2020.

[38] M.J.M. Chowdhury, M.S. Ferdous, K. Biswas, N. Chowdhury, A. Kayes, M. Alazab, and P. Watters. A comparative analysis of distributed ledger technology platforms. *IEEE Access*, 7: 167930–167943, 2019.

[39] K. Bonawitz, H. Eichner, W. Grieskamp, D. Huba, A. Ingerman, V. Ivanov, C. Kiddon, J. Konečnỳ, S. Mazzocchi, H.B. McMahan, and T. Van Overveldt. Towards federated learning at scale: System design. *arXiv preprint arXiv:1902.01046*, 2019.

[40] K. Bonawitz, V. Ivanov, B. Kreuter, A. Marcedone, H.B. McMahan, S. Patel, D. Ramage, A. Segal, and K. Seth. Practical secure aggregation for privacy preserving machine learning. *In proceedings of the 2017 ACM SIGSAC Conference on Computer and Communications Security*, pp. 1175–1191, 2017.

[41] Q. Yang, Y. Liu, T. Chen, and Y. Tong. Federated machine learning: Concept and applications. *ACM Transactions on Intelligent Systems and Technology (TIST)*, 10(2): 1–19, 2019.

[42] W.Y.B. Lim, N.C. Luong, D.T. Hoang, Y. Jiao, Y.-C. Liang, Q. Yang, D. Niyato, and C. Miao. Federated learning in mobile edge networks: A comprehensive survey. *IEEE Communications Surveys & Tutorials*, 22(3): 2031–2063, 2020.

4

Ground Point Filtering and Digital Terrain Model Generation using LiDAR Data

Arshad Husain[1,*] and *Rakesh Chandra Vaishya*[2]

ABSTRACT

In recent years, geospatial feature extraction has become a very widely recognized and actively pursued research area. Various geospatial feature extraction algorithm exsist which involve the filtering of ground points from Light Detection and Ranging (LiDAR) point cloud datasets as the basic and imperative step. In the case of the LiDAR dataset, the accuracy of the generated Digital Terrain Model (DTM) is dependent on the accuracy of the ground filtering method. The objective of this research paper is to propose a novel approach for automated ground point filtering and generation of Digital Terrain Model (DTM) using the LiDAR point cloud dataset. The Proposed approach involves five steps such as segmentation of the LiDAR point cloud, vertical slicing, slope based filtering, circular growing, and DTM generation. ArcGIS 10.3 has been used for the generation of DTM using filtered ground points and also a Least Significant Bit (LSB) based image steganography technique is applied to secure the DTM. The proposed method has been tested at two different datasets. Dataset 1 is captured using mobile LiDAR, while Dataset 2 is captured using terrestrial LiDAR. Ground points of both datasets are filtered out with an average value of completeness and correctness are 98.11%, 94.71% respectively and corresponding DTM is generated.

1. Introduction

Light Detection And Ranging (LiDAR) is an operational remote sensing device that measures the range between the target and source by computing the travel time of a fired laser pulse back towards the LiDAR sensor [1]. The device also captures the

---

[1] DIT University, Dehradun, India-248009.
[2] Motilal Nehru National Institute of Technology, Allahabad, Prayagraj, India-211004.
   Email: rcvaishya@mnnit.ac.in
* Corresponding author: arshad.husain18@gmail.com

scan angle of the target from the sensor. These two parameter ranges and scan angles are further used to find out the local co-ordinate values of the target point using a mathematical transformation called geo-location [2, 3]. With the help of an in-built Global Positioning System (GPS) in the LiDAR device, local coordinate values of the target are transformed into global coordinate values and finally, a three-dimensional dense geo-referenced point cloud is generated [4, 5]. LiDAR technology offers a prompt, accurate, and precise technique for map wide landscapes at a high resolution as compared to traditional surveying techniques such as photogrammetric systems, GPS surveys, etc. [5–7]. It was not always feasible for the mapping of the adjoining corridor, trees crown, change detection, and transmission lines to get the scale of damages to buildings after a disaster with traditional survey techniques and LiDAR technology has good performance in such a case [8]. LiDAR offers less human and atmospheric interaction irrespective of mapping systems and conventional surveying [6, 9]. LiDAR delivers geometric information as well as extraneous information such as a return number, number of returns, intensity, GPS Time, etc., which are all greatly beneficial for various geospatial feature identification, classification, and extraction. Datasets captured with the help of the LiDAR device is in vector format and the size of the captured dataset is huge in size and is termed as Big Data in computer science engineering. Therefore, it becomes very tedious to perform the geo-spatial and geo-statistical analysis of captured data [10]. Processing of the LiDAR dataset is extremely labor-intensive and can take weeks because it can be spent on data that took a couple of hours to capture. The congestion that occurs in the workflow has moved from the data acquisition stage to the processing stage [11]. There are many problems that are faced to analyze the individual geospatial features by using the entire point cloud dataset at once which maybe overcome by using a time-efficient Geospatial feature extraction technique [4]. Almost all LiDAR applications comprise ground point filtering which is an essential phase to define which LiDAR pulse returns are from the ground surface and which are from the non-ground surface. Filtering of ground points from the LiDAR dataset is a primary aspect for various geospatial feature extraction algorithms such as detection of vertical linear objects (trees, pole-like objects), road surface, etc. [12]. Ground point filtering from the LiDAR dataset is also an essential part of the generation of various models like Digital Terrain Model, Digital Elevation Model (DEM), and Digital Surface Model. The accuracy of these generated models depends upon the accuracy of the ground filtering method [4]. However, in the case of non-ground points are filtered accurately before interpolation to a raster DEM then only is an accurate DEM acquired [13]. In the case of geospatial feature extraction algorithms, lots of processing time is consumed in the filtering of ground points and it becomes quite tedious to handle large amounts of LiDAR data. To generate DEMs and DTMs, LiDAR technology is progressively being espoused as the primary method [14–16]. Some European countries and the United States of America have initiated the use of LiDAR technology to generate regional to national DEM products [17] because these generated DEMs are much more accurate and superior to DEMs which are generated by traditional methods. LiDAR data has been widely used in several other important applications apart from the model generation (DEM and DTM) such as object detection [18], 3D visualization [19], coastal monitoring, hydrological monitoring, land-use and land-cover classification, forest inventory [20]. A large number of researchers and scientists have been fascinated with the LiDAR data since its emergence, and their area of interest is LiDAR data filtering. Many filtering algorithms and pipelines have been suggested since then. The basic notion of all kinds of ground filtering algorithms is that ground and non-ground are unalike in the local geometry characteristics and elevation such as local smoothness, slope, and structure. Ground points usually belong to the lowermost surface features in a local extent (bare-earth topography) in LiDAR data, while Non-ground points are captured from the above bare-earth topography object, like bridges, shrubs, trees, buildings, and other man-made objects. A widely adopted reformist filter for ground points from LIDAR data is TIN (Triangulated Irregular Network) based method [21–25]. At first, a granular terrain model is created. To steadily enhance the terrain model, new ground points are seeded based on their slope and distance to the existing terrain model. The generated results by the use of TIN based reformist filtering method [22] have the best filtering results and adaptation ability among different filtering algorithms [26]. Mongus and Žalik (2012) [27] proposed a thin plate spline-based iterative filtering (non-parametric) method as an alternative of the TIN based filtering method by choosing local nethermost points of input data as control points. Belkhouche and Buckles (2011) [28] proposed a TIN based method to generate a local ground model in which only non-edge triangles persisted and edge triangles from TIN using slope was suppressed. The proposed algorithm was not noise-resistant. Errors were accumulated simply through the progressive procedure. A standard slope based ground filtering procedure was proposed by Vosselman (2000) [17]. Point clouds are used to estimate the local maximum slope and to distinguish the ground points and non-ground points individually. The threshold for the radius and slope were defined initially. The threshold value for the radius was kept marginally higher than the building size while the slope threshold was set as the maximum slope of the captured test dataset. An improved version of Vosselman (2000) [17] was proposed by Sithole (2001) [3]. The method calculated the slope threshold for the test point cloud dataset adaptively. Shan and Sampath (2005) [2] proposed a bidirectional classification method for distinguishing ground point and non-ground point from the LiDAR point cloud. Neighborhood analysis was performed based on elevation and slope difference to filter out the ground points. Small features such as shrubs, bushes, and parked vehicles were accurately identified by the proposed method. A Multi-directional Ground Filtering (MGF) technique was proposed by Meng et al. (2009) [1]. Apart from the geometric information of point cloud data, scanning geometry (across the scan line and along the scan line) was also used. According to the topography of the input point cloud dataset, the threshold value for the elevation difference and slope were designated. The proposed method was dependent on the present noise of test data and calculated the ground control point individually. Few segmentation based methods for the filtering of ground points were proposed [29–32]. These methods were either based on plane fitting segmentation or object-based segmentation. Filin (2002) [29] recommended a segmentation-based process for segmenting and classifying the LiDAR point cloud. They selected a seed point and analyzed the elevation difference of the chosen point with corresponding neighbors. At last, a relationship with a tangent plane was established to complete the segmentation process. To segment the LiDAR data, E-cognition was used by Jacobsen and Lohmann (2003) [30]. Further, the elevation difference was used to carry out the classification process. Region growing was applied by Tóvári and Pfeifer (2005) [31] for segmentation purposes and a local weighted plane fitting algorithm was executed iteratively to filter the ground points from the whole point cloud. Smooth regularization based segmentation method was proposed by Rabbani et al. (2006) [32]. In order to store and handle the huge amount of data (Big Data) Apache Hadoop is a leading software framework. Occasionally these data contain sensitive information and its required to secure such information. A HeABAC model referred as attribute-based access control model for the Hadoop ecosystem is introduced to extend the security of sensitive information [33]. The proposed model provides an extension to HeAC referred as Hadoop access control model. For Hadoop ecosystem HeAC, a formal multi-layer access control model (called HeAC) was also presented [34, 35]. Further authors have extended this base model (HeAC) to OT-RBAC model referred as cohesive object-tagged role-based access control model [34]. None or few of the researches have merged the concept of segmentation, elevation difference, and slope to accurately and time efficiently to filter out the ground points. In this research, all these concepts are conceded together. The objective of this chapter is to detail a novel method for ground point filtering and corresponding DTM generation using LiDAR data.

In this study, a time-efficient automated method for filtering of ground points and generation of DTM from filtered ground points using LiDAR data has been proposed. The proposed method incorporates five successive steps; in the first step segmentation of input, the LiDAR dataset is performed to divide the dataset into regular square grids. The second step deals with the vertical slicing of each grid to generate the area of interest layer. Slope based filtering and circular growing are performed to accurately filter out the ground points from the generated area of interest layer in the third and fourth steps respectively. In the last step, DTM is generated using filtered ground points using ArcGIS 10.3 and also a Least Significant Bit (LSB) based image steganography technique is applied to secure the DTM. The organization of the manuscript as in Section 2, describes the comprehensive description of test data. The proposed method and corresponding results are discussed in Section 3 and Section 4 respectively. Discussion about the result and conclusion part is deliberated in Section 5 and Section 6 respectively.

2. Test Data

2.1 Dataset 1

In the present study, The FARO Focus 3D X 330 TLS used to captured the Dataset 1 image from the MG Marg, Civil Lines, Prayagraj, Uttar Pradesh, India (25°26'55.5"N, 81°50'43.5"E). The Terrestrial Laser Scanner (TLS) offers –60° to +90° vertical and 360° horizontal fields of view range from 0.6 meters up to 330 meters with a distance accuracy up to ± 2 mm, delivers high precision coverage and performance. An inbuilt exclusive touch screen Liquid Crystal Display (LCD) display enables the user to customize the data capture parameter and also show the status information accordingly. In the captured area of dataset 1, power lines and streets are densely blocked by trees, low-slope in the direction of horizontal streets as it has an urban behavior and nonurban behavior. The maximum elevation difference within the dataset 1 is 16.81 meters. The length of the street is 209.43 meters. The comprehensive depiction of the dataset along with the perspective view of the captured dataset itself shows below in Figure 1(a,b,c, and d). Table 1 represents the statistical specification of dataset 1.

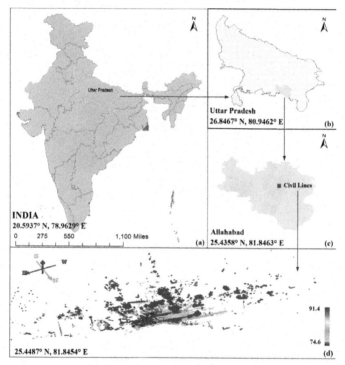

Figure 1: **(a,b,c,d)** Represents respectively maps of India Country, Uttar Pradesh State, Praygraj district, perspective view of the captured dataset.

Table 1: Statistical specification of the Dataset 1 and Dataset 2.

Dataset	File Size	No. of Points	Area (meter²)	Point Density (per meter²)
Dataset 1	0.35 GB	7247998	101985.20	71.0691
Dataset 2	1.14 GB	21417231	23778.1068	900.7122

2.2 Dataset 2

In the present study, the Optech Lynx mobile mapper used to captured the Dataset 2 image of an inside corridor of parking yard at 30 Commerce St, Concord, Ontario L4K 5C3, Canada as shown below in Figure 2 (43° 47' 24.5652" N, 79° 31' 54.6888" W). The 3D perspective view of the captured dataset shows below in Figure 2(b) and google earth image of the corresponding location in Figure 2(a). The parking yard captured shown in Figure 2(a) by the red square of the Google Earth image.

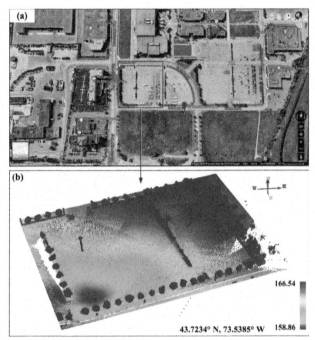

Figure 2: **(a)** Test site Google Earth image and, **(b)** Dataset 2 perspective view.

Table 1 represents the statistical specification of dataset 2. The captured dataset is freely accessible at the Terrasolid official website which includes features like roads, traffic signs, utility poles, parked vehicles, a similar type of trees inside, and around the yard.

The entire covered area by the captured dataset is measured in meter square (meter^2) and size of the file is in gigabytes (GB) while the density of point is in per meter square (/meter^2).

3. Proposed Method

The proposed method for DTM generation using LiDAR point cloud data and ground point filtering is divided into five steps as shown below in Figure 3. A detailed description of all the steps involved is discussed below.

3.1 Segmentation

3.1.1 Two Dimensional Projection

The two-dimensional projection has been performed at the geometric coordinate (X,Y, Z) of each LiDAR point taken as an input dataset. For doing so, the XY plane is considered as a projection plane for projecting the input dataset. The Z coordinate values for each MLS point have been set to zero because of the consideration of XY as a project plane. Now, Each MLS point has only X coordinates and Y coordinates, i.e., in the XY plane. The Z coordinate information for each MLS point has been stored in such a manner so that it could be reassociated with the corresponding

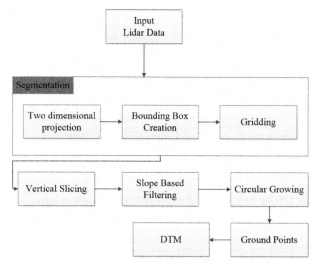

Figure 3: The process sequence of the proposed method.

point. The 2D project plane is considered to be a projection plane for projecting the input dataset in order to create a minimum bounding box at the input dataset. Since the XY plane has less distortion in the area of input dataset as compared to others, therefore it was chosen. Figure 4(a), represents the 2D projected dataset and Figure 4(b) represents a closer view of the projected dataset. 2D projected tree points are represented by dark spots in Figure 4(b).

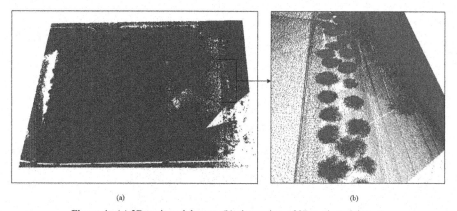

(a)   (b)

Figure 4: **(a)** 2D projected dataset, **(b)** closer view of 2D projected dataset.

3.1.2 Bounding Box Creation

Bounding Box creation at the projected dataset, first of all, identifies the four points of the 2D project dataset having max X, max Y, min X, min Y as shown below in Figure 5 by points a,b,c and d. The bottom left point P having coordinate (min X, min Y) and top right point r having coordinate (max X, max Y) of the bounding box has been specified with the support of these four identified points. Likewise, the other

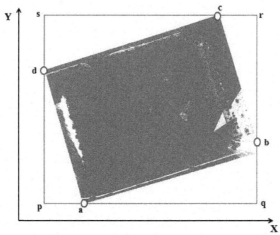

Figure 5: Bounding box (p, q, r, s) at 2D projected dataset.

two corners Q and S at location bottom right and top left having coordinate (max X, mini Y) and (min X, max Y) respectively has been also specified with the support of these four identified points. Point indicated by $p,q,r,$ and s in Figure 5, represent these corners.

3.1.3 Gridding

To create successive regular square grids, the projected data set has been divided after the creation of bounding box as shown in Figure 6. The length and width of the grids have been defined by Gx and Gy respectively to divide the projected dataset in regular grids. The grid size in X and Y dimensions has been denoted by length Gx and width Gy respectively. Point depicted by p in Figure 5 at bottom left

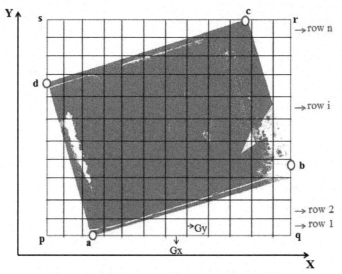

Figure 6: Grid formation of the projected dataset (2D).

corner of the bounding box has been chosen as a seed point for grid formation. In Figure 6, the first row grids are created by increasing the value of the X-coordinate of the previous seed pointed by *Gx*. In the second row, the coordinate of the seed point for the first grid will be $(P_x, P_y + Gy)$, where P_x and P_y are located at bottom left corner of the bounding box in X and Y direction. The second row grids are created in similar fashion as like the first row grids by increasing the seed point X coordinate likewise, bounding box rows are divided into regular square grids depicted below in Figure 6.

3.2 Vertical Slicing

Initially, The Z coordinate value of each grid point is re-associated with the corresponding one. Now each grid point has all the three X, Y, and Z coordinate values and all the points of each grid are taken as an input iteratively. Now, vertical slicing has been performed by selecting the minimum Z value from the n points of the chosen grid and Z mean value, i.e., Z_{mean} is calculated. Z_{mean} value is used as a minimum value of Z for the selected grid for further calculation in order to eliminate the effect of the outliers from the grid. It might be possible that actual minimum Z value associated with the point may belong to an outlier. Now, for further processing, the point of vertical slice height from (z_{mean}) to $(z_{mean} + h)$ is taken because of the area of interest (ground points, Figure 7). To improve the run time performance of the proposed method, Vertical slicing is used to eliminate the extraneous point from each grid that doesn't belongs to the area of interest. Vertically sliced layered points of the area of interest shown below in Figure 8.

All the points belonging to the area of interest are processed further at vertically sliced points for ground point filtering in two more successive steps.

3.3 Slope Based Filtering

The point id of the maximum elevated ground point (*map*) for each grid is taken as input. Further, the slope between the maximum elevated ground point and point having the minimum Z (minimum elevated ground point, *mip*) of the corresponding grid is calculated (T_{dslope}) (1). T_{dslope} will act as the threshold slope for ground point filtering because each ground point cannot have a greater slope than T_{dslope} (calculation of T_{dslope} is based on maximum and minimum elevated ground points). Now, each point of the selected grid is taken iteratively, the slope between the ith (selected point) and minimum elevated ground point (Z_{min}, D_{slopei}) is calculated (2). If $D_{slopei} > T_{dslope}$, labels the point as non-ground point, and otherwise labels it as ground point (3). Likewise, all the points of each grid are processed iteratively.

$$T_{dslope} = cos^{-1} \left(\frac{\sqrt{(map_x - mip_x)^2 + (map_y - mip_y)^2}}{\sqrt{(map_x - mip_x)^2 + (map_y - mip_y)^2 + (map_z - mip_z)^2}} \right) \quad (1)$$

$$D_{slopei} = cos^{-1} \left(\frac{\sqrt{(i_x - mip_x)^2 + (i_y - mip_y)^2}}{\sqrt{(i_x - mip_x)^2 + (i_y - mip_y)^2 + (i_z - mip_z)^2}} \right) \quad (2)$$

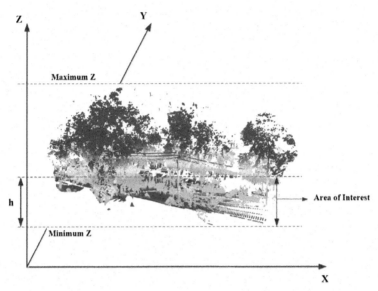

Figure 7: Vertical slicing for finding area of interest.

Figure 8: Vertical sliced layer of an area of interest.

$$\forall point(i): \begin{cases} if \ \left(D_{slopei} > T_{dslope}\right) & NGP \\ else & GP \end{cases} \tag{3}$$

Where map_x, map_y, map_z, mip_x, mip_y, mip_z are the X, Y, and Z coordinate value of the maximum elevated point and a minimum elevated ground point. Similarly, i_x, i_y, and i_z are the X, Y, and Z coordinate value of selected i^{th} seed point.

3.4 Circular Growing

After slope based filtering, there might be a possibility of the presence of vertical linear structures such as tree trunk and pole like objects located at low down areas.

The objective of this step is to suppress these individual vertical structure points. In this step, the entire slope based filtered points of each grid are chosen iteratively and a bounding box is created (Section 3.1.2). The seed point has been selected of the bounding box at bottom left corner depicted by point S in Figure 9. A circle has been created with a user-defined radius (r). Points lying under the created circle have been extracted with the help of a K-Dimensional (K–D) tree data structure.

In order to identify the structure of these points, Principal Component Analysis (PCA) is performed. In order to perform PCA, the calculation of variance-covariance matrix $(Cov)_{3\times3}$ denoted by equation 4 and performed. The calculated value of the covariance matrix is further used for the calculation of the eigenvalue matrix $(\lambda_{3\times1})$ denoted by equation 5. The eigenvalue matrix included eigenvalues λ_{max}, λ_{mod}, and λ_{min} denoted by equation 6. Therefore, PCA involves the three eigenvalues in normalized form and also corresponding eigenvectors. Two parameters, α_{max} (maximum normalized eigenvalue) and θ (angle between the Z-axis and eigenvector $V\alpha_{max}$ corresponding to the α_{max}) are used for the identification of vertical linear objects. The calculation has been performed for $V\alpha_{max}$ and angle θ in equation 8 and equation 9 respectively. Unit vector $\hat{k}$ represent the Z axis whereas angle θ has been calculated by taking the dot product between the Z axis and $V\alpha_{max}$. Now, Compare the calculated value of α_{max} and θ with the pre-defined thresholds as shown below in Table 2. The extracted circle points only belong to vertical linear features such as pole-like objects or tree trunks if the calculated values are greater than the pre-defined thresholds. After they finalized the computed extracted points of circle, the base layer seed point has been shifted by the value r in X dimension as shown in Figure 9. Now, a circle of radius r has been created at new seed point. A similar procedure has been

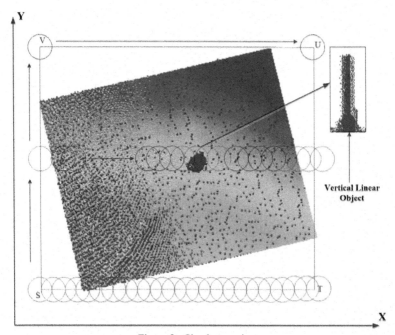

Figure 9: Circular growing.

Table 2: Proposed method steps along with Parameters and used value.

Steps	Parameters	Used Value
Segmentation	Gx, Gy	1 meter, 1 meter
Vertical Slicing	n, h	100, 1 meter
Circular Growing	α_{max}, θ, r	0.3 meter, 0.8, 75°

applied for those extracted points which lying under the circle. Now, the seed point has been shifted by the value r in the Y direction depicted in Figure 9 by point T when reached the bottom right corner of the base layer. Therefore, a circular growth has been performed row wise from top to bottom and terminates when reached at the top right corner of the bounding box depicted by point U in Figure 9. Likewise, circular growth has been performed at the slope based filtered points of each grid. The reason for using the K–D tree for neighborhood searching is because of its lesser time complexity.

$$Cov = \begin{pmatrix} \sigma_x^2 & \sigma_{xy} & \sigma_{xz} \\ \sigma_{xy} & \sigma_y^2 & \sigma_{yz} \\ \sigma_{xz} & \sigma_{yz} & \sigma_z^2 \end{pmatrix} \tag{4}$$

$$(Cov)_{3\times3} - (\lambda_{3\times1} \times I_{3\times3}) = 0 \tag{5}$$

$$\lambda = \begin{pmatrix} \lambda_{max} \\ \lambda_{mod} \\ \lambda_{min} \end{pmatrix} \tag{6}$$

$$\alpha_{max} = \frac{\lambda_{max}}{\lambda_{max} + \lambda_{mod} + \lambda_{min}} \tag{7}$$

$$_{max} = a\hat{i} + b\hat{j} + c\hat{k} \tag{8}$$

$$\theta = \cos^{-1}\left(\frac{c}{\sqrt{(a^2 + b^2 + c^2)}}\right) \tag{9}$$

where the X, Y, and Z coordinate variances are denoted by σ_x^2, σ_y^2 and σ_z^2 respectively and the covariance between X–Y, Y–Z, and Z–X coordinate values are denoted by σ_{xy}, σ_{yz}, and σ_{xz} respectively, a, b and c represent respectively the coefficients of unit vectors in X, Y, and Z direction and λ_{max}, λ_{mod} and λ_{min} respectively denoted the maximum, moderate, and minimum eigenvalues.

3.5 DTM Generation

In oder to complete the DTM generation process three foremost steps have been followed (Figure 10). Initially filtered ground points are taken as the input (.las file format) in ArcMap 10.3 (ESRI's ArcGIS 10.3). Further, in second step the .lasd file format has been created to visualize and further processing of LAS file using ArcCatalog. In particular of ArcCatalog, LAS Dataset layer tool has been used from the ArcToolbox. This .lasd is a LAS dataset file pointer for LAS files and does not import the lidar point data, it merely stores the reference of the LAS file and surface constraints. Finally, with the use of Las Dataset tools, an elevation (Z coordinate) based Inverse Distance Weight (IDW) interpolation technique (10) is applied in ArcMap in order to generate a raster of three-dimensional Digital Terrain Model (Figure 11, Figure 12).

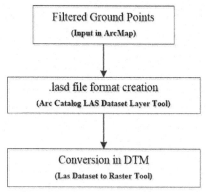

Figure 10: DTM generation process workflow.

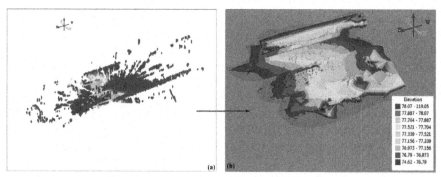

Figure 11: (a) Filtered ground points and, **(b)** generated DTM for Dataset 1.

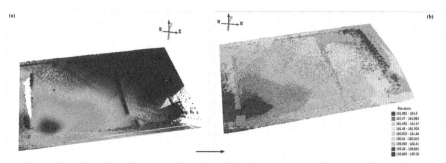

Figure 12: (a) Filtered ground points and, **(b)** generated DTM for Dataset 2.

$$\hat{V} = \frac{\sum_{i=1}^{n}\left(\dfrac{V_i}{d_i^p}\right)}{\sum_{i=1}^{n}\left(\dfrac{1}{d_i^p}\right)} \tag{10}$$

where, $\hat{V}$ represents the value of the point to be estimated, d_i is the distance from the ith point to the estimated point, V_i is the value of ith point, p is the real number (only positive) called as the power parameter of distance and n is the total number of points.

3.5.1 Implementing Security

Due to the emergence of the internet as a widely accepted communication medium there is a strong need to secure the transmitted digital content. As attackers may wish to get the secret information that is being transmitted in the form of output image (DTM). For security purposes there are numerous availabilities of image steganography techniques such as Spatial Domain data hiding algorithms, Pixel Value Difference (PVD), Least Significant Bit (LSB) based image steganography, Filtering Algorithms, Discrete Wavelet Transformation, and Discrete Cosine Transformation. Further, to enhance the security of the generated output image a LSB based image steganography has been applied [36]. Typically, an image is represented as a two-dimensional matrix with rows and columns ($r*c$) for a greyscale image and a three-dimensional matrix for colour images ($r*c*3$) in memory (where r and c are representing, matrix dimension, rows and columns respectively). In the matrix each entry represents the Digital Number (DN) value of a pixel. Typically, the image steganography technique has been utilised to embed a message into an image by modifying the DN values of few pixels. Selection of pixels depends upon the applied encryption algorithm. The image's recipient must be aware of the same applied algorithm in order to know the modified pixels to extract the embedded message.

Therefore, with the implementation of image steganography techniques generated DTM (output image) could be secured and if so the output image has been accessed by someone else would not be able to get the exact information.

4. Results

The proposed approach has been tested at captured LiDAR point cloud datasets, i.e., Dataset 1 and Dataset 2 described in Section 2. The statistical specifications of these datasets are given in Table 1. Numerous parameters such as G_x, G_y, n, h, α_{max}, θ, r, and their used values have taken in different steps of the proposed approach for the present study as listed below in Table 2.

4.1 Method Parameters Setting

In the segmentation of the input point cloud dataset (Section 3.1.3), *Gx* and *Gy* parameters are used for dividing the dataset into regular square grids. The used values of both parameters are 3 meters each. This value has been chosen based on completeness, correctness, and run time analysis of the proposed method (Figure 13, Figure 14). Steps included in the vertical slicing of the proposed methods explained in Section 3.2 involved two parameters n and h. The value of variable n is fixed to be 100 for the calculation of Z_{mean}, by considering maximum 100 points it will belong to the outlier for each grid in the captured dataset. For the creation of a vertical slice in which the area of interest points must lie, the value h is set to 1 meter because in a grid of 1×1 meter², all the ground points must lie in the layer from (Z_{mean}) to $(Z_{mean} + 1)$ meter. Three parameters α_{max}, θ, and r described respectively by the maximum normalized eigen value, the angle between the eigen vector corresponding to maximum normalized Eigen value and Z-axis ($\hat{k}$), radius of the circle are used in the circular growing step of the proposed method (Section 3.4). To identify the vertical linear objects, the value of α_{max} and θ is set to 0.8 and 7;5° respectively (El-Halawany and Lichti 2011). The radius r of circle is fixed to 0.3 meter, slightly greater than the average diameter of pole-like objects in the captured dataset.

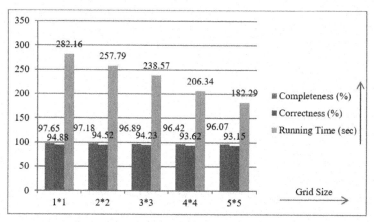

Figure 13: Statistical analysis among Completeness, Correctness, and Running time at different grid sizes for Dataset 1.

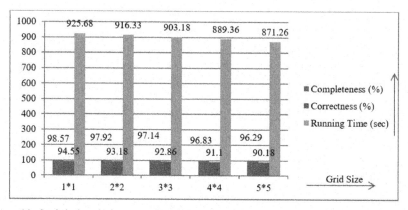

Figure 14: Statistical analysis among Completeness, Correctness, and Running time at different grid sizes for Dataset 2.

4.2 Reference Data

Global Mapper 18 has been used to generate the reference datasets from the captured test datasets. Overlapping of generated reference dataset with a corresponding output dataset has been performed to find out the True Positive (TP), False Positive (FP), and False Negative (FN) points.

4.3 Output Dataset

The proposed method applied at both the captured dataset, i.e., dataset 1 and dateset 2 and corresponding ground points are filtered out at parameter value shown in Table 2. Results obtained of average completeness (11) and correctness (12) are 98.11% and 94.71% respectively. Figure 11 and Figure 12, shows the filtered ground points with the corresponding generated DTM for Dataset 1 and Dataset 2 respectively. Reference datasets are used for statistical analysis of output datasets. Table 3 and Table 4, show the accuracy statistics for Dataset 1 and Dataset 2 respectively.

$$Completeness = \frac{Detected Ground\ points}{Reference\ Ground\ points} = \frac{TP}{TP + FN} \quad (11)$$

$$Correcteness = \frac{Ground\ points\ detected}{Ground\ points\ detected + Nonground\ points\ detected} = \frac{TP}{TP + FP} \quad (12)$$

Table 3: Accuracy statistics of Dataset 1.

Entire points in output dataset 1	6084777
Ground points in output dataset 1	5773236
Non-Ground points in the output file	311541
Entire points in reference data	5912172
Completeness	97.65 %
Correctness	94.88%

Table 4: Accuracy statistics of Dataset 2.

Entire points in output dataset 2	20537956
Ground points in output dataset 2	19418637
Non-Ground points in the output file	1119319
Entire points in reference data	19700352
Completeness	98.57 %
Correctness	94.55 %

5. Discussion

The proposed method uses only the geometric information (X, Y, and Z coordinate) values of each LiDAR point. Additional information such as intensity, a number of returns, return numbers, scanning geometry, etc., are not required in the proposed method. The proposed method is also independent of the point density of the LiDAR dataset. The method is implemented on a Sony Vaio E Series notebook having the following configuration (windows 7, 64 bit, Intel core i3@2.4 GHz, 3 GB RAM) at installed software Matlab2013. The average execution time of the proposed method at parameter values as shown in Table 2, is 810.63 GB per second. Accuracy parameters such as completeness, correctness, and execution time of the proposed method depend upon the grid size parameter calculated by $Gx*Gy$. If the size of the grid decreases, execution time of the method increases because by decreasing the grid size, more grids will be formed and it will take supplementary time for the creation of an additional number of grids (Figure 13 and Figure 14). The completeness and correctness of the method increases by decreasing the grid size. If the size of the grid decreases, there will be fewer points in each grid and it will be easy to pick the maximum elevated ground point from fewer points (Figure 13 and Figure 14).

5.1 Compare with the Existing Method

Existing literature regarding the filtering of ground points using the Lidar point cloud uses different kinds of LiDAR datasets for their algorithm testing. Due to the differences in the tested dataset, evaluation of completeness and correctness of the proposed method in the present study with existing literature is not forthright. Therefore, for comparison purposes, three methods (Table 5) are coded in the same environment in which the proposed method is coded and tested with both datasets (Dataset 1 and Dataset 2).

Execution time and correctness of the proposed method is slightly better than the compared literature. However, completeness of the proposed method is a little higher or nearly equal to compared literature except Husain and Vaishya 2016 [4], for Dataset 2.

Table 5: Completeness, Correctness, and Running time of different literature at Dataset 1 and Dataset 2.

Literature	LiDAR Dataset	Completeness (%)	Correctness (%)	Running Time (sec)
El-Halawany, 2013 [37]	Dataset 1	88.34	90.07	1531.96
	Dataset 2	92.68	91.79	2988.81
Ishikawa et al., 2013 [38]	Dataset 1	91.49	90.27	1014.43
	Dataset 2	96.38	93.78	2047.18
Husain and Vaishya, 2016 [4]	Dataset 1	96.49	77.56	945.43
	Dataset 2	98.38	81.75	3078.18

6. Conclusions and Future Trends

In the present study, a novel, and automated, and time-efficient method for the filtering of ground points and DTM generation using filtered ground points from the LiDAR point cloud dataset is proposed. The proposed method performs in five steps for DTM generation and filter ground points. The proposed method only includes the geometric information of each LiDAR point and does not include any radiometric information of point cloud data point. Segmentation of input LiDAR dataset is performed by dividing the dataset into regular grids. The vertical linear features have been identified by PCA and K–D trees have been used for a time efficient range search. ArcGIS 10.3 has been used in order to generate the DTM from the filtered ground points. Only 100 points will belong to outliers to consider as an initial assumption of the proposed method. Knowledge-based information is used for setting the value of range search radius (r). Matlab2013a is used for the implementation and run time analysis of the proposed method, tested on two different LiDAR point cloud datasets and corresponding ground points are filtered with average completeness and correctness of 98.11% and 94.71% respectively. In addition of DTM generation a Least Significant Bit (LSB) based image steganography technique is applied to secure the generated DTM. The extension of the proposed work may include limitations such as software dependency for DTM generation and also improve the accuracy level of completeness and correctness. Generated DTM could be further used for the calculation of water runoff. The extension of the manuscript may be the automated determination of the optimized value of the used parameter as a future aspect.

Acknowledgement

This paper and the research behind it would not have been possible without the exceptional support of the Optech Lynx mobile mapper, Canada for capturing MLS dataset and also express deep gratitude to Mr. Friederike Schwarzbach, technical support assistant of Terrasolid, who provided us with the data for this research work.

Conflict of Interest: None

On behalf of all authors, the corresponding author states that there are no conflicts of interest.

References

[1]   X. Meng, L. Wang, J.L. Silván-Cárdenas, and N. Currit. A multi-directional ground filtering algorithm for airborne LIDAR. *ISPRS J. Photogramm Remote Sens*, 64: 117–124, 2009.

[2]   J. Shan, and A. Sampath. Urban DEM generation from raw LiDAR data: A labeling algorithm and its performance. *Photogramm Eng. Remote Sens*, 71: 217–226, 2005.

[3]   G. Sithole. Filtering of laser altimetry data using a slope adaptive filter. *Int. Arch. Photogramm. Remote Sens*, 34-3/W4: 203–210, 2001.

[4]   A. Husain, and R.C. Vaishya. A time efficient algorithm for ground point filtering from mobile LiDAR data. *International Conference on Control Computing Communication and Materials (ICCCCM)*, 978-1-4673-9084-2/16/$31.00 ©2016 IEEE.

[5]   A. Kukko, and J. Hyyppä. Small-footprint laser scanning simulator for system validation, error assessment, and algorithm development. *Photogramm Eng. Remote Sens*, 75: 1177–1189, 2009.

[6]   X. Liu. Airborne LiDAR for DEM generation: Some critical issues. *ProgPhysGeog.*, 32: 31–49, 2008.

[7]   A. Baligh, M.J. ValadanZoej, and A. Mohammadzadeh. Bare earth extraction from airborne lidar data using different filtering methods. *In Proceedings of Commission III ISPRS Congress Beijing China*, 2008.

[8]   B. Lohani. *Airborne AltimetricLiDAR: Principle, Data collection, processing and Applications.* 2010http://home.iitk.ac.in/~blohani/LiDAR_Tutorial/Airborne_AltimetricLidar_Tutorial.htm.

[9] D. Gonzalez-Aguilera, E. Crespo-Matellan, D. Hernandez-Lopez, and P. Rodriguez-Gonzalvez. Automated urban analysis based on LiDAR-derived building models. *IEEE Trans Geosci. Remote Sensing*, 51: 1844–1851, 2013.

[10] J. Carter, K. Schmid, K. Waters, B. Betzhold, B. Hadley, R. Mataosky, and J. Halleran. An introduction to lidar technology, data, and applications. *National Oceanic and Atmospheric Administration (NOAA) Coastal Services Center NOAA Coastal Services Center 2234 S Hobson Ave Charleston SC*, 29405(843): 740–1200, 2012.

[11] S.I. El-Halawany. Detection of road furniture from mobile terrestrial laser scanning point clouds. *A Thesis Submitted to the Faculty of Graduate Studies in Partial Fulfillment of the Requirements for The Degree of Doctor of Philosophy Department of Geomatics Engineering Calgary Alberta*, 2013.

[12] J. Zhao, and S. You. Road network extraction from airborne LiDAR data using scene context. *Computer Vision and Pattern Recognition Workshops (CVPRW) IEEE Computer Society Conference*, 2012.

[13] K. Zhang, and D. Whitman. Comparison of three algorithms for filtering airborne LiDAR data. *Photogramm Eng. Remote Sens*, 71: 313–324, 2005.

[14] J.M. Hill, L.A. Graham, R.J. Henry, D.M. Cotter, A. Ping and P. Young. Wide-area topographic mapping and applications using airborne light detection and ranging (LiDAR) technology. *Photogramm Eng. Remote Sens*, 66: 908914, 2000.

[15] U. Lohr. Digital elevation models by laser scanning. *Photogramm Rec.*, 16: 105–109, 1998.

[16] J. Kilian, N. Haala and M. Englich. Capture and evaluation of airborne laser scanner data. *Int. Arch. Photogramm Remote Sens Spatial InfSci.*, 31: 383–388, 1996.

[17] G. Vosselmann. Slope based filtering of Laser altimetry data. *Int. Arch. Photogramm Remote Sens*, XXXIII 935–942, 2000.

[18] R. Ma, and W. Meyer. DTM generation and building detection from Lidar data. *Photogramm Eng. Remote Sens.*, 71: 847–854, 2005.

[19] K. Kraus, and J. Otepka. DTM modelling and visualization-the SCOP approach. *In Proceedings of Photogrammetric Week* 05: 241–252, 2005, Heidelberg Germany.

[20] S. Popescu, and K. Zhao. A voxel-based lidar method for estimating crown base height for deciduous and pine Trees. *Remote Sens Environ.*, 112: 767–781, 2008.

[21] H.S. Lee, and N.H. Younan. DTM extraction of LiDAR returns via adaptive processing. *IEEE Trans. Geosci. Remote Sensvol.* 41: 2063–2069, 2003.

[22] P. Axelsson. Processing of laser scanner data-algorithms and applications. *ISPRS J. Photogramm Remote Sensvol.*, 54: 138–147, 1999.

[23] N. Pfeifer, T. Reiter, C. Briese, and W. Rieger. Interpolation of high quality ground models from laser scanner data in forested areas. *Int. Arch. Photogramm Remote Sens Spatial InfSci.*, 32: 31–36, 1999.

[24] W. Schickler, and A. Thorpe. Surface estimation based on LiDAR. *In Proceedings of the ASPRS Annual Conference St Louis Missouri*, 2001.

[25] C. Briese, and N. Pfeifer. Airborne laser scanning and derivation of digital terrain models. *In Proceedings of Fifth Conference on Optical 3-D Measurement Techniques Vienna Austria*, 2001.

[26] G. Sithole, and G. Vosselman. Experimental comparison of filter algorithms for bare-earth extraction from airborne laser scanning point clouds. *Photogramm Eng. Remote Sens*, 59: 85–101, 2004.

[27] D. Mongus, and B. Žalik. Parameter-free ground filtering of LiDAR data for automatic DTM generation. *ISPRS J. Photogramm Remote Sens*, 67: 1–12, 2012.

[28] M.Y. Belkhouche, and B. Buckles. Iterative TIN-based automatic filtering of sparse LiDAR data. *Remote Sensing Letters* 2: 231–240, 2011.

[29] S. Filin. Surface clustering from airborne laser scanning data. *Int. Arch Photogramm Remote Sens Spatial InfSci.*, 34: 119–124, 2002.

[30] K. Jacobsen, and P. Lohmann. Segmented filtering of laser scanner dsms. *In Proceedings of the ISPRS Working Group I/3 workshop 3-D Reconstruction from Airborne Laserscanner and InSAR Data Dresden Germany*, 2003.

[31] D. Tóvári, and N. Pfeifer. Segmentation based robust interpolation a new approach to laser filtering. *Int. Arch Photogramm Remote Sens Spatial InfSci.*, 36: 79–84, 2005.

[32] T. Rabbani, F.A. Van den Heuvel, and G. Vosselman. Segmentation of point clouds using smoothness constraint. *Int. Arch Photogramm Remote Sens Spatial InfSci.*, 36: 248–253, 2006.

[33] M. Gupta, F. Patwa, and R. Sandhu. An attribute-based access control model for secure big data processing in hadoop ecosystem. *Proceedings of the Third ACM Workshop on Attribute-Based Access Control Tempe AZ USA.* 2018. https://doi.org/10.1145/3180457.3180463.

[34] M. Gupta, F. Patwa, and R. Sandhu. Object-tagged RBAC model for the hadoop ecosystem. *In:* Livraga, G. and Zhu, S. (eds.). *Data and Applications Security and Privacy XXXI. DBSec* 2017. *Lecture Notes in Computer Science*, vol. 10359. Springer, Cham. 2017. https://doi.org/10.1007/978-3-319-61176-1_4.

[35] M. Gupta, F. Patwa, and R. Sandhu. Access control model for the hadoop ecosystem. *Proceedings of the 22nd ACM on Symposium on Access Control Models and Technologies, Indianapolis, IN, USA.* 2017. http://dx.doi.org/10.1145/3078861.3084164.

[36] D. Neeta, K. Snehal, and D. Jacobs. Implementation of LSB steganography and its evaluation for various bits. *1st International Conference on Digital Information Management*, 173–178, 2006, 10.1109/ICDIM.2007.369349.

[37] S.I. El-Halawany, and D.D. Lichti. *Detection of Road Poles from Mobile Terrestrial Laser Scanner Point Cloud.* 978-1-4244-9404-0/11/$26.00 ©2011 IEEE.

[38] K. Ishikawa, F. Tonomura, Y. Amano, and T. Hashizume. Recognition of road objects from 3D mobile mapping data. *International Journal of CAD/CAM*, 13: 41–48, 2013.

5

Predictive Big Data Analytics and Privacy based Decision Support System

*Lakshita Aggarwal** and *Puneet Goswami*

ABSTRACT

In the era of technological development, Big Data is not simply "business as usual" and the decision to adopt Big Data must take into account many businesses and technology considerations. It's an accumulation of data that is too large and complex for processing by traditional database management tools. Data retrieved from different sources is analyzed by Operation Analysts or Business Intelligence (BI) analyst's to take decisions appropriately for desired results. Big data has been pushing current technologies and infrastructure to its limit where the traditional ways of processing really didn't work anymore. Predictive analysis is one of the buzz areas of research especially in healthcare. Predictive analysis is done to accelerate the diagnostic process before the situation worsens. It will also help in developing new norms and standards to curtail the spread of a pandemic like coronavirus and helps us in caring for those affected by using proper measures against the virus The aim of predictive driver analysis is to provide better facilities and services to the patients and medical practitioners to know what treatment or an asset a person needs based on the study of their past data set. Knowing prior allows our healthcare provider to quickly recommend the right health facility so that correct actions and measures can be taken. This chapter involves a sincere attempt to analyze the predictive analysis of the data sets and then further sort the data sets using some deep learning based tools. Data sets have been analyzed on the basis of V's of big data. The data of occupancy in different hospitals located at various geo-locations is taken in consideration and is analyzed on the IBM Cognos software to understand the predictive analysis of the model. As the data is accumulated from varied areas therefore its confidentiality was a major concern, so a few techniques have been devised for preserving privacy of the data.

Department of Computer Science & Engineering, SRM University Delhi-NCR Sonepat (Haryana), India.
    Email: goswamipuneet@gmail.com
* Corresponding author: lakshitaaggarwal31@gmail.com

1. Introduction

Healthcare is a connected set of anything, anyone, anytime, anyplace, any services and any network. Medical care and health care represents one of the most attractive application areas. Compliance with treatment and medication at home and other healthcare providers is an important application. According to R&D activities in the field of healthcare diseases like the coronavirus (COVID-19) during a pandemic spares no cities or nations causing extensive damage and increased mortality rate in all age groups. Coronaviruses are the largest group of RNA (Ribonucleic Acid) viruses having an immense range of natural hosts. Newly evolved, COVID-19 is a global threat to mankind. The immune response against COVID-19 is essential to control and eliminate infection. If some correct and preventive measures are taken against the pandemic the situation even can be controlled using home based remedies or the mild clinical treatments. Big data deals with a huge amount of data sets to analyze it, process it or create it and then "acts" upon it. Big data in healthcare includes Electronic Health Records (EHR's), medical imaging, sequencing, and other medical devices. This will help in 360° analysis of patient's health care data analysis. It helps in creating holistic 360° view of patients and helps physicians to analyze the patient's needs deeply. This chapter discusses the data of various age groups and tries to show the results according to different age groups that are the most prone to COVID-19. The main aim of contributing this chapter is to discuss some of the predictive techniques during the pandemic and also to devise some privacy based mechanisms.

2. Literature Review

The physical and environmental entities around us streams a large amount of data, whereas the combined scale of data from various devices seems destined to continue to grow. Application of big data involves analytics. Data analysis is the process of deriving new insights from data or generating new knowledge from data, i.e., turning raw data into actionable insights. The chapter points towards the review work done in the field of big data analytics from the perspective of their utility in making effective, efficient and innovative things or developing unique services that proves to be ubiquitous for a wide spectrum of domain. The broad vision for big data has been reviewed as it is shaped in various communities, examines its applications of data analysis across various domains. This will help researchers in developing newer insights on the appropriateness of the analytical techniques like pattern recognition, Qualitative analysis, quantitative analysis, data mining, etc., and understanding its need accordingly to its requirements to facilitate society.

Big data is gaining momentum in both the industry and research communities due to an explosion in the number of devices, sensors and the applications that produce a large amount of data from a large spectrum of domains.

Analytics is actually a science, method or process that helps in examining anything complex. Data analytics is the process of deriving or fetching (the analysis step) from the data the knowledge or actionable insights out of (something complex). Data analytics is not a new concept it is initiated from past historic times.

In [1] Tukey, defined data analysis as procedures for analyzing data, and techniques for interpreting the results, data gathering that makes analysis easier, more precise and accurate, and finally he involves all the related machinery and statistical methods used in data analysis process.

Some researchers, also included the concept of "data mining" that helps in fetching useful insights out of big data and the other useful patterns out of it.

Then in the twentieth century, researchers introduced analytics as quantitative, statistical or predictive model to analyze business problems or used it as a tool in management systems. Then, came the phase when Varian in 2009, understood it as "an ability to take data understand it, process it, extract value from it, visualize it and communicate it as hugely important skill in the coming ten years.

In 2013 [2], Davenport include the analytics as:-

1.0 = Traditional Analytics
2.0 = Development of Big data technology
3.0 = Big data + analytics

Hu Yun et al. [21] worked on laboratory data analysis screening 2510 patients. They collected nucleic acid and haematology data from 2510 patients for identifying the COVID-19 infection for retrospective analysis. They tried to calculate the results of the influenza virus. In their chapter, they decided to examine the effects of faecal matter. They proposed medical and clinical treatment by just introspecting 2510 patients, but the data could vary from one location to another. Also the immunity and many other factors inside the body also differ from one region to the other. This chapter doesn't takes into account number of factors such as: that people of different countries consuming varied nutritional foods, may show a diverse nature against the virus and moreover they did not include the preventive measures in the chapter. This chapter also does not discuss predictive analytics taking the number of patients in cause affected.

Faizora et al. [23] stated that with COVID-19 it is still an unclear infectious disease, i.e., we can obtain an accurate SEIR (Susceptible, Exposed, Infectious, and Removed or Recovered) predictions only when the epidemic ends. In this, they made a corona tracker, which will identify based on the prediction model. But, other factors such as medical treatment analysis and preventive measures were not discussed that may help in flattening the curve.

Palash et al. [22] worked on growth models where they worked on the Daily Infection Rate (DIR). They concluded that the data may vary according to the state or the area we are analysing as the number of factors in the particular region also vary from one to another. They worked on state-wise analysis showing different DIR at different intervals of time, and varied results are cumulatively shown for each state. They also discussed some preventive measures where we can try making the DIR reach zero so that we can flatten the curve and maybe one day the pandemic ends.

Vinay et al. [24] have studied clinical features and transmission mechanisms of past pandemics like: such as the Spanish flu, Asian flu, Hong Kong flu, Swine flu. The chapter also discussed various economic impacts and other risk factors on relevant statistics related to COVID-19. The authors have also taken into account signs and symptoms of patients to assess their cases carefully. In their work, they summarized their studies providing a brief overview on diagnosis, treatment and their prevention. The chapter also discussed the pathway for the transmission of the disease of COVID-19 from the nasal passage till the lungs. The chapter also discussed factors of AI, machine learning, & block-chain to flatten the curve.

Aggarwal et al. [19] discussed the approach of Multi criterion decision support system. In their work multiple factors are considered such as medicinal/clinical treatment, country/state wise analysis, nutritive values and many more. But the chapter does not highlight predictive big data analytics.

Samrat et al. [25] analysed exploratory visual data through which they explained how early detection could help in better response in fighting the SARS virus. This chapter investigated visual data where they studied three different categories: confirmed cases, recovered cases and the number of people died in different countries. This chapter also stressed upon the need of vaccines and other treatments for viral diseases since birth. But their observations lacked in areas where the need to stress upon medical treatment or the preventive measures to be undertaken in the cause. Below, the comparative analysis clearly shows the idea.

Table 1: Comparative analysis.

Author	Study Domain	Method
Tukey [1]	Data Gathering and analyzing	Statistical Methods
Daven Port [2]	Traditional Analysis	Big Data Analytics
Hu et al. [21]	Retrospective Analysis	Data Analysis
Fairoza et al. [23]	Prediction model	SEIR Modelling
Palash et al. [22]	Growth Models	DIR
Vinay et al. [24]	Comprehensive Review	AI+ ML
Aggarwal et al. [19]	Multi-criteria decision support system	Data Analysis
Samrat et al. [25]	Visual exploratory data analysis	Need of vaccines, treatment & other observatory features
Proposed Model	Predictive Data Analysis	IBM Cognos + Data Science

3. Analysis

IBM actually in 2013 came up with the 4V's [26] also known as the four characteristics of big data. The challenges that big data has imposed on the infrastructure and technologies. So, these 4V'S are:-

- Volume
- Variety
- Veracity
- Velocity

Volume—Scale of data is always growing. We have always had data growth in past, but what is happening in the recent years with the onset of big data, this growth is happening at unprecedented rate. Data at rest is large. We are generating over 2.5 petabytes of data a day currently. And as we have already seen, due to the large volume of data much of that data is unstructured as well as structured.

Velocity—Velocity means data in motion. It refers to the speed at which data is moving. We often talk about the fire horse of data coming and accumulating day by day to us and data is being available and utilized at very large speed. Data is often streaming at large frequencies. And we have to quickly make some sense of the data, possibly do some quick analysis to be able to provide an intelligent answer often times within seconds or milliseconds of time.

Variety—Variety states the different forms the data is available in. It could be social media data, types of audio and video data, music, structured and unstructured data and the huge variety of data available is challenging existing analytics algorithm.

Veracity—The more data we have the dirtier the data it is. No matter how clean we think our data is, there are always numerous issues with the data available to us. And when we talk about big data or data accumulating at fast speed in such a large variety of formats, veracity becomes a big issue. When data comes in large volumes, issues starts prevailing such as inconsistency, latency, missing data, data that may not be as accurate as we would like it to be.

So, these 4V's describes really well the different challenges that are posed by the onset of big data.

Shift from 4V'S TO 6V'S

Two V's are added to solve complex business problems to solve the uncertainty of data and make the data more useful for mankind. So, two more V's are added:-

- Variability
- Value

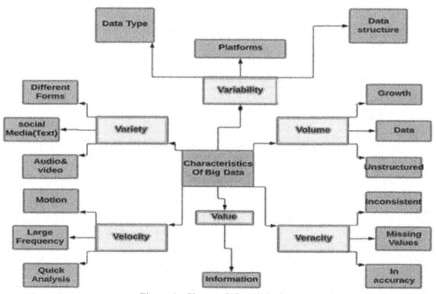

Figure 1: Characteristics of big data.

Variability is data to be understood, find and to navigate federated big data in a structured or unstructured format.

Value is the time to build important applications that are designed for big data.

3.1 Functional Requirements of Big Data

We always capture data, which is whatever is available around us through devices, sensors and many more things. Researchers try to capture data always which is not as easy task, then organize that data in a meaningful way. Being able to integrate these different desperate data sources that are coming at different granularities with different formats and different speeds. And then as we bring those data sets together, oftentimes we want to layer them in order to be able to analyze them, create some insights and then make it able to act.

Figure 2: Step wise requirements.

By the time, we go through this flow, more data has arrived and we need to keep going through this iterative process over and over again until we gather enough insights. And the data often times in this process will change the formats, the size and the types of data. It is a very dynamic iterative process that doesn't seem to ever stop. It shows that once the raw data is analyzed, it is processed to prepare the final solutions out of it. It becomes ready to help power the world with ubiquitous knowledge and results.

3.2 The Sphere has Changed in Significant Ways

❖ In how we engage the data from millions of PC's to billions of devices used around the globe.

❖ The devices we carry with structured data processed from huge amounts of unstructured data.

❖ The type of data we use to move from a static approach to a dynamic approach and the insights we gain out of it.

❖ The rigid and fast growing speed we adapt from a file's rigid structure to cloud infrastructure.

❖ Securing data with high encryption methods, i.e., moving from a reactive approach to the intelligent proactive protection of data.

Digital technologies have been major forces to make a shift to a future that recognizes itself making a new converging ecosystem.

4. Different Types of Analytics

We can combine unstructured data and structured data together to form information and gain a deeper understanding of what they would like to interact with.

This data layering and augmentation of data are one of the greatest benefits of big data. We can now leverage machine generated data to improve a business's effectiveness. We can use that data to enable and monitor cyber security, fraud and many more in real time analytics. Anyone can detect, prevent & stop frauds from happening in real time which was nearly an impossible task in the past. Having access to large, real-time complex data for data analysis is the real benefit of big data.

In traditional data analysis, the past usually indicated that your business may have had some amount of data, and the data coming from different formats may be accumulated in tons of capacity out of which we wished to make some sense. So, this requires different approaches for analysis depending on the problem that we are trying to solve. Some of the analysis might use the traditional approach like we have data in a data lake and we wish to make an advanced predictive analytics approach to create some predictive and advanced models.

Managing big data to an extent requires many different approaches to help the business and other investments to successfully plan for the future.

Instead of just having a data, in a repository and taking a sub sample of that data we are now going into the era of large data when our traditional approaches of taking a sub-sample are not working anymore and the data's new paradigm shift where we have large complex streaming data from massive unstructured data to informative structured data.

The coupled way of using unstructured data, structured data and semi-structured data and the predictive analytics model is the new way of analyzing big data with some new insights.

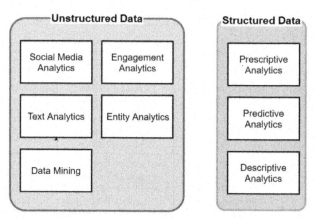

Figure 3: Analytics of different data structures.

4.1 Unstructured Data

❖ **Social Media Analytics:** it measures and collects interactions on different social media platforms and collects data for various analyses process.

- ❖ **Engagement Analytics:** it measures raw data from different systems software and application software and uses those data sets to process in decision analysis.
- ❖ **Text Analytics:** it analyzes unstructured data, i.e., the data which is just collected from different sources but has never been analyzed and sometimes due to lack of space it is just discarded without even processing.
- ❖ **Entity Analytics:** it helps in finding relevant data for entities and persons to help in the specific domain of knowledge.
- ❖ **Data Mining:** Huge amounts of data gets stored in a data warehouse to use this data we need to process the data sets by applying various data mining algorithms and use them in a meaningful and reasonable ways.

4.2 Semi-structured Data

Semi-structured data is easy to generate. It lacks explicit structure. But, semi-structured data is hard to browse, query and optimize. It is a textual database that appears with patterns and analysis. Like: XML files, log files, etc.

4.3 Structured Data

- ❖ **Prescriptive Analytics:** it takes us straight through the decision and into taking of action based on the insights found. This is the level of automation that tries several different types of predictive algorithms to see the results under a certain set of circumstances, a particular algorithm or the model would create the best most optimized results for us. It tells to "recommend an action".
- ❖ **Predictive Analytics:** this is where machine learning and deep learning comes into play. These types of analytics typically enables us to answer questions like "what will happen in the future?"

Table 2: Different analytics.

Analytics	Prescriptive	Predictive	Descriptive
What Happened	Should	Could	Has
Users Need to Do	Optimize resources and increase utilization	Predict failures and Forecast demands	Increase reliability and trust
Users need to know	Optimization and long term utilization	Consolidate under-utilized facilities to improve services	Maintain asset failures
How analytics is answered	Optimization, i.e., the best possible results Variable/Random optimization-variability in specified areas	Alert (Action Needed) → Simulate (What Could happen) → Forecast (will this continue) →Predict (What happens next)	Standard report making (What had happened)→ Drill down (Data Mining)→ where problem exists→ How often and where
Possible analysis	Business rules, models and optimization	Prediction and statistical analysis	Alerts, reports and business intelligence

❖ **Descriptive Analytics:** it enables us to answer questions like "what has happened in the future? It also tries to report what happened and why? Business analysts are great at doing this and sometimes for this we need to perform additional analysis to see what the trend might have been in the past. We still have a room for correction where we can refine the decisions before taking insights to action.

The diagram below depicts the various stages in which the prediction occurs:

1. Predict the behaviour and preference on the basis of a past event that has already occurred.

2. Produce real time issues and think of the potential before they really make a difference in society.

3. Generate, visualize and predict models.

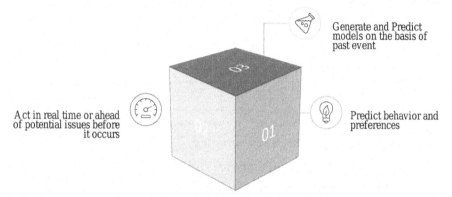

Generate and Predict models on the basis of past event

Act in real time or ahead of potential issues before it occurs

Predict behavior and preferences

Figure 4: Illustrating stages of predictive analytics.

So, we add diagnostic and cognitive analytics as well to the structured data for data analysis at great insights.

❖ **Diagnostic analytics:** this is to analyze "Why something happened?" Sometimes, we perform root cause analysis and perform some deeper analytics on the data we have to produce better and desired outcomes.

❖ **Cognitive Analytics:** Cognitive analytics add on the disciplines of smart and intelligence to the preprocessed data sets through experiences, surveys and past records. It includes answers like "what did I learn, what is best".

5. Shift from Traditional Approach to Big Data Analytics

In past times, using traditional approaches it is difficult to analyze all of the data collected from different sources and it sometimes is not even analyzed as a whole and only a few parts of it was analyzed and other data is just discarded from the data source even without processing. But, as the big data analysis comes into play it analyses the complete data set by processing it into information. So, big data tries to leverage all the data being captured by analyzing all the information.

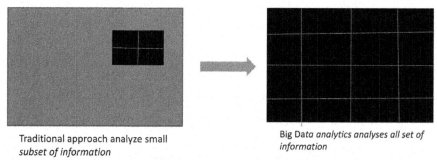

Traditional approach analyze small   Big Data *analytics analyses all set of*
subset of information   *information*

Figure 5: Traditional v/s Big Data approach.

Table 3: Gartner's hype cycle of technologies [3, 4, 5, 6, 7, 8, 9, 10].

Technology	Parameters	Year	Expected Outcome	Proposed Outcomes
Predictive Analysis	Peak Growth	2010–2013	Scope of Enlightenment	No steep increase
IoT Platform	Model + Taxonomy	2011–2015	Innovation Trigger	Plateau of Productivity
Big Data	Growth of Data	2011–onwards	In petabytes	In Zettabyte's
Internet of Things	Devices	2011–onwards	Innovative devices	Hit market with growing curves

6. Analytics of Different Technologies

Map view of different technologies that are booming in our market and spreading widespread its wings in serving mankind from past 10 years.

Predictive Analysis: This answers the question "What will happen in future?" predictive analysis may be employed to the business processes to further boom the on-going business processes. As it helps in predicting the future by learning from past events. The predictive analysis is powered by learning from data to discover models or actions by the process of data-mining patterns. It will help in benefitting society by providing large observations from past data sets. It was assumed from 2010–2013 that peak growth in data analytics will be observed but steeper curves of growing analysis are not observed. Scope of enlightenment with the growing time is not seen.

IoT Platform: IoT platforms initiated its roots in the market from 2011 onwards. The model and taxonomical structure for IoT was developed. The IoT platform triggered the innovation with the help of a larger number of smart devices that are able to be deployed in the market for benefitting human-kind.

Big Data: As technological development takes place, more data from more devices, large sensors, applications and many more keep accumulating as piles of data. The big piles created the problem of processing those data sets and fetches us better insights out of it. So, better tools and techniques were required to analyze those data sets.

Internet of Things: Then, came the phase of Internet of Things that were the large number of devices were equipped using IoT platforms. IoT has a huge potential to enhance its wings in multiple domains and gain momentum along with broader vision.

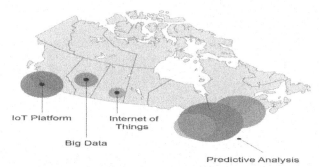

Figure 6: Map view of technologies spreading around globe.

From the above table, we can say that not only big data but also the associated technologies with it are also growing its curve be it IoT or big data. The advent of IoT and big data, steady growth, expansion and creation of new areas.

Big data is the data that is too big (volume), too diverse (variety), too fast (velocity), too different forms (variety), too different platforms (variability), too different information (value). In 2014, a survey of data scientists reveals that 71% of interviewed people claim that analytics is becoming increasingly difficult due to the diverse types of data sources.

Predictive Analysis

Predictive analytics involves a variety of techniques such as statistics of data, mining the data, machine learning, Artificial intelligence (AI) to analyze a large amount of data and discover new patterns and relationship between various associated attributes. The ability to discover new patterns and relationships from the pre-existing data accumulated so as to make predictions on future behavior or some unknown events. These techniques helps in pro-actively identifying various risks and opportunities.

7. Framework on Decision Support System

For taking a decision the typical expert system is deployed. The main modules of an expert system are:

1. Data : External & Internal data
2. Knowledge management
3. Dialog management
4. Data management
5. Model management
6. Decision maker
7. Information system
8. Security

Data: It constitutes external and internal data constituting attribute data, i.e., the data with characteristics and spatial data concerned with geo-location of data. Data is the primary basis which deals with the other architectural layers of the model.

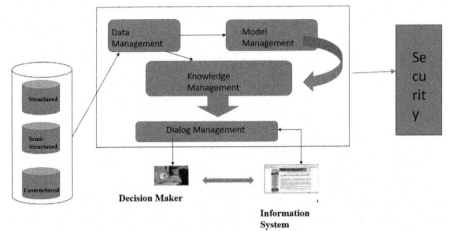

Figure 7: Decision Support System (DSS).

Knowledge Management: The main module of any expert system is its knowledge management (KM). It is a warehouse of the domain knowledge that is captured from the expert analysis of humans through knowledge acquisition models. The [11] Knowledge in knowledge management comes from the past experiences or the results from past data sets. It uses the knowledge of "being told" mechanism.

Dialog Management: It acts as a user interface to the decision support system (DSS). The decision maker communicates with the DSS and performs analysis. The dialog manager makes queries and reports based on DSS. It makes the spatial query management and produces output by interacting with the knowledge management and decision maker. It acts as the "gateway" for uses to communicate with the DSS. It is like the menu icons for user's better and effective communication.

Data Management: Data management deals with spatial and non-spatial data. It holds the data to be used in decision making. The data in the data manager is managed by the database management system (DBMS). This data interacts with all other architectural layers like model management, knowledge management, and dialog management [11].

The data and its related information are crucial in the decision making progress. Generally, we have two main sources of data internal sources (that are within the organization) and external sources (that are outside the organization). We also deal with geographical based or location based data, i.e., spatial or non-spatial data. Collection of data from these models and properly organizing it leads to the intelligent phase model to predict the information.

Model management: Model is the relationship between the various parameters of the system. It is the description of "reality". By understanding the various activities of model management it becomes easy to formulate models and use them effectively. It holds all the necessary models for the further analysis process. Model management deals with knowledge management, data management and dialog management.

Decision maker: Decision maker is interactive, flexible and adaptable computer based information that utilizes decision rules, model and model based system with comprehensive database management system [12]. The decision maker fetches insights leading to implementable decision in decision-making progress. Decision maker takes the complex decision making progress and increases its effectiveness. The Decision maker acts as an assistant to the problems of all levels whether structured, semi-structured or unstructured data. Decision maker acts as the first-line interface and then the data moves in hierarchy to the middle and top level management system.

Information system: Information system fetches results from the decision maker which then passes it onto the dialog manager. It facilitates decision making by the team of decision makers providing effective communication, brainstorming sessions are carried out so the collective pool of ideas and opinions gives final shape to the decision support system.

Security: The issue of security or privacy to data is discussed in a separate section of the chapter giving some techniques that we can use to safeguard our sensitive information from alteration.

8. Decision Support System Process

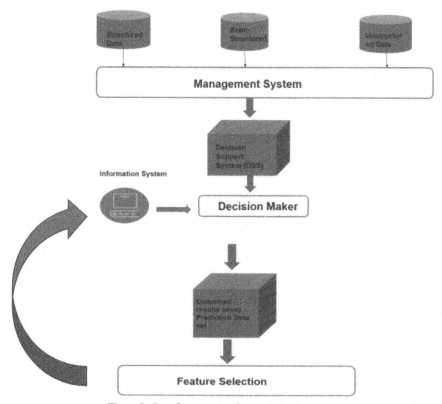

Figure 8: Data flow process of proposed DSS model.

Decision support system (DSS) is modified in a manner such that optimum results for a person can be taken seeing all the perspectives of domain. This system can work efficiently in diseases like COVID-19 or even it can be used for other industries by making some modifications in it. This helps in providing support to the man-kind.

9. Algorithm

```
{
   Start
   Initialize data structure as 'x(t)';
i = 0;
{
Model_i = Model[i] & Model_i in management system;
   Assign data in Decision Support sytem;
   Train data set results using predictive analytics;
}
Fetching results from information system;
{
   Combining all values [i] after reducing in prediction driver analysis;
   Reduce data sets into feature selection;
}
End;
}
```

10. Decision Making Life Cycle Methodology

The decision making life cycle is the sequential steps undergone to take all the study characteristics of the problem. It is also done to understand the scope and extent of the problem. In this, we also account for the amount of resources needed. It identifies

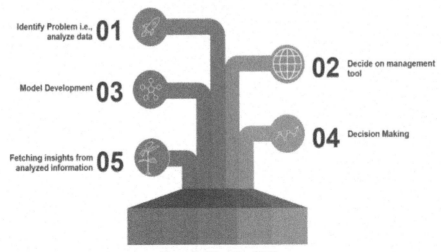

Figure 9: Life cycle of DSS.

the problem analyzing process. It takes raw data sets from external and internal data and other knowledge management systems.

Then, we decide on the management tool or the characteristics of the tool to decide the language or the tool used to analyze the process.

To develop the model, [13] concepts are needed for the solution making process and also the knowledge acquisition making progress. It also analyzes the methods of knowledge representation. At last, the whole testing of the system takes place while developing the model.

Decision making is the additional interaction between multiple decision makers. It also requires heavy planning and management analysis of data on various parameters. Then the implementation scheme comes after decision making.

Then, in [15] the last insights are fetched from analyzed information sets from basic resource requirement at the fulfilled site on pace. Full testing of the software takes place before the deployment of the software. Security of subsystems takes place at the final layer.

11. Exploratory Data Analysis (EDA)

We have analyzed the data set of different hospitals in particular states including both the rural and public. Then, these data sets are analyzed on IBM Cognos software that if the pandemic grows the same manner then what needs to be done to improve infrastructure in such a manner that humans should not suffer. Although, we know in our country India, the healthcare sector contributes less to the GDP. If we want to fight a deadly disease like COVID-19. The urgent need is to improve infrastructure and for that predictive driver analysis is performed.

The data analyzed on Cognos software after driver analysis predicts the results of different states having different district hospitals as depicted in Uttar Pradesh with its 174 while it varies to just 32 in Chhattisgarh with the help of this analysis we can predict the number of hospitals [17] located at different locations and the varied steps to be taken in this regard to improve efficiency for the people below the poverty line (BPL) as these people use most of the government healthcare centers.

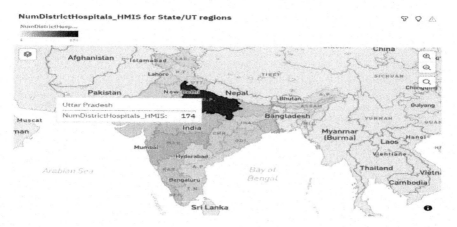

Figure 10: District hospital in Uttar Pradesh.

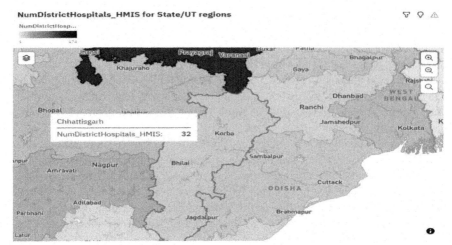

Figure 11: District hospital in Chhattisgarh.

12. Different Age Groups Affected

When different age groups are studied it is predicted that the working or independent age group is more prone to virus which is depicted by the graphs [14].

The people most affected are the age groups of 20–29 and 30–39 are the most important categories of age groups with the total percentage out of affected ones. This population constitutes 46% of the total.

Out of Total cases 20–29 and 30–39 are the most important categories of the age group with a total value of 318 (46% of the total).

The sum of total cases for all values of age groups is 692.

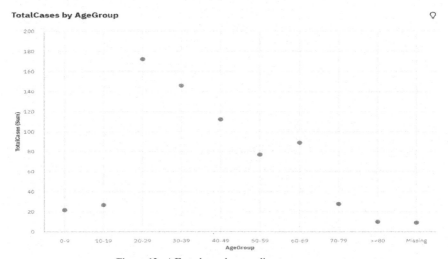

Figure 12: Affected people according to age group.

AgeGroup for TotalCases

Column values
Increase Decrease Sum

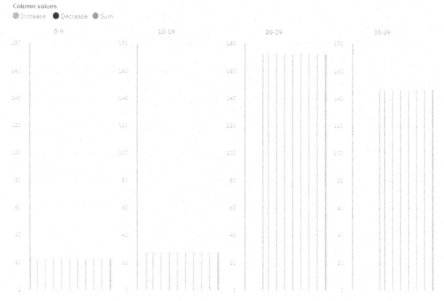

Figure 13: Total cases.

The summed values of total cases over all combinations of the inputs range from a minimum of 9 to a maximum of 172.

The above graphs depicts the value of total cases in different age groups of 0–9, 10–19, 20–29, 30–39 years of age. After analyzing it on a prediction model we had controlled the cases on the masses by applying various preventive measures on the growing number of cases.

This proves that using a prediction mechanism along with big data may prove instrumental for the world to demolish such diseases.

13. Privacy to Data

As the data grows there is an urgent need to provide privacy to this sensitive information. For providing privacy to data we have varied models and algorithms. Data security has always been the major issue in IT sector. As the data grows the concern of security [18–21] also grows because the data is located at different locations in and around the globe.

So, the word privacy by itself means that when the raw data or information is excluded from people and is just confined or known to some set of the population that keeps its safe from unauthorized threats.

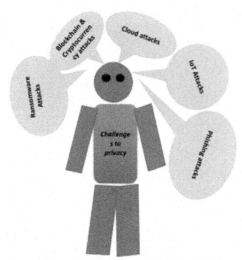

Figure 14: Challenges User's Face.

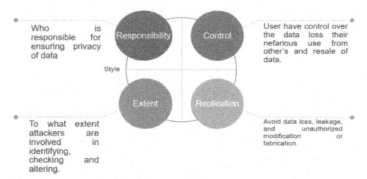

Figure 15: Key elements of privacy.

The above figure depicts that if the CRER (Control, Replication, Extent and Responsibility) of the data is taken in consideration then we may prove instrumental in providing security to the data. Data Security has been envisioned as the urgent paradigm in computation.

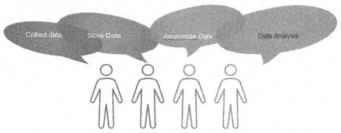

Figure 16: Flow process of data.

The usefulness of processing big data is mainly unquestioned. There are broadly two aspects of big data analysis: First, the larger the amount of data, the higher the probability is of identifying risks associated with it.

Secondly, big data analysis is able to infer that personal data is much more critical and sensitive and is not intended to be affected by attackers.

The data is collected at a pool storage and out of that storage the data is anonymized and from that anonymized data some part of the data is analyzed for further processing.

Some common anonymized methods are

1. Suppression: Suppression refers to removing the values of an attribute completely or replacing those attributes with some dummy values or some special symbols. This technique is generally used in the areas of sensitive medical information.

Table 4: General data.

Name	Dob	Sex	Blood Count
Alice	1/21/76	M	53715
Cathy	4/13/86	F	53703
Bob	2/28/76	M	53704
Andy	1/21/76	M	53715
Dan	4/13/87	F	53706
Ellen	2/05/89	F	53708

So, irrespective of giving the correct blood count we may insert some dummy or special symbols so that data does not get attacked by attackers.

Table 5: Suppressed table.

Name	Dob	Sex	Blood Count
Alice	1/21/76	M	5371*5
Cathy	4/13/86	F	537*3
Bob	2/28/76	M	537*4
Andy	1/21/76	M	537*5
Dan	4/13/87	F	537*6
Ellen	2/05/89	F	537*8

Now, the data is encrypted which has chances of elimination from attackers.

2. Generalization: Generalization refers to replacing values with more general or more abstract values inside the taxonomical attributes.

For example: In date of birth (DOB) age must be in years rather than specifying the correct age, a range of years may be specified.

Table 6: Generalized data.

Name	Dob	Sex	Blood Count
Alice	Jan-76	M	5371*5
Cathy	Apr-86	F	537*3
Bob	Feb-76	M	537*4
Andy	Jan-76	M	537*5
Dan	Apr-87	F	537*6
Ellen	May-89	F	537*8

This kind of alterations generally helps in quasi-identifiers.

3. Permutation: Permutation refers to partitioning the data into groups and shuffling the sensitive values within each group so that they cannot be manipulated by the attackers.

Table 7: General data.

Name	Dob	Sex	Blood Count
Alice	1/21/76	M	53715
Cathy	4/13/86	F	53703
Bob	2/28/76	M	53704
Andy	1/21/76	M	53715
Dan	4/13/87	F	53706
Ellen	2/05/89	F	53708

Table 8: General data.

Dob	Sex	Zip code	Profession
1/21/76	M	53715	Teacher
4/13/86	F	53703	Doctor
2/28/76	M	53704	Businessman
1/21/76	M	53715	Engineer
4/13/87	F	53706	Bank manager
2/05/89	F	53708	Clerk

Table 9: Extracted data.

Dob	Sex	Zip Code	Profession
1/21/76	M	53715	Teacher

Table 10: Extracted data.

Name	Dob	Sex	Zipcode
Alice	1/21/76	M	53715

So, this is the most common technique wherein we just partition the data into disjoint transactions such that the two tables when combined may yield appropriate response

4. Perturbation: Perturbation refers to replacing values in a way such that linkage to the original data is removed but keeping the logic and statistical properties similar. That is we add some extra values to the data that are just noisy factors to keep it protected from the attackers.

Table 11: Perturbed data.

Name	Dob	Sex	Profession	Blood Count
Alice	1/21/76	M	Business	53715
Cathy	4/13/86	F	Navy	53703
Bob	2/28/76	M	Teacher	53704
Andy	1/21/76	M	Doctor	53715
Dan	4/13/87	F	Homemaker	53706
Ellen	2/05/89	F	Army Officer	53708

So, these are the few techniques that may be added into the data to keep the data secured from the attackers or invaders. So, the data needs to be protected using some above stated methods to keep it secure.

14. Inference and Results

After obtaining the above results we can infer that the spread of COVID-19 can be controlled up to an extent if we implement the above proposed Decision support system and the decision making life cycle as it will help us to identify and analyze the problem first then we can decide upon the best tool by searching within system the best remedy situation that can be provided for now and then, then we can implement our decision support model that will help doctors to analyze the patient's past history or the number of symptoms that arise or it will also help in asymptomatic control by analyzing the knowledge management tool for taking the best action possible. Some privacy techniques for the sensitive data are also discussed and they may prove instrumental in providing privacy to the data.

References

[1] J.W. Tukey. The future of data analysis. *Ann. Math. Stat.*, 33(1): 1–67, 1962. Retrieved from DOI:https:// doi.org/10.1214/aoms/1177704711.
[2] T. Davenport. *Analytics 3.0.*, 2013. Retrieved from https://hbr.org/2013/12/analytics-30.
[3] A.A. Forni and R. Meulen. *Gartner's 2016 Hype Cycle for Emerging Technologies*, 2016. Retrieved from https://www.gartner.com/newsroom/id/3412017.
[4] K. Rahul, R.K. Baniyal, and P. Goswami. Analysis and processing aspects of data in big data applications "published in *Taylor and Francis Journal of Discrete Mathematical Sciences and Cryptography*, Vol. 23, 2020 - Issue 2: *Sustainable Engineering for Science and Technology*, Pages 385–393 | published online: 14 May 2020. DOI: https://doi.org/10.1080/09720529.2020.1721869.

[5] K. Panetta. *Top Trends in the Gartner Hype Cycle for Emerging Technologies*, 2017. Retrieved from http://www.gartner.com/smarterwithgartner/top-trends-in-the-gartner-hype-cycle-for-emerging-technologies-2017/.

[6] C. Pettey. *Gartner's 2010 Hype Cycle Special Report*, 2010. Retrieved from http://www.gartner.com/newsroom/id/1447613.

[7] C. Pettey, and L. Goasduff. *Gartner's 2011 Hype Cycle Special Report*, 2011. Retrieved from http://www.gartner.com/newsroom/id/1763814.

[8] S. Madan, and P. Goswami. K-DDD measure and map reduce based anonymity model for secured privacy-preserving big data publishing" published in *International Journal of Uncertainty, Fuzziness and Knowledge-Based Systems a SCI(E) and Scopus indexed journal with ISSN* (print): 0218-4885 | ISSN (online): 1793–6411, 27(02): 177–199, 2019 https://doi.org/10.1142/S0218488519500089.

[9] C. Pettey, and R. van der Meulen. *Gartner's 2012 Hype Cycle For Emerging Technologies*, 2012. Retrieved from http://www.gartner.com/newsroom/id/2124315.

[10] J. Rivera, and R. Meulen. *Gartner's 2013 Hype Cycle For Emerging Technologies*, 2013. Retrieved from http://www.gartner.com/newsroom/id/2575515.

[11] J. Rivera, and R. Meulen. *Gartner's 2014 Hype Cycle For Emerging Technologies*, 2014. Retrieved from http://www.gartner.com/newsroom/id/2819918.

[12] J. Rivera, and R. Meulen. *Gartner's 2015 Hype Cycle For Emerging Technologies*, 2015. Retrieved from http:// www.gartner.com/newsroom/id/3114217.

[13] A. Pavlo, G. Angulo, J. Arulraj, H. Lin, J. Lin, L. Ma, P. Menon, T.C. Mowry, M. Perron, I. Quah, S. Santurkar, A. Tomasic, S. Toor, D. Van Aken, Z. Wang, Y. Wu, R. Xian, and T. Zhang. Self-driving database management systems. In *Proceedings of the 8th Biennial Conference on Innovative Data Systems Research*, 2017. Retrieved from http://pelotondb.io/publications/.

[14] A. Mosavi. A multi-criteria decision making environment for engineering design and production decision-making. *International Journal of Computer Applications*, 69(1), 2013.

[15] J. Yin, A. Kulkarni, S. Purohit, I. Gorton, and B. Akyol. Scalable real-time data management for smart grid. In *Proceedings of the Middleware 2011 Industry Track Workshop*. 2021. Retrieved from DOI: https://doi.org/10.1145/2090181.2090182.

[16] L. Aggarwal, and S. Madan. A technological survey on privacy preservation data mining techniques. *International Journal for Research in Engineering Application & Management* (IJREAM). ISSN: 2454-9150, 04(07), Oct. 2018. http://ijream.org/chapters/IJREAMV04I0743056.pdf.

[17] H. Chen, J. Guo, C. Wang, F. Luo, X. Yu, W. Zhang, J. Li, D. Zhao, D. Xu, Q. Gong, J. Liao, H. Yang, W. Hou, and Y. Zhang. Clinical characteristics and intrauterine vertical transmission potential of COVID-19 infection in nine pregnant women: A retrospective review of medical records. *Lancet*, 395(10226): 809_815, Mar. 2020.

[18] M. Gupta, F. Patwa, and R. Sandhu. An attribute-based access control model for secure big data processing in Hadoop ecosystem. *In Proceedings of the Third ACM Workshop on Attribute-Based Access Control*, pp. 13–24, 2018.

[19] M. Gupta, F. Patwa, and R. Sandhu. Object-tagged RBAC model for the Hadoop ecosystem. In *IFIP Annual Conference on Data and Applications Security and Privacy*, pp. 63–81. Springer, Cham, 2017.

[20] M. Gupta, F. Patwa, J. Benson, and R. Sandhu. Multi-layer authorization framework for a representative Hadoop ecosystem deployment. *In Proceedings of the 22nd ACM on Symposium on Access Control Models and Technologies*, pp. 183–190, 2017.

[21] F.M. Awaysheh, M. Alazab, M. Gupta, T.F. Pena, and J.C. Cabaleiro. Next-generation big data federation access control: A reference model. *Future Generation Computer Systems* 108: 726–741, 2020.

[22] L. Aggarwal, P. Goswami, and S. Sachdeva. Multi-criterion intelligent decision support system for COVID-19. *Applied Soft Computing*, Vol. 101, 107056, ISSN 1568-4946, 2021, https://doi.org/10.1016/j.asoc.2020.107056. Elsevier (http://www.sciencedirect.com/science/article/pii/S1568494620309947).

[23] K. Rahul, R.K. Banyal, and P. Goswami. Machine learning algorithms for big data analytics. *Computational Methods and Data Engineering*, Springer, Singapore, 2021.

[24] Y. He, X. Wang, and J.Z. Huang. Recent advances in multiple criteria decision making techniques. *Clinica Chimica Acta*, 507: 94–97, 2020.

[25] P. Ghosh, R. Ghosh, and B. Chakraborty. COVID-19 in India: State-wise analysis and Prediction. On May 19, 2020. https://doi.org/10.1101/2020.04.24.20077792doi: medRxiv preprint.

[26] S.K. Dey, Md. M. Rahman, U.R. Siddiqi, and A. Howlader. Analyzing the epidemiological outbreak of COVID-19: A visual exploratory data analysis approach. Journal of Medical Virology, Wiley, 2020.

[27] L. Kharb, L. Aggarwal, and D. Chahal. A contingent exploration on big data tools. *In*: V. Bindhu, J. Chen and J. Tavares (eds.). *International Conference on Communication, Computing and Electronics Systems. Lecture Notes in Electrical Engineering*, Vol 637. Springer, Singapore, 2020. https://doi.org/10.1007/978-981-15-2612-1_71.

[28] M. Gupta, F.M. Awaysheh, J. Benson, M. Al Azab, F. Patwa, and R. Sandhu. An attribute-based access control for cloud-enabled industrial smart vehicles. *IEEE Transactions on Industrial Informatics*, 2020.

[29] S. Sontowski, M. Gupta, S.S.L. Chukkapalli, M. Abdelsalam, S. Mittal, A. Joshi, and R. Sandhu. Cyber attacks on smart farming infrastructure. *UMBC Student Collection*, 2020.

[30] M. Gupta, J. Benson, F. Patwa, and R. Sandhu. Secure V2V and V2I communication in intelligent transportation using cloudlets. *IEEE Transactions on Services Computing*, 2020.

[31] A.J. Yadav, and M.L. Garg. Docker containers versus virtual machine-based virtualization. In *Emerging Technologies in Data Mining and Information Security*, pp. 141–150. Springer, Singapore, 2019.

[32] A. Yadav, Ritika, and M.L. Garg. Monitoring based security approach for cloud computing. *Ingénierie des Systèmes d'Information*, 24(6): 611–617, 2019. https://doi.org/10.18280/isi.240608.

6

Fingerprinting Based Positioning Techniques Using Machine Learning Algorithms
Principles, Approaches and Challenges

Safar Maghdid Asaad,[1,3] *Kayhan Zrar Ghafoor,*[2]
Halgurd Sarhang,[3] *Aos Mulahuwaish*[4,]* *and Abbas M Ali*[5]

ABSTRACT

The demand for using location-based services (LBSs) has rapidly increased, specifically in the last decade. Most people's daily activities are related to LBS services, including navigation, billing address, tracking stuff, transportation, and other point-of-interest (POI). In the same manner, many solutions are widely available to process the positioning from outdoors to indoors. One of the most utilized positioning solutions is using fingerprinting-based techniques via different technologies, including WiFi, Bluetooth, 3G/4G, and UWB. Many attempts have been made to enhance fingerprinting-based positioning and then to provide an accurate solution. These recent attempts which are referred to use modern machine learning algorithms as fingerprinting matching process. However, there is no single

[1] Department of Information System Engineering Techniques, Erbil Technical Engineering College, Erbil Polytechnic University, Erbil, Kurdistan Region-F.R., Iraq.
Emails: safar.dei20@epu.edu.iq, safar.maghdid@koyauniversity.org
[2] Department of Computer Science, Knowledge University, University Park, Kirkuk Road, 44001 Erbil, Iraq.
Email: kayhan.zrar@knu.edu.iq
[3] Department of Software Engineering, Faculty of Engineering, Koya University, Koya KOY45, Kurdistan Region-F.R. Iraq.
Email: halgurd.maghdid@koyauniversity.org
[4] Department of Computer Science and Information Systems, Saginaw Valley State University, MI, USA.
[5] Department of Software Engineering, Salahaddin University-Erbil, Iraq.
Email: abbas.mohamad@su.edu.krd
* Corresponding author: amulahuw@svsu.edu

solution to provide an accurate, low-cost, on-the-go, and seamless positioning solution. Therefore, this article aims to address the issues of using fingerprinting-based positioning. A new taxonomy for the recent solutions, which are related to fingerprinting-based techniques, is also designed. Accordingly, machine learning algorithms which have been used in the fingerprinting-based technique and their challenges are investigated.

1. Introduction

Nowadays, one of the world's most prominent innovations is LBSs. Global navigation satellite systems (GNSS) [1–4] the European Geostationary Navigation Overlay Service (EGNOS) including (1) Global positioning systems (GPS), (2) BeiDou navigation satellite systems (BDS), (3) GLONASS, and (4) Galileo are applicably utilized when users are outdoors. Due to the GNSS suffering from obstruction of signals by objects like trees, roofs, walls, and buildings, their performances deteriorate, and they cannot be used in the indoor environment. To fill this gap in the urban or indoor environments, numerous researches have been conducted recently. Among these researches, many of these technologies have attracted the researchers to propose new indoor localization solutions based on some of the already available technologies including, ZigBee, cellular, Bluetooth, infrared, Ultra-Wide Band (UWB), radio frequency identification (RFID), Micro-electromechanical systems (MEMS), geomagnetic field, pseudo files (PL) and Wireless Fidelity (WiFi).

Because of the availability of WiFi signals in almost all indoor environments for accessing the internet and the increasingly growing number of smartphone users, several measurements, including (1) angle-of-arrival (AoA) [5], (2) received signal strength (RSS) [6], and (2) time-of-arrival (ToA) [7] have been derived from establishing fingerprint databases. Besides, based on these fingerprint databases, many algorithms have been designed to estimate indoor locations accurately. Typical fingerprinting positioning techniques consist of two phases, which are Offline and online phases, as illustrated in Figure 1. In the first phase, the fingerprint database is constructed, containing the measurements derived from the power of WiFi signal values in preferred points via the applicable device. After that, to represent the mapping relationship between the signal information and positions, a position model can be trained based on the collected data. After that, the positioning model can be used to predict the desired point's location during the online process.

Most of the current indoor WiFi localization techniques are concentrated on fingerprints based on the received signal strength (RSS) [8–11] multipath propagation characteristics and interferences in indoor environment cause variability of Received Signal Strength (RSS). This is because; the RSS can be extracted from some common WiFi devices. However, the RSS signal is sensitive to the environment changing and heterogeneous hardware. To overcome the drawbacks of the technologies and fingerprinting data, machine learning algorithms have been applied to improve the mapping accuracy. However, to find the drawbacks and to suggest new models, and improve the performance of indoor positioning solutions, such research needs to be surveyed. Therefore, this article aims to compare existing approaches and solutions in indoor positioning using fingerprinting techniques via machine learning algorithms.

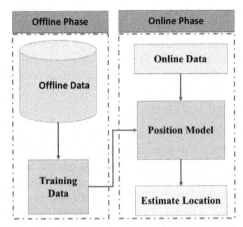

Figure 1: Sample structure of fingerprint-based indoor positioning system.

Therefore, the main contribution of this chapter is to present recent fingerprinting-based positioning techniques via using Machine Learning Algorithms. The chapter also investigates the issues of WiFi indoors, positioning it in terms of time and space complexity, Big data, privacy, and security. Finally, the main purpose of this chapter is to make a guideline for the reader to know about the recent progress of indoor positioning challenges and approaches.

The remainder of the chapter is structured such, the current fingerprinting-based positioning technique using machine learning algorithms are discussed in Section 2. This is accompanied by a contrast between all the solutions grouped into classical techniques and Modern Techniques categories. When advanced machine learning methods are used, Section 3 addresses the recent research challenges and potential solutions. Finally, the research is concluded in Section 4.

2. Literature Review

The increasing expectations for applications based on LBSs have encouraged investigators to introduce a pool of opinions to ensure these systems' effectiveness. Besides, these concepts are not without limitations. Thus, so many machine learning techniques are applied to improve them. The existing solutions that propose using machine learning algorithms to provide more significant relativity are examined in this research to highlight the available challenges and provide recommendations to be explored in future works. As shown in Figure 2, the current Machine learning algorithms for the purpose of localization are categorized into two categories, which are (1) classical algorithms and (2) modern algorithms.

2.1 Classical Machine Learning based Solutions

Machine learning algorithms are still used in various fields, including tracking systems, image recognition, speech recognition, recommendation systems, and so on. Further, because of their effectiveness in solving available problems. As

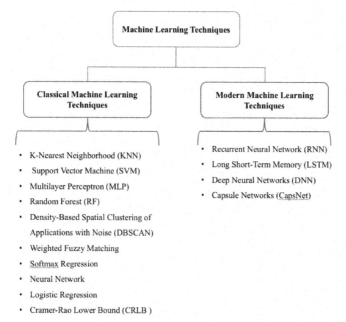

Figure 2: Taxonomy of machine learning algorithms for the purpose of localization.

presented in Table 1, the latest localization solutions based on classical machine learning techniques are explained.

Walls and many obstacles in the indoor environment are some factors that affect the accuracy of indoor navigation. Therefore, many applications have been used to tackle these types of issues. These kinds of applications are based on communication technologies, including the Internet of Things (IoT), Artificial Intelligence (AI), Bluetooth, UWB, and WiFi. The authors in [16] proposed an algorithm based on WiFi technology to improve indoor location tracking accuracy. Essentially, the fingerprinting database is established via measuring and collecting the RSSI values for each RP. Afterward, a weighted fuzzy matching algorithm is used to track the user's location. The weighted fuzzy matching algorithm matches the user's RSSI value with the pre-stored RSSI values in the fingerprinting database. Finally, Particle Swarm Optimization (PSO) algorithm is applied to improve indoor localization accuracy further. The study performs a simulation with assuming an (8 m x 8 m) empty room with four WiFi Access Points (APs) at each vertex. The Simulation results verified that the accuracy of the location tracking could be improved when the weighted fuzzy matching and PSO algorithms are used together. Approximately obtained results determine that the average position error is about 2 m when the PSO algorithm is not applied, while the average position error is about 1.2 m when the PSO algorithm is applied. However, only 4 APs are used, which are not enough for real environments. The multi-floor, environmental movement, and different object availability concerns have remained as future challenges.

In a similar study, authors in [17] investigated a new indoor localization prototype based on the WiFi (RSS) fingerprinting, but with employing Machine

Table 1: Comparisons of existing indoor localization solutions based on the classical machine learning algorithms.

Year	Solutions	Fingerprint	Methods	Environments	Accuracy	Characteristics
2020	[16]	WiFi (RSS)	- Weighted fuzzy matching - PSO	(8 m × 8 m) Simulation empty Room	1.2 m	Combined weighted fuzzy matching and PSO algorithms to achieve higher position accuracy.
2020	[17]	WiFi (RSS)	- KNN - SVM - MLP	(3170 M) floor	- 1.2 m - 5.88 m - 3.06 m	The performance of the localization is further improved by training multiple classifiers.
2019	DBSCAN-KRF [18]	WiFi (RSS)	- DBSCAN - KNN - RF	- Two (8.8 m × 5.6 m) offices - Two corridors	N/A	- DBSCAN detect insensitive region of the RSS fingerprint signal from the fingerprint Library and delete the noise sample - KNN and RF obtain the positioning when the region is sensitive and insensitive respectively.
2018	[19]	Cellular (RSS)	- WKNN - Neural Network	- Two urban environments - One rural environment	- 5.9 m - 5.1 m - 8.7 m	- division the environment into small clusters - estimating the position within each cluster
2018	[20]	Bluetooth (RSS)	- SVM - Logistic regression	Corridor	50 cm	Used Bluetooth as low cost and ease of use technology.
2017	DoA-LF [21]	WiFi (RSS + DoA Info of APs)	- WKNN - CRLB	(100 m × 100 m) Simulation indoor environment	N/A	- DoA information of APs working on mm Wave spectrum reduce the positioning failer in comparison to fingerprinting based positioning with signal below 6 GHz. - The mm Wave can reduce the positioning error.

learning techniques. In the offline phase, the authors measured the RSSI values of MikroTik APs signals via Smartphones to establish the fingerprint database. Later on, in the online phase, the proposed prototype uses various classifiers including, (1) Support Vector Machine (SVM). (2) K-Nearest Neighborhood (KNN), and (3) Multilayer Perceptron neural network (MLP). Figure 3 presents the block diagram of the proposed prototype. The classifiers are trained and tested in the same training dataset. A part of the dataset is used as a validating dataset to assess the achievement of the proposed prototype. The experimental area is the third floor of a building with the placing of five APs. The experiments' obtained results express that the performance of the KNN is better than the other classifiers. However, the KNN requires an absolutely large database fingerprint, and its performance deteriorates when the RSS values fluctuate.

Since the instability of Wi-Fi signals, the conventional distance-based calculation techniques fail to evaluate the RSS fingerprints of some adjacent reference positions accurately. KNN algorithm cannot obtain accurate positioning when RSS fingerprints are clustered into only one region. To this end, the authors in [18] propose a new algorithm named DBSCAN-KRF and a new concept called "the insensitive region of the RSS fingerprint." The DBSCAN-KRF is an integration of three models. (1) the "Density-Based Spatial Clustering of Applications with Noise (DBSCAN)" model. It is used to detect the RSS fingerprint signal's insensitive region from the fingerprint Library and delete the noise sample. (2) The KNN model is used to obtain the positioning when the region is sensitive. (3) "Random Forest (RF)" model is selected to obtain the positioning when the region is insensitive. The study conducted many experiments considering two important factors that affect the accuracy of indoor positioning models. These factors are the number of APs and the number or density of RSS records. The experimental findings present that the DBSCAN-KRF algorithm's accuracy is notably higher than the baseline algorithms when the number of APs and the quantity of RSS samples in each reference point are 8 and 40, respectively. However, with owning the simplicity characteristic, the performance of WKNN declines with RSS fluctuations, and the WKNN requires a massive dataset. Additionally, the change of environment, the positioning target movement, multi-floor localization, and the positioning environment factors' area size are not considered in the proposed algorithm.

Another study [19] and does not require knowledge of the cellular base transceiver station (BTS focused on received signal strength (RSS) from cellular signals to build an indoor localization model. The study employs Weighted K-Nearest Neighbor (WKNN) to split the large cluster into tinier ones. Then, WKNN is integrated with a multi-layer neural network to benefit from the robust clustering ability of WKNN. The flowchart of the suggested model is shown in Figure 4. Another benefit of the integrated model is that the implemented multi-layer neural network can predict the indoor location within each cluster. Three experiments are conducted, including two urban environments and an individual rural environment. The obtained results are 5.9 m, 5.1 m, and 8.7 m in the urban environments and the rural environment, respectively, within the mean distance localization error. These results present that the accuracy of the integrated approach is better than the WKNN-only algorithm.

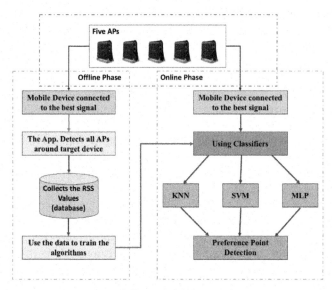

Figure 3: Block diagram of the proposed prototype.

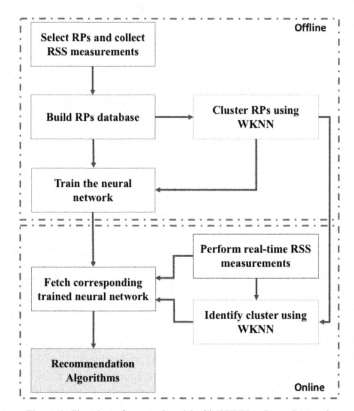

Figure 4: Flowchart of proposed model with WKNN and neural network.

However, the cellular base transceiver station (BTS) and RSS mathematical model are not considered.

Cost and installation are other issues in indoor positioning systems. The studies in [20] used Bluetooth Low Energy (BLE) for fingerprinting-based indoor positioning. That is because of the ease of using it and the low-cost characteristics of Bluetooth. The authors prepared the fingerprint database by deploying 14 Bluetooth beacons in a corridor. The RSSI values are collected from the k nearest to BLE devices to a mobile device. The architecture of the proposal is demonstrated in Figure 5. Accordingly, two popular machine learning algorithms are implemented to evaluate the accuracy of indoor positioning estimation, including (1) SVM and (2) logistic regression. The achieved results from a set of trial experiments show that the SVM technique is more accurate than Logistic Regression. Approximately, the average error of SVM is 50 cm. In contrast, the average error of logistic regression is 90 cm. However, the performance of the SVM is limited to such big and complex data. Moreover, other concerns are overlooked, including the environment movement objects and multi-floor localization.

The millimeter-wave (mmWave) has some characteristics that can help reduce the positioning error in an indoor environment. These characteristics are narrow beam, rapid signal attenuation, broad bandwidth, and so forth. A new location fingerprint positioning solution based on the narrow beam and rapid signal attenuation characteristics of mmWave is proposed in [21] the existing studies on LF mostly focus on the fingerprint of Wi-Fi below 6 GHz, bluetooth, ultra wideband, and so on. The LF with millimeter-wave (mmWave). The solution is called (DoA-LF). The fingerprint dataset of DoA-LF contains RSSI information and direction of arrival (DoA) information of APs operating on the mmWave spectrum, which is achieved via the multiple signal classification (MUSIC) method. Figure 6 depicts the proposed DoA-LF solution.

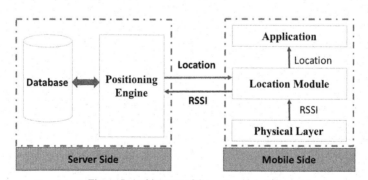

Figure 5: Architecture of the proposed model.

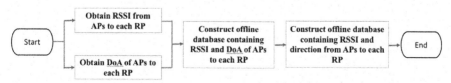

Figure 6: Proposed DoA-LF solution.

Subsequently, the weighted K nearest neighbor (WKNN) technique is engaged to calculate the weighted mean of the chosen K candidate RPs with the most similar features. Afterward, the Cramer-Rao Lower Bound (CRLB) tool is applied to analyze the influence of the quantity of APs, the interval of RPs, the channel type of mmWave, and the failure of the DoA prediction model on positioning error. The simulation results from a 100 m x 100 m indoor environment are verified that (1) the positioning error is minimized notably when an optimal K is selected (2) the DoA information of APs working on mmWave spectrum band can significantly reduce the positioning error in comparison to fingerprinting based positioning with signal below 6 GHz (3) since the mmWave has a more extensive path loss exponent and more petite variance of shadow fading contrasted with low-frequency signals, the mmWave can be utilized to decrease the positioning error.

2.2 Modern Machine Learning based Solutions

Due to existing challenges associated with classical machine learning techniques, a range of solutions are proposed to improve the accuracy of indoor positioning based on modern machine learning algorithms. The comparisons between existing solutions using advanced machine learning algorithms are provided in Table 2.

Classical matching algorithms, utilized in the Fingerprinting technique, regularly suffer from restricted performance in analyzing complex and noisy data. Equally, deep learning algorithms are more powerful at analyzing very complicated and noisy values. Therefore, a local feature-based deep long short-term memory (LF-DLSTM) is proposed for this purpose [22] conventional machine learning algorithms often suffer from limited performance. Recently developed deep learning algorithms have been shown to be powerful for the analysis of complex data. In this paper, we propose a local feature-based deep long short-term memory (LF-DLSTM). Classical localization systems collect the RSSI data via smartphones. The smartphones are used to scan for WiFi routers signals and collect RSSI data. However, within the initial step, the proposed algorithm faced the problems of low sampling rate and the high battery-power drain of smartphones. To address this issue, the authors are focused on the advantages of a passive scanning system. A huge amount of RSSI data is collected in a passive scanning system by employing WiFi routers for scanning smartphones with a high sampling rate. The proposed technique reduces the noise effect in RSSI and obtains robust local features from the row RSSI data via the local feature extractor. Accordingly, for final accurate localization, the DLSTM network is applied to encode temporal dependencies and generate a more discriminatory representation. In the proposed model, two practical experiments have been carried out. The first one has been in a research lab, and the second one has been in an office. The results present that the proposed model outperforms the state-of-art methods for indoor localization. The achieved localization performance of mean localization errors is 1.48 and 1.75 meters within the research laboratory and office environments. However, multi-floor localization and change of environmental concerns have not been addressed.

Authors in [14] used WiFi-RSS in indoor environments to suggest a modern WiFi-based indoor localization method known as WiFiNet. The proposed method

Table 2: Comparisons of existing indoor localization solutions based on the modern machine learning algorithms.

Year	Solutions	Fingerprint	Methods	Environments	Accuracy	Characteristics
2021	WiFiNet [14]	WiFi (RSS)	CNN	(3600 m²) real world environment (university area)	3.3 m	- Achieves the greatest generalization and adaptation to practical environments, with an RMSE of 3.3 m when measured during walking around the real environment. - The processing time in a medium area (30 locations and 113 APs) as opposed to baseline WiFi indoor positioning algorithms including SVM.
2020	LF-DLSTM [22]	WiFi (RSS)	DLSTM	- Lab - Office	- 1.48 m - 1.75 m	Reduces the noise effect in RSSI and obtains robust local features from the row RSSI data via the local feature extractor.
2020	CapsLoc [23]	WiFi (RSS)	CapsNet	(460 m²) a corridor with three IoT labs	0.68 m	- extracting higher level features from the WiFi RSS fingerprint dataset via CapsNet.
2020	[24]	Wi-Fi (RSS) Magnetic field	- Resnet	- Indoor and outdoor test sites (divided into dozens of grids	- 97.1 %	- It is smart enough to learn key features from a large fingerprint image dataset.
2019	[25]	CSI	- DNN - Softmax regression - KWNN	(40 m X 40 m) urban microcell environment	0.8349 m	- Depending on "multipath MIMO CSI in the time domain" instead of the frequency domain, and using coarse-to-fine process increases the localization accuracy.
2019	[26]	Geomagnetic sensor signal	- Basic RNN - LSTM	- (94 m x 26 m) indoor testbed - (608 m x 50 m) indoor testbed	- 1.2 m, 4.1 m - 0.51 m, 1.04 m	- Geomagnetic signal is available everywhere in the environment. - Objects have a unique sequence of the geomagnetic field signals as long as the objects are moving. - Data collection process based Geomagnetic signal on is simpler than to be based on the RF signal.

aims to get advantages of Convolutional Neural Networks' superior capability to solve classification problems. The authors compare three strategies, a new architecture called WiFiNet that was developed and built specifically to address this challenge, and the most common pre-trained networks that use both transfer learning and feature extraction. Furthermore, the top-performing traditional architectures for WiFi-based indoor localization were tested as a benchmark. The experiments were conducted in a realistic environment, 3600 m², at a university campus. WiFiNet achieves the greatest generalization and adaptation to practical environments, with a Root Mean Square Error (RMSE) of 3.3 m when measured during walking around the real environment. The processing time in a medium area (30 locations and 113 APs) notably reduced as compared with baseline WiFi indoor positioning algorithms, including SVM. However, with the increasing number of APs, the processing time is increasing as well.

Another proposed work [23] is known as the CapsLoc system, as presented in Figure 7. The CapsLoc is based on the RSS fingerprinting data to estimate indoor locations. Authors employ Capsule Networks (CapsNet) by considering the fingerprinting wireless positioning scheme to predict indoor positions accurately. The CapsNet model extracts a convolutional layer, a primary capsule layer, plus a feature

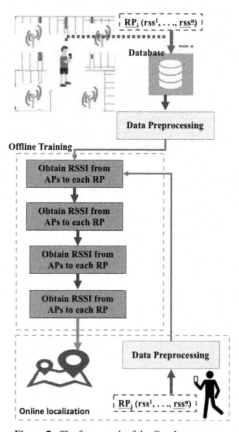

Figure 7: The framework of the CapsLoc system.

capsule layer from the WiFi fingerprint to establish its hierarchical structures. Real experimental tests are conducted on a corridor with three IoT labs on the third floor using 6 APs (two APs in each lab) to deal with an area of 460 m^2. The achievements indicate that applying the CapsLoc model can provide better indoor positioning accuracy with an averaged error of 0.68 m. The results also express that the model outperforms KNN, SVM, and CNN.

Another paper [24] presented a deep learning-based Wi-Fi and magnetic field fingerprint-based localization framework. Since magnetic field strength (MFS) is difficult to discriminate over wide regions, the unsupervised learning density peak clustering algorithm is initially utilized to choose multiple MFS center points as geotagged features to aid indoor positioning. Where the unsupervised learning density peak clustering algorithm is based on the comparison distance (CDPC) technique. Authors create a position fingerprint picture for localization using Wi-Fi and magnetic field fingerprints, considering the state-of-the-art use of deep learning in image classification. The suggested deep residual network (Resnet), which is smart enough to learn key features from a large fingerprint image dataset, is used to perform the localization. An MLP-based transferred learning perfect localizer is applied to refine the pre-trained Resnet coarse localizer by using the prior knowledge of the pre-trained Resnet coarse localizer. Many data enhancement techniques have been used and dynamically modified the learning rate (LR) to improve the robustness of our localization scheme. The proposed method achieves adequate localization efficiency including both indoor and outdoor settings, according to experimental findings.

One of the main issues of fingerprinting-based localization systems is to extract valid features from the utilized technologies. This is to establish the fingerprint database that contains the mapping between the Reference Points and their corresponding signal features. Authors in [25] proposed a hierarchical localization approach which was based on multipath "multiple-input multiple-output (MIMO) channel state information (CSI)" fingerprints. The approach is based on time domain-based multipath MIMO CSI instead of the frequency domain-based multipath MIMO CSI. Two deep neural networks (DNN) are trained for coarse and fine positioning in the offline phase. The coarse positioning is used to reduce the training time when the targeted region is wide. A softmax regression classifier follows this to generate soft information on the classified output data. Two machine learning algorithms, softmax regression classifier, and K, weighted the nearest neighbor (KWNN), enhanced localization accuracy in the online phase. The simulation outcomes demonstrate that the localization accuracy can be increased when multipath MIMO CSI in the time domain is considered instead of the frequency domain. As well as, the coarse-to-fine process can obtain a more reliable performance compared to the present approaches.

Several factors influence the localization accuracy of the existing Radio Frequency (RF) fingerprinting-based techniques such as WiFi, Bluetooth Low Energy (BLE). These factors include (1) the number of available AP, (2) physical obstructions and complexity of the indoor space, (3) moving objects in the environment, and (4) physical scale. Specifically, the value of the RSS fluctuates when the indoor space becomes complicated, and the physical scale is enlarged. To overcome the issue of RSS fluctuation, the authors in [26] which is enlarged with the increased physical scale and the complexity of the indoor space. In this paper, instead of RF signal we use the geomagnetic sensor signal for indoor localization, whose signal strength is more stable than RF RSS. Our approach using the geomagnetic field is as follows. Although similar geomagnetic field values exist in indoor space, an object movement would experience a unique sequence of the geomagnetic field signals as the movement continues. We can locate the position of the object by tracking the geomagnetic field signal sequence sensed with the object movement by using a deep neural network model called recurrent neural network (RNN proposed a solution based on the geomagnetic field signal for indoor positioning instead of the RF signal. Since the geomagnetic sensor signal is available everywhere in the environment, the objects have a unique sequence of the geomagnetic field signals as long as the objects are moving. The proposed work establishes the fingerprinting database via collecting geomagnetic field signals in many locations from two large testbed environments. The first environment is the first floor of Incheon International Airport, with a selected (608 m x 50 m) area known as a large-scale testbed. The Second environment is the first floor of the Korea University Science and Engineering campus. The testbed size is (94 m x 26 m) area, and it is called a medium-scale testbed. Collecting the geomagnetic field stable signal is more manageable than collecting the unstable radio signals from multiple beacons or APs. Two DNN models, including basic recurrent neural network (basic RNN) and Long Short-Term Memory (LSTM), are applied to map between a precise position and the previously collected geomagnetic field signals. After training the DNNs, the obtained results present that achieved average localization accuracy via LSTM is notably higher than the RNN in both environments. The achieved results are 1.2 m, 4.1 m, 0.51 m, and 1.04 m with RNN and LSTM, respectively, in both environments medium-scale and large-scale testbeds. However, the proposed technique might suffer from measuring the same geomagnetic field signal value that might arise in multiple locations. That is due to installing differently characterized magnetometers by manufacturers in the devices, including smartphones. Furthermore, the magnetometers are disturbed by several factors including, electronic devices and ferromagnetic architectural features.

3. Challenges

In this section, the most common challenges that face the researchers who have been working on localization, specifically fingerprint-based localization systems, are addressed.

A. Time Consuming

Constructing the fingerprint database and training the model takes a long time. Consequently, the number of measurements and the size of the reallocation environment, and the time to predict the intended locations are increasing linearly. We consider that by monitoring user trajectories, the data can be obtained dynamically, but other procedures are further required to minimize the training period. Using crowd-sourcing technology as the method for solving this issue would be superior.

B. Environment Complexity

One of the necessities for positioning based on radio frequency signals is line-of-sight communication connecting the transmitter and transceiver. Sometimes signals attenuate through occlude obstacles. Besides, the signals might be prevented by obstacles and cannot be accessed by the receiver. For example, the WiFi Access Point signal cannot penetrate an obstacle to access the receiver. To tackle these issues, high-precision receivers are required to be utilized, which maximizes the indoor positioning technology cost but adds to the accuracy of positioning within tens of meters. Other points affect the signal's strength, including the spatiotemporal changes of signals and the geometric changes of the environment.

C. Storage Capacity and Computing Power

Other limitations belong to the receiver devices, including storage size and computing power. The recording of RSS from many nearby APs and the storing of this data in a database along with the client device's identified locations in an offline phase is the basic process for wireless fingerprinting-based localization. Big data would be collected in a big enough space for an appropriate amount of APs, which necessitates a very large storage capacity, which linearly raises the expense and complicates the computing method. Furthermore, the capacity and processing ability of the clients' devices have a significant impact on the success of the proposed solutions. For example, many algorithms are implemented on smartphones, and their computing power is varied according to their model and manufacture. Therefore, the positioning accuracy is linearly increased when the more powerful smartphone is used to estimate the local position based on the machine learning techniques. In terms of energy consumption, clients' electronic devices cannot continue to execute or position algorithms at high speeds, so that the battery will easily drain. Remote terminal processing activities can be offloaded to local cloud data centers owing to IoT technology. Smartphones are only utilized to gather signals and obtain positioning results in order to prolong their life cycle. However, the other big data issue could be handled via implementing a distributed database system. This is to solve the issue of reducing the time delay of retrieving location information and avoiding space complexity. Since the data is distributed in many servers/sources, the users will easily contact the servers/sources to export the required location information.

D. Security and Privacy

Real-life individuals gain great benefits from Location-based services [27–29] but still, some issues have been faced by the individuals. When the background applications collect the location information from the individuals, this information might be used to reveal their privacy for attackers' benefit. Additionally, some proposed indoor positioning algorithms utilize cloud computing to store the fingerprint data and store the implemented model. In that case, the related positioning data must be transmitted between the user's phone and the cloud. During this transmission process, there may be some vulnerable points to attack, specifically MITM. To overcome these vulnerabilities, robust cryptographic approaches have to be implemented to encrypt the data before being transmitted. So, the service provider should implement protecting algorithms that prevent the man-in-the-middle attack (MITM). Usually, MITM is defended by authentication techniques such as Public Key Infrastructures (PKI) mutual authentication, stronger mutual authentication like secret keys or passwords. If the attacker knows secret key information, although the cryptography mechanism is done, it is useless. So secret key management also a very important issue [15].

To propose a robust solution, many machine learning algorithms have been suggested to establish a model to predict a real-time indoor location with acceptable accuracy. Some of them require a huge amount of data to be trained.

4. Conclusion

Recently, LBSs attracted the attention of a huge number of researchers. This is because the services can be used in a variety of applications, both indoors and outdoors. Correspondingly, many solutions have been conducted to improve the positioning accuracy, specifically for indoor environments. Using fingerprinting-based techniques through various technologies, including WiFi, Bluetooth, Geomagnetic, 3G/4G, and UWB, is one of the most used positioning solutions. Several attempts have been made to improve positioning based on fingerprinting and then to provide reliable solutions. A detailed overview of the recent fingerprinting-based position techniques using machine learning algorithms is presented in this work. The early achievements are referred to as the fingerprinting matching method using advanced machine learning algorithms. However, to provide a reliable, low-cost, on-the-go, and seamless positioning solutions, there is no single solution. This chapter, therefore, attempted to address the issues of using positioning based on fingerprinting. The issues involve the storage size of the receiver device, computing power, and security aspects issues. A new taxonomy is also being developed for the latest solutions relating to fingerprinting-based techniques. Machine learning algorithms that have been used in fingerprinting-based techniques are then investigated, and their limitations are discussed.

References

[1]   C. Tiberius, and E. Verbree. GNSS positioning accuracy and availability within location based services: The advantages of combined GPS-Galileo positioning. *NaviTec*, no. 1, 2004.

[2]   C. Stallo, A. Neri, P. Salvatori, A. Coluccia, R. Capua, G. Olivieri, L. Gattuso, L. Bonenberg, T. Moore, and F. Rispoli. GNSS-based location determination system architecture for railway performance assessment in presence of local effects. *In 2018 IEEE/ION Position, Location and Navigation Symposium (PLANS)*, pp. 374–381, 2018, https://doi.org/10.1109/PLANS.2018.8373403.

[3]   K. Zhang, M. Spanghero, and P. Papadimitratos. Protecting GNSS-based services using time offset validation. *In 2020 IEEE/ION Position, Location and Navigation Symposium (PLANS)*, Apr. 2020, pp. 575–583, 2020, doi: 10.1109/PLANS46316.2020.9110224.

[4]   J. Paziewski. Recent advances and perspectives for positioning and applications with smartphone GNSS observations. *Meas. Sci. Technol.*, 31(9): 2020, doi: 10.1088/1361-6501/ab8a7d.

[5]   S. Tomic, M. Beko, R. Dinis, and L. Bernardo. On target localization using combined RSS and AoA measurements. *Sensors (Switzerland)*, 18(4): 1–25, 2018, doi: 10.3390/s18041266.

[6]   L. Kanaris, A. Kokkinis, A. Liotta, and S. Stavrou. Fusing bluetooth beacon data with Wi-Fi radiomaps for improved indoor localization. *Sensors (Switzerland)*, 17(4): 1–15, 2017, doi: 10.3390/s17040812.

[7]   A.G. Ferreira, D. Fernandes, A.P. Catarino, and J.L. Monteiro. Performance analysis of ToA-based positioning algorithms for static and dynamic targets with low ranging measurements. *Sensors (Switzerland)*, 17(8): 9–11, 2017, doi: 10.3390/s17081915.

[8]   N.A.M. Maung and W. Zaw. Comparative study of RSS-based indoor positioning techniques on two different Wi-Fi frequency bands. *17th Int. Conf. Electr. Eng. Comput. Telecommun. Inf. Technol. ECTI-CON 2020*, pp. 185–188, 2020, doi: 10.1109/ECTI-CON49241.2020.9158211.

[9]   J. Golenbiewski and G. Tewolde. Wi-Fi based indoor positioning and navigation system (IPS/INS). *IEMTRONICS 2020 - Int. IOT, Electron. Mechatronics Conf. Proc.*, 2020, doi: 10.1109/IEMTRONICS51293.2020.9216376.

[10] L. Chen, I. Ahriz, and D. Le Ruyet. CSI-based probabilistic indoor position determination: An entropy solution. *IEEE Access*, 7: 170048–170061, 2019, doi: 10.1109/ACCESS.2019.2955747.

[11] M. Alfakih, M. Keche, H. Benoudnine, and A. Meche. Improved Gaussian mixture modeling for accurate Wi-Fi based indoor localization systems. *Phys. Commun.*, 43: 101218, 2020, doi: 10.1016/j.phycom.2020.101218.

[12] L. Ma, A.Y. Teymorian, X. Cheng, T. George, and W. Dc. A hybrid rogue access point protection framework for commodity Wi-Fi Networks. *Proc. - IEEE INFOCOM*, vol. 2018-April, pp. 1894–1902, 2008.

[13] S.H. Fang and T. Lin. Principal component localization in indoor wlan environments. *IEEE Trans. Mob. Comput.*, 11(1): 100–110, 2012, doi: 10.1109/TMC.2011.30.

[14] N. Hernández, I. Parra, H. Corrales, R. Izquierdo, A.L. Ballardini, C. Salinas, and I. García. WiFiNet: WiFi-based indoor localisation using CNNs. *Expert Syst. Appl.*, 177: 114906, 2021, https://doi.org/10.1016/j.eswa.2021.114906.

[15] R. Daş, A. Karabade, and G. Tuna. Common network attack types and defense mechanisms. *2015 23rd Signal Process. Commun. Appl. Conf. SIU 2015 - Proc.*, pp. 2658–2661, 2015, doi: 10.1109/SIU.2015.7130435.

[16] H.K. Yu, S.H. Oh, and J.G. Kim. AI based location tracking in WiFi indoor positioning application. In *2020 International Conference on Artificial Intelligence in Information and Communication (ICAIIC)*, Feb. 2020, pp. 199–202, 2020, doi: 10.1109/ICAIIC48513.2020.9065227.

[17] A.A. Careem, W.H. Ali, and M.H. Jasim. Wirelessly indoor positioning system based on RSS Signal. *Proc. 2020 Int. Conf. Comput. Sci. Softw. Eng. CSASE 2020*, pp. 238–243, 2020, doi: 10.1109/CSASE48920.2020.9142111.

[18] K. Wang, X. Yu, Q. Xiong, Q. Zhu, W. Lu, Y. Huang, and L. Zhao. Learning to improve WLAN indoor positioning accuracy based on DBSCAN-KRF Algorithm from RSS Fingerprint Data. *IEEE Access*, 7: 72308–72315, 2019, https://doi.org/10.1109/ACCESS.2019.2919329.

[19] A.A. Abdallah, S.S. Saab, and Z.M. Kassas. A machine learning approach for localization in cellular environments. *2018 IEEE/ION Position, Locat. Navig. Symp. PLANS 2018 - Proc.*, pp. 1223–1227, 2018, doi: 10.1109/PLANS.2018.8373508.

[20] P. Sthapit, H.S. Gang and J.Y. Pyurr. bluetooth based indoor positioning using machine learning algorithms. *2018 IEEE Int. Conf. Consum. Electron. - Asia, ICCE-Asia 2018*, pp. 3–6, 2018, doi: 10.1109/ICCE-ASIA.2018.8552138.

[21] Z. Wei, Y. Zhao, X. Liu, and Z. Feng. DoA-LF: A location fingerprint positioning algorithm with millimeter-wave. *IEEE Access*, 5(c): 22678–22688, 2017, doi: 10.1109/ACCESS.2017.2753781.

[22] Z. Chen, H. Zou, J.F. Yang, H. Jiang, and L. Xie. WiFi fingerprinting indoor localization using local feature-based deep LSTM. *IEEE Syst. J.*, 14(2): 3001–3010, 2020, doi: 10.1109/JSYST.2019.2918678.

[23] Q. Ye, X. Fan, G. Fang, H. Bie, X. Song, and R. Shankaran. CapsLoc: A robust indoor localization system with WiFi fingerprinting using capsule networks. *In ICC 2020 - 2020 IEEE International Conference on Communications (ICC)*, Jun. 2020, pp. 1–6, 2020, doi: 10.1109/ICC40277.2020.9148933.

[24] D. Li, Y. Lei, X. Li, and H. Zhang. Deep learning for fingerprint localization in indoor and outdoor environments. *ISPRS Int. J. Geo-Information*, 9(4): 2020, doi: 10.3390/ijgi9040267.

[25] J. Fan, S. Chen, X. Luo, Y. Zhang, and G.Y. Li. A machine learning approach for hierarchical localization based on multipath MIMO fingerprints. *IEEE Commun. Lett.*, 23(1): 1, 2019, doi: 10.1109/LCOMM.2019.2929148.

[26] H.J. Bae and L. Choi. Large-scale indoor positioning using geomagnetic field with deep neural networks. *IEEE Int. Conf. Commun.*, vol. 2019-May, pp. 1–6, 2019, doi: 10.1109/ICC.2019.8761118.

[27] F.M. Awaysheh, M. Alazab, M. Gupta, T.F. Pena, and J.C. Cabaleiro. Next-generation big data federation access control: A reference model. *Future Generation Computer Systems*, 108(2020): 726–741.

[28] M. Gupta, J. Benson, F. Patwa, and R. Sandhu. Secure V2V and V2I communication in intelligent transportation using cloud lets. *IEEE Transactions on Services Computing*, 2020.

[29] M. Gupta, J. Benson, F. Patwa, and R. Sandhu. Dynamic groups and attribute-based access control for next-generation smart cars. *In Proceedings of the Ninth ACM Conference on Data and Application Security and Privacy*, pp. 61–72, 2019.

[30] A. McDole, M. Abdelsalam, M. Gupta, and S. Mittal. Analyzing CNN based behavioural malware detection techniques on cloud IAAS. In *International Conference on Cloud Computing*, pp. 64–79. Springer, Cham, 2020.

[31] M. Gupta, F. Patwa, and R. Sandhu. POSTER: Access control model for the Hadoop ecosystem. *In Proceedings of the 22nd ACM on Symposium on Access Control Models and Technologies*, pp. 125–127, 2017.

[32] M. Gupta, F.M. Awaysheh, J. Benson, M. Al Azab, F. Patwa, and R. Sandhu. An attribute-based access control for cloud-enabled industrial smart vehicles. *IEEE Transactions on Industrial Informatics*, 2020.

[33] A.K. Yadav, and M.L. Garg. Docker containers versus virtual machine-based virtualization. *In Emerging Technologies in Data Mining and Information Security*, pp. 141–150. Springer, Singapore, 2019.

[34] A.K. Yadav, Ritika, and M.L. Garg. *SecHMS- A Secure Hybrid Monitoring Scheme for Cloud Data Monitoring*. EAI Endorsed Transactions on Scalable Information Systems, 8(30): 2020. e8. ISSN 2032-9407.

[35] A. Yadav, A., Ritika, and M.L. Garg. Monitoring based security approach for cloud computing. Ingénierie des Systèmes d'Information, 24(6): 611–617, 2019. https://doi.org/10.18280/isi.240608.

7

Recent Advancements in Network and Cyber Security using RNN

Gokul Yenduri and *Thippa Reddy Gadekallu**

ABSTRACT

Cybercrime is at an all-time high, prompting day-to-day difficulties in administration. Intruders strive to discover loopholes despite the various approaches used to prevent attacks and protect records. The recurrent neural network can solve both supervised and unsupervised tasks. RNNs are designed to analyze data sources using hidden information, making them suitable for cyber protection. RNN is used in a variety of fields, including natural language, image, and voice processing, and it has made considerable progress. The usage of RNN and other strategies in several applications, such as event detection, fraud detection, and malware detection, is assessed in this chapter.

1. Introduction

Malware is a common danger to all in today's data environment, from prominent companies to ordinary users, and therefore we must protect our infrastructure, networks, and valuable data. With frequent leaks, identity stealing, and other cyber-attacks, cyber-crime has hit a whole new level. Through leveraging security flaws, hackers obtain access to sensitive records, passwords, and other useful material. While the number of applications on social networking sites has evolved, so has the number of malicious attacks. Entities, on the other hand, can simply build numerous malicious attacks and distribute them through social media using third-party apps. E-mails, executable files, applications, and other tools may be used in attacks. Criminals take advantage of security vulnerabilities to exploit their adversaries. As a consequence, security service vendors are primarily relying on the deep learning technique and machine learning technique, in which an algorithm depends on the

School of Information Technology and Engineering, Vellore Institute of Technology, India.
* Corresponding author: thippareddy.g@vit.ac.in

fundamental knowledge from a vast acquisition of security-related data and predict based on given data. Hackers are forced to come up with innovative ways to evade detection systems. Deep learning algorithms have been used to overcome emerging security challenges for the past few decades [67]. These methods may be used to detect new malware, act as anomaly detection systems, safeguarding against information leakage, as well as other protection concerns.

Deep Learning (DL) methods outperformed prior approaches in several AI challenges. It can identify cyber-attacks by studying the dynamic underlying framework, concealed sequential relationships, and hierarchical functions representation from a vast collection of protection data. In this research, we take a look at how machine learning, artificial intelligence, soft computing, and deep learning may be used to address cyber-security challenges. A collection of steps taken to secure computer networks, applications, and data is referred to as cyber protection. Based on previous studies, this study provides an overview of cyber security techniques with the goal of determining which technique is the most prevalent among existing techniques and RNN is most often used because it does well in time series forecasting. Section 2 of this chapter discusses the current state-of-the-art literature, while Section 3 discusses how models may be applied to cyber-security issues. Section 4 is devoted to problems, while Section 5 is dedicated to the conclusion

2. State-of-the-Art Literature Survey

2.1 Popular Machine Learning Algorithms used in Cyber Security

2.1.1 Support Vector Machine

SVM is the most commonly and powerful machine learning technique used in security, especially for intrusion detection. SVM will classify and divide the data groups into two based on the details to the margin on each side of the hyper-plane [68]. The placement of data points can be improved by increasing the margin and distances between hyper-planes. The data points on edge of hyper plane's are called support vectors or support vectors points. Based on the kernel SVM can be further

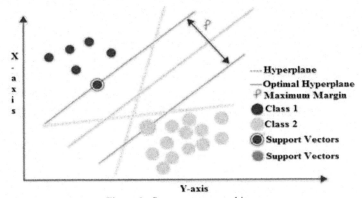

Figure 1: Support vector machine.

classified into two types, linear and non-linear. It may be single-class or multiple-class depending on the detection type. SVM is memory intensive and takes a long time to train. To understand the complex user's actions, SVM requires training at distinct intervals. The kernel feature and parameters have an impact on the classifier's efficiency.

2.1.2 Decision Tree

One of the most commonly used predictive modeling algorithms for cyber security tasks is decision trees [69]. Some of the most important advantages of using decision trees in several classification and prediction applications, as well as some typical drawbacks, are mentioned below.

- It can be simple to read and understand non-technical people.
- Users can efficiently and simply prepare data for decision trees.
- Nonlinear relationships between parameters have no effect on tree growth.
- Indirectly, decision trees perform vector filtering or feature selection.

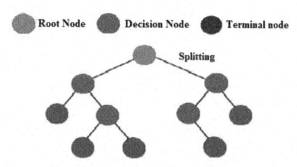

Figure 2: Decision tree.

2.1.3 K nearest Neighbor

K-nearest neighbor is an unsupervised learning algorithm (KNN). It determines the difference/dissimilarity between two data instances using a distance function. It needs less time to train than other classifiers. Its computation time, on the other hand, is overhead during the classification process. This classifier works under the assumption that data points that are equivalent in the same space are closer together than dissimilar data points. There are two types of KNN based on anomaly levels [70]. The anomaly scores are calculated in one of two ways: (1) by calculating the gap between the kth neighbor and the data point, or (2) by measuring the density of each data instance. The value of the kth data point affects the classifier's overall performance. Noisy details and the distance feature used to calculate the distance between data points makes the classifier insecure. KNN is computationally expensive and needs a large amount of storage to manipulate. Using the Euclidean formula for distance, the distance function d(x, y) is commonly used to calculate the distance between data points x and y.

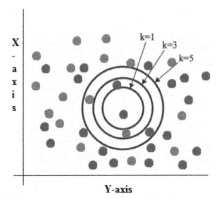

Figure 3: K-nearest neighbor.

2.2 Popular Deep Learning Algorithms used in Cyber Security

2.2.1 Artificial Neural Networks

ANN's are conceptual or designed based on the influence of the human nervous system, which has the capability of recognizing patterns and, also support machine learning. Since the nervous systems of animals are more complicated than those of humans, systems built in this manner would be able to solve more complex problems. In general, artificial neural networks are depicted as assets of massively integrated "neurons" that can calculate values from inputs. A neural network is similar to a website network with interacting neurons that can amount in the millions [71]. Both parallel processing in the body is achieved with the aid of these integrated neurons, and the perfect representation of Parallel Processing is the human or animal body. Artificial neural networks are now made up of clusters of artificial neurons. The clustering is based on forming layers that are then linked. The "craft" solving complicated challenges in the real world are dependent on how these layers link. As a result, their superior capacity to infer meaning from abstract or imprecise data, neural networks may be used to identify patterns and identify trends that are too complex for humans or other computational techniques to find.

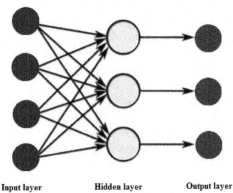

Figure 4: Artificial neural network.

2.2.2 Recurrent Neural Network

A feed-forward neural network with internal memory can be called a recurrent neural network. Since it conducts the same procedure for every data input and the present input's performance is based on previous output, RNN is a kind of neural network that is repetitive in nature. After the output is generated, it is then copied and sent into the recurrent network [72]. It considers both the new input and the output obtained from the previous data when making a decision. In contrast to feed-forward neural network, RNN uses its internal state to produce sequences of inputs. As a consequence, things like unfermented signature recognition and speech recognition are now possible. All inputs are autonomous of one another. All of the inputs in an RNN, on the other hand, are bound to one another. Initially it extracts X (0) from the series of inputs, then followed by outputs h (0), which serves as the input for the next phase along with X (1). So, the inputs for the next phase are h (0) and X (1). Likewise, h (1) and X (2) are the next, and so on. During training, it remembers the background within its internal memory.

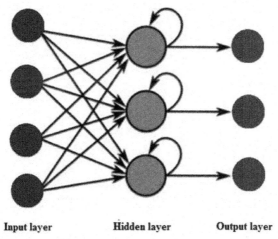

Input layer   **Hidden layer**   **Output layer**

Figure 5: Recurrent neural network.

2.2.3 Convolution Neural Networks

CNN is a deep neural network designed specifically for image processing. It has recently been discovered to have exceptional skills in the study of sequential results. CNN always employs two basic operations: convolution and pooling [73]. In the convolution operation, several filters are used to remove features (feature selection) from the data set, while keeping the spatial details associated with them. Pooling, also known as sub-sampling, is a method for reducing the dimensionality of features generated by convolution. Full pooling and average pooling are the two most popular pooling operations used in CNN. Relu is a well-known option for the activation of CNN for back-propagation gradient transfer in training.

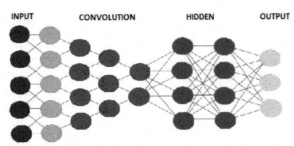

Figure 6: Convolution neural networks.

2.2.4 Deep Belief Network

They are a type of deep neural network which learns in an unsupervised greedy manner. It was created in order to imitate the capacity of the human brain and also designed to recognize dynamic patterns. DBN is a generative stack of Restricted Boltzmann Machines (RBM). On the other hand, it does not enable peer-to-peer connectivity inside the network layer, unlike RBM. Every node in the deep-belief network is linked to every other node in the layers before and after it. Probabilistic data is accepted as input by DBN [74]. Before a DBN can generate output, each layer of the network must understand all of the information. Until the training stage is completed to the required degree, each layer continues to generate optimal choices at each step, as seen in Figure 7.

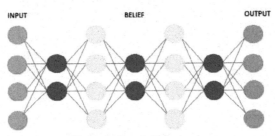

Figure 7: Deep belief network.

2.3 Popular Evolutionary Algorithms Used in Cyber Security

2.3.1 Genetic Algorithm

Nature has always been a fantastic source of inspiration for people. Genetic Algorithm is a search-based algorithm that follows the concept of natural selection. GA is a subset of Evolutionary Computation and is a somewhat broader computational branch. GA has a community or several possible solutions to a problem. These possibilities are then exposed to recombination and mutation to produce offspring and the mechanism is repetitive over generations. Each candidate solution is assigned a fitness value based on objective feature value, and the fitter candidate solution has a higher probability of mating and creating a "fitter" candidate solution. It follows Darwin's theory of "Survival of the Fittest". In this process, better individuals or candidate solutions continue to "evolve" until we find an ideal solution [74]. Genetic

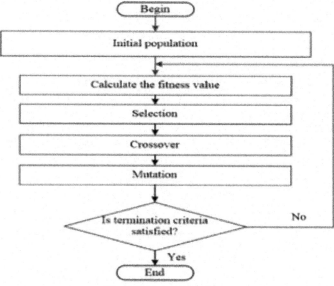

Figure 8: Genetic algorithm.

algorithms are generally random in nature, but since they often use historical data, they are better when compared to random local searches in which we literally test different solutions.

2.3.2 Differential Evolution

It is a population based meta-heuristic search algorithm that uses evolutionary mechanism to improve a candidate response. This technique makes limited predictions

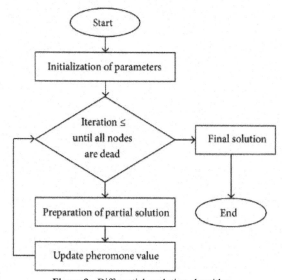

Figure 9: Differential evolution algorithm.

about the underlying optimization problem and can explore huge spaces quickly. DE is a multi-modal problem and a robust population-based search algorithm that is one of the most efficient and reliable algorithms available [75].

2.3.3 Artificial Bee Colony (ABC) Algorithm

DervisKaraboga proposed the Artificial bee colony algorithm optimization in [3], which was motivated by a honey bee swarms' intelligent actions in locating a food source. In ABC algorithm models, scout bees arbitrarily discover all food supply locations depending on the dances, employed bees exploit a source of food that comes from scout bees, and onlooker bees decide on the food quality. ABC has been used in a variety of applications in a broad spectrum of areas [76].

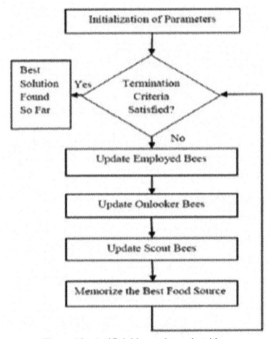

Figure 10: Artificial bee colony algorithm.

2.3.4 Ant Colony Optimization

Ants utilize pheromone tracks to communicate with one another. A running ant leaves differing quantities of pheromone on the land to mark its route. An ant encountering a previously laid trail will sense it and decide to pursue it with a large likelihood, thus strengthening the trail with its pheromone. As a result, the accumulated behavior appears as constructive feedback: the more ants that pursue a trail, the more suitable track becomes the most followed route; therefore, the chance that an ant may select a route rises with the total number of ants that have previously chosen the same route. Based on this ant's operation, Marco Dorigo developed ant colony optimization, a computational technique that belongs to a class of related meta-heuristic methods [77–85].

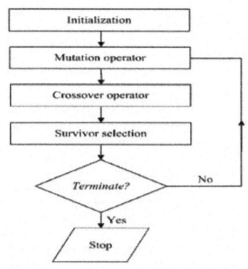

Figure 11: Ant colony optimization.

3. Application of Different ML/AI Techniques for Cyber Security

3.1 RNN Over other Traditional Models

RNN accepts missing information and does not conclude over linear relationship. There is no need of interaction between the observations many times. It supports multivariate analysis since certain real-world problems necessitate a large number of input variables. Concentrate on multi-step forecast which helps in long-term predictions.

Table 1: Application of ML/AI techniques for cyber-security.

Method [Ref]	Reference	Applications
RBM	[1–11, 15, 32–36, 92]	Malware Detection, Intrusion Detection, Spam Identification, False Data Injection
RBM & Auto encoder	[12]	Intrusion Detection
RBM & RNN	[13]	Intrusion Detection
GAN	[14]	DGA
RNN	[16–31, 60–66, 86–89]	Malware Detection, DGA, Intrusion Detection, Border Gateway Protocol, Anomaly Detection, Keystroke Verification, Contamination attack, Zero-day attack
Auto encoder	[37–54, 59]	Malware Classification, Intrusion Detection, Internal Dataset, Network Traffic, Impersonation Attacks, User Authentication.
CNN	[55–58, 93]	Malware Classification, DGA, Drive-by Download Attack, Malware Detection

4. Challenges

4.1 Artificial Intelligence is used in both Cyber-attacks and Cyber-prevention

Artificial Intelligence has changed the world by working not just on the defensive side, but also on the offensive side. One definition of Artificial Intelligence is biometric login. Through a lot of testing and modeling, AI will learn anomalies in behavior patterns that can be used as a defense weapon but sadly, hackers, phishers, and robbers can use the same tactics to carry out a cyber-attack.

4.2 Less Technically Skilled Workers

When attackers can quickly copy an identity for any scam and can manipulate any loophole, then the problem can only get worse until there are enough resources with the right expertise to deal with it. Companies must invest in current personnel preparation to hire additional resources to analyze network threats to deter cyber-attacks. Companies would risk millions in money if this does not happen.

4.3 Risk While Shifting to Cloud

Because of the flexibility and risks associated with legacy data centers, organizations are migrating their critical data to the cloud. Moving data to the cloud necessitates careful setup and protection precautions, or else you risk falling into a pit. Online service providers just secure their platform; protecting a company's infrastructure from theft and deletion in the cloud is the duty of the company. Firewalls, multi-factor authentication, virtual private networks (VPNs), and other cloud protection technologies are available. In brief, the organization must implement protocols and technologies to protect it against both external and internal risks.

4.4 Ransom Ware Threats on Illegal Software

Ransom ware encrypts data or prevents access to users on a computer or a network. After the hacker has gained entry, he demands money depending on the importance of the data. In these situations, claimants can face financial and productivity damages, as well as increased expenses.

4.5 Lack of End Security to IOT

As the Internet of Things (IoT) is more widely adopted, DDoS attacks [90, 91] and ransomware are some of the examples of security attacks that may be used by invaders to steal sensitive data. To carry out cyber threats, attackers may take advantage of the weakness in IoT networks.

5. Conclusion and Future Work

Attacks on cyber networks are evolving at a quicker rate than the capacity of cyber defenses, to write and execute modern signatures to track them. This, along with advances in machine learning algorithm creation, expands the possibilities for utilizing neural network-based deep learning methods in cyber-security applications to identify new malware variants and zero-day assaults. We addressed different approaches that can be used to tackle a variety of security concerns within this research. We also discussed the uses of different approaches as well as the possible problems that have been posted. RNN is the most commonly used method for most researchers, and RNN ensemble models often produce promising results. Soft computing methods have just recently begun to demonstrate their importance, and combining them with common techniques like RNN would aid in the potential reduction of cybercrime. This work has presented how RNN exceeds traditional models and which algorithms may be adopted for cyber defense. It will be left to future investigations to compare the performance of ensemble models and advanced models with RNN.

References

[1] D. Zhu, H. Jin, Y. Yang, D. Wu, and W. Chen. Deep Flow: Deep learning-based malware detection by mining Android application for abnormal usage of sensitive data. *In Proceedings of the 2017 IEEE Symposium Computers and Communications (ISCC).* Heraklion, Greece, 3–6 July 2017; pp. 438–443, 2017.

[2] Y. Ye, L. Chen, S. Hou, W. Hardy, X. Li, A.M. Deep. A heterogeneous deep learning framework for intelligent malware detection. *Knowl. Inf. Syst.,* 54: 265–285, 2018.

[3] N. Gao, L. Gao, Q. Gao, and H. Wang. An intrusion detection model based on deep belief networks. *In Proceedings of the 2014 2nd International Conference Advanced Cloud and BigData (CBD).* Huangshan, China, 20–22 November 2014; pp. 247–252, 2014.

[4] M.Z. Alom, V. Bontupalli, and T.M. Taha. Intrusion detection using deep belief networks. *In Proceedings of the 2015 National Aerospace and Electronics Conference (NAECON).* Dayton, OH, USA, 15–19 June 2015; pp. 339–344.

[5] B. Dong, and X. Wang. Comparison deep learning method to traditional methods using for network intrusion detection. *In Proceedings of the 8th IEEE International Conference Communication Software and Networks (ICCSN).* Beijing, China, 4–6 June 2016; pp. 581–585, 2016.

[6] M.J. Kang, and J.W. Kang. Intrusion detection system using deep neural network for in-vehicle network security. *PLoS ONE* 2016, 11: e0155781, 2016.

[7] K.K. Nguyen, D.T. Hoang, D. Niyato, P. Wang, P. Nguyen, and E. Dutkiewicz. Cyber attack detection in mobile cloud computing: A deep learning approach. *In Proceedings of the 2018 IEEE Wireless Communications and Networking Conference (WCNC).* Barcelona, Spain, 15–18 April 2018; pp. 1–6, 2018.

[8] G. Tzortzis, and A. Likas. Deep belief networks for spam filtering, in tools with artificial intelligence. *In Proceedings of the 2007 19th IEEE International Conferenceon ICTAI.* Patras, Greece, 29–31 October 2007; Volume 2, pp. 306–309, 2007.

[9] Y. He, G.J. Mendis, and J. Wei. Real-time detection of false data injection attacks in smart grid: A deep learning-based intelligent mechanism. IEEE Trans. Smart Grid 2017, 8: 2505–2516, 2017.

[10] Y. Chen, Y. Zhang, and S. Maharjan. Deep learning for secure mobile edge computing. arXiv 2017, arXiv:1709.08025.

[11] Y. Ding, S. Chen, and J. Xu. Application of deep belief networks for opcode based malware detection. *In Proceedings of the 2016 International Joint Conference on Neural Networks (IJCNN).* Vancouver, BC, Canada, 24–29 July 2016; pp. 3901–3908, 2016.

[12] Y. Li, R. Ma, and R. Jiao. A hybrid malicious code detection method based on deep learning. Methods, 9: 205–216, 2015.

[13] L.F. Maimó, A.L.P. Gómez, F.J.G. Clemente, and M.G. Pérez. A self-adaptive deep learning-based system for anomaly detection in 5G networks. IEEE Access 2018, 6: 7700–7712, 2018.

[14] H.S. Anderson, J. Wood bridge, B. Filar. Deep DGA: Adversarially-tuned domain generation and detection. *In Proceedings of the 2016 ACM Workshop on Artificial Intelligence and Security.* Vienna, Austria, 28 October 2016; pp. 13–21, 2016.

[15] K. Alrawashdeh, and C. Purdy. Toward an online anomaly intrusion detection system based on deep learning. *In Proceedings of the 15th IEEE International Conference Machine Learning and Applications (ICMLA).* Miami, FL, USA, 9–11 December 2015; pp. 195–200, 2015.

[16] R. Pascanu, J.W. Stokes, H. Sanossian, M. Marinescu, and A. Thomas. Malware classification with recurrent networks. *In Proceedings of the 2015 IEEE International Conference Acoustics, Speech and Signal Process (ICASSP).* Brisbane, Australia, 19–24 April 2015; pp. 1916–1920, 2015.

[17] T. Shibahara, T. Yagi, M. Akiyama, D. Chiba, and T. Yada. Efficient dynamic malware analysis based on network behavior using deep learning. *In Proceedings of the 2016 IEEE Global Communications Conference (GLOBECOM).* Washington, DC, USA, 4–8 December 2016; pp. 1–7, 2016.

[18] J. Woodbridge, H.S. Anderson, A. Ahuja, and D. Grant. Predicting domain generation algorithms with long short-term memory networks. arXiv 2016,arXiv: 1611.00791.

[19] P. Lison, and V. Mavroeidis. Automatic Detection of Malware-Generated Domains with Recurrent Neural Models.arXiv 2017, arXiv:1709.07102.

[20] D. Tran, H. Mac, V. Tong, H.A. Tran, and L. G. Nguyen. A LSTM based framework for handling multiclass imbalance in DGA botnet detection. *Neurocomputing,* 275: 2401–2413, 2018.

[21] P. Torres, C. Catania, S. Garcia, and C. G. Garino. An analysis of recurrent neural networks for botnet detection behavior. *In Proceedings of the 2016 IEEE Biennial Congress of Argentina (ARGENCON),* Buenos Aires, Argentina, 15–17 June 2016; pp. 1–6, 2016.

[22] J. Kim, J. Kim, H.L.T. Thu, and H. Kim. Long short term memory recurrent neural network classifier for intrusion detection. *In Proceedings of the 2016 International Conference Platform Technology andService (PlatCon).* Jeju, Korea, 15–17 February 2016; pp. 1–5.

[23] J. Kim, and H. Kim. Applying recurrent neural network to intrusion detection with hessian free optimization. *In Proceedings of the International Conference on Information Security Applications.* Jeju Island, Korea, 20–22 August 2015; pp. 357–369, 2015.

[24] G. Kim, H. Yi, J. Lee, Y. Paek, and S. Yoon. LSTM-Based System-Call Language Modeling and Robust Ensemble Method for Designing Host-Based Intrusion Detection Systems. arXiv 2016,arXiv:1611.01726.

[25] G. Loukas, T. Vuong, R. Heartfield, G. Sakellari, Y. Yoon, and D. Gan. Cloud-based cyber-physical intrusion detection for vehicles using Deep Learning. *IEEE Access,* 6: 3491–3508, 2018.

[26] M. Cheng, Q. Xu, J. Lv, W. Liu, Q. Li, and J. Wang. MS-LSTM: A multi-scale LSTM model for BGP anomaly detection. *In Proceedings of the IEEE 24th International Conference Network Protocols (ICNP),* Singapore, 8–11 November 2016; pp. 1–6, 2016.

[27] P. Kobojek, and K. Saeed. Application of recurrent neural networks for user verification based on keystroke dynamics. *J. Telecommun. Inf. Technol.,* 3: 80–90, 2016.

[28] C.D. McDermott, F. Majdani, and A. Petrovski. Botnet detection in the internet of things using deep learning approaches. *In Proceedings of the 2018 International Joint Conference on Neural Networks (IJCNN).* Rio de Janeiro, Brazil, 8–13 July 2018; pp. 1–8, 2018.

[29] R.B. Krishnan, and N.R. Raajan. An intellectual intrusion detection system model for attacks classification using RNN. *Int. J. Pharm. Technol.,* 8: 23157–23164, 2016.

[30] R.C. Staudemeyer. Applying long short-term memory recurrent neural networks to intrusion detection. *S. Afr. Comput. J.,* 56: 136–154, 2015.

[31] C.L. Yin, Y.F. Zhu, J.L. Fei, and X.Z. He. A deep learning approach for intrusion detection using recurrent neural networks. *IEEE Access,* 5: 21954–21961, 2017.

[32] Z. Yuan, Y. Lu, Z. Wang, Y. Xue. Droid-sec: Deep learning in android malware detection. *ACMSIGCOMM Comput. Commun. Rev.,* 44: 371–372, 2014.

[33] Z. Yuan, Y. Lu, and Y. Xue. Droid detector: Android malware characterization and detection using deep learning. *Tsinghua Sci. Technol.,* 21: 114–123, 2016.

[34] S. Hou, A. Saas, Y. Ye, and L. Chen. Droid delver: An android malware detection system using deep belief network based on API call blocks. *In Proceedings of the International Conference Web-Age Information Manage, Nanchang.* China, 3–5 June 2016; pp. 54–66, 2016.

[35] L. Xu, D. Zhang, N. Jayasena, and J. Cavazos. HADM: Hybrid analysis for detection of malware. *In Proceedings of the SAI Intelligent Systems Conference.* London, UK, 21–22 September 2016; pp. 702–724, 2016.

[36] R. Benchea, and D.T. Gavrilut. Combining restricted Boltzmann machine and one side perceptron for malware detection. *In Proceedings of the International Conference on Conceptual Structures.* Iasi, Romania, 27–30 July 2014; pp. 93–103, 2014.

[37] X. Wang, and S.M. Yiu. A multi-task learning model for malware classification with useful file access pattern from API call sequence. arXiv preprint arXiv:1610.05945, 2016.

[38] W. Wang, M. Zhu, X. Zeng, X. Ye, and Y. Sheng. Malware traffic classification using convolutional neural network for representation learning. *In Proceedings of the IEEE 2017 International Conference on Information Networking (ICOIN).* Da Nang, Vietnam, 11–13 January 2017; pp. 712–717, 2017.

[39] T. Ma, F. Wang, J. Cheng, Y. Yu, and X. Chen. A hybrid spectral clustering and deep neural network ensemble algorithm for intrusion detection in sensor networks. *Sensors,* 16: 1701, 2016.

[40] M.E. Aminanto, and K. Kim. Deep learning-based feature selection for intrusion detection system in transport layer. *In Proceedings of the Korea Institutes of Information Security and Cryptology Conference,* pp. 740–743, 2016.

[41] A.A. Diro, and N. Chilamkurti. Deep learning: The frontier for distributed attack detection in Fog-to-Things computing. *IEEE Commun. Mag.,* 56: 169–175, 2018.

[42] S. Chawla. *Deep Learning Based Intrusion Detection System for Internet of Things*; University of Washington: Seattle, WA, USA, 2017.

[43] J.A. Cox, C.D. James, and J.B. Aimone. A signal processing approach for cyber data classification with deep neural networks. *Procedia Comput. Sci.,* 61: 349–354, 2015.

[44] Z. Wang. *The Applications of Deep Learning on Traffic Identification.* BlackHat: Washington, DC, USA, 2015.

[45] M. Lotfollahi, M.J. Siavoshani, R.S.H. Zade, and M. Saberian. Deep packet: A novel approach for encrypted traffic classification using deep learning. *Soft Computing,* 24(3), 1999–2012, 2020.

[46] G. Mi, Y. Gao, and Y. Tan. Apply stacked auto-encoder to spam detection. *In Proceedings of the International Conference in Swarm Intelligence.* Beijing, China, 26–29 June 2015; pp. 3–15, 2015.

[47] G. Loukas, T. Vuong, R. Heartfield, G. Sakellari, Y. Yoon, and D. Gan. Cloud-based cyber-physical intrusion detection for vehicles using Deep Learning. *IEEE Access,* 6: 3491–3508, 2018.

[48] A. A. Diro, and N. Chilamkurti. Leveraging LSTM networks for attack detection in fog-to-things communications. *IEEE Commun. Mag.,* 56: 124–130, 2018.

[49] C. Shi, J. Liu, H. Liu, Y. Chen. Smart user authentication through actuation of daily activities leveraging WiFi-enabled IoT. *In Proceedings of the 18th ACM International Symposium on Mobile AdHoc Networking and Computing.* Chennai, India, 10–14 July 2017; ACM: New York, NY, USA, p. 5, 2017.

[50] M. Yousefi-Azar, V. Varadharajan, L. Hamey, U. Tupakula. Autoencoder-based feature learning for cyber security applications. *In Proceedings of the 2017 International Joint Conference Neural Networks (IJCNN).* Anchorage, AK, USA, 14–19 May 2017; pp. 3854–3861, 2017.

[51] R. Abdulhammed, M. Faezipour, A. Abuzneid, and A. AbuMallouh. Deep and machine learning approaches for anomaly-based intrusion detection of imbalanced network traffic. *IEEE Sens. Lett.,* 2018.

[52] Nadeem, Mutahir, Ochaun Marshall, Sarbjit Singh, Xing Fang, and Xiaohong Yuan. Semi-supervised deep neural network for network intrusion detection, 2016. Available online:https://digitalcommons.kennesaw.edu/ccerp/2016/Practice/2/.

[53] M.Z. Alom, and T.M. Taha. Network intrusion detection for cyber security using unsupervised deep learning approaches. *In Proceedings of the 2017 IEEE National Aerospace and Electronics Conference (NAECON).* Dayton, OH, USA, 27–30 June 2017; pp. 63–69, 2017.

[54] Mirsky, Yisroel, Tomer Doitshman, Yuval Elovici, and Asaf Shabtai. Kitsune: An ensemble of autoencoders for online network intrusion detection. arXiv preprint arXiv:1802.09089, 2018.

[55] D. Gibert. Convolutional Neural Networks for Malware Classification; UniversitatPolitècnica de Catalunya: Barcelona, Spain, 2016.

[56] F. Zeng, S. Chang, X. Wan. Classification for DGA-Based malicious domain names with deep learning architectures. *Int. J. Intell. Inf. Syst.,* 6: 67–71, 2017.

[57] K. Yamanishi. *Detecting Drive-By Download Attacks from Proxy Log Information Using Convolutional Neural Network.* Osaka University: Osaka, Japan, 2017.

[58] N. McLaughlin, J. Martinez del Rincon, B. Kang, S. Yerima, P. Miller, S. Sezer, Y. Safaei, E. Trickel, Z. Zhao, A. Doupé, and G. Joon Ahn. Deep android malware detection. *In Proceedings of the Seventh ACM on Conference on Data and Application Security and Privacy*, pp. 301–308, 2017, March.

[59] W. Hardy, L. Chen, S. Hou, Y. Ye, X. Li. DL4MD: A deep learning framework for intelligent malware detection. *In Proceedings of the International Conference Data Mining (ICDM)*. Barcelona, Spain, 12–15 December 2016; p. 61, 2016.

[60] M. Nabil, M. Ismail, M. Mahmoud, M. Shahin, K. Qaraqe, E. Serpedin. Deep learning-based detection of electricity theft cyber-attacks in smart grid AMI Networks. *In*: Alazab, M. and M. Tang (eds.). *Deep Learning Applications for Cyber Security. Advanced Sciences and Technologies for Security Applications*. Springer, Cham, 2019, https://doi.org/10.1007/978-3-030-13057-2_4.

[61] Z. Lipton, J. Berkowitz, and C. Elkan. A critical review of recurrent neural networks for sequence learning, 2015, ArXiv preprintarXiv:1506.00019.

[62] T. Young, D. Hazarika, S. Poria, and E. Cambria. Recent trends in deep learning based natural language processing. *IEEE Computational intelligenCe magazine*, 2018 Jul 20; 13(3): 55–75, 2018.

[63] H. Salehinejad, S. Sankar, J. Barfett, E. Colak, and S. Valaee. Recent advances in recurrent neural networks. arXiv preprint arXiv:1801.01078. 2017 Dec 29.

[64] S. Venkatraman, M. Alazab, and R. Vinayakumar. A hybrid deep learning image-based analysis for effective malware detection. *Journal of Information Security and Applications*, 47: 377–389, 2019, ISSN 2214–2126.

[65] R. Vinayakumar, M. Alazab, K.P. Soman, P. Poornachandran and S. Venkatraman. Robust intelligent malware detection using deep learning. *In IEEE Access*, 7: 46717–46738, 2019, doi: 10.1109/ACCESS.2019.2906934.

[66] E.M. Raybourn, M. Kunz, D. Fritz, and V. Urias. A zero-entry cyber range environment for future learning ecosystems. *In*: Koç, Ç. K. (eds.). *Cyber-Physical Systems Security*. Springer, *Cham.*, 2018, https://doi.org/10.1007/978-3-319-98935-8_5.

[67] D. Gümüşbaş, T. Yıldırım, A. Genovese, and F. Scotti. A comprehensive survey of databases and deep learning methods for cybersecurity and intrusion detection systems. *In IEEE Systems Journal*, 15(2): 1717–1731, June 2021, doi: 10.1109/JSYST.2020.2992966.

[68] J. Bajard, P. Martins, L. Sousa and V. Zucca. Improving the efficiency of SVM classification With FHE. *In IEEE Transactions on Information Forensics and Security*, 15: 1709–1722, 2020, doi: 10.1109/TIFS.2019.2946097.

[69] T.P. Vuong, G. Loukas, D. Gan and A. Bezemskij. Decision tree-based detection of denial of service and command injection attacks on robotic vehicles. *IEEE International Workshop on Information Forensics and Security (WIFS)*, pp. 1–6, 2015, doi: 10.1109/WIFS.2015.7368559.

[70] M.S. Sarma, Y. Srinivas, M. Abhiram, L. Ullala, M.S. Prasanthi and J.R. Rao. Insider threat detection with face recognition and KNN user classification. *IEEE International Conference on Cloud Computing in Emerging Markets (CCEM)*, pp. 39–44, 2017, doi: 10.1109/CCEM.2017.16.

[71] M.R. Habibi, H.R. Baghaee, T. Dragičević and F. Blaabjerg. *False Data Injection Cyber-Attacks Mitigation in Parallel DC/DC Converters Based on Artificial Neural Networks. In IEEE Transactions on Circuits and Systems II: Express Briefs*, 68(2): 717–721, Feb. 2021, doi: 10.1109/TCSII.2020.3011324.

[72] S. Kwon, H. Yoo and T. Shon. IEEE 1815.1-based power system security with bidirectional RNN-based network anomalous attack detection for cyber-physical system. *In IEEE Access*, 8: 77572–77586, 2020, doi: 10.1109/ACCESS.2020.2989770.

[73] R. Hu and S. Xiang. CNN prediction based reversible data hiding. *In IEEE Signal Processing Letters*, 28: 464–468, 2021, doi: 10.1109/LSP.2021.3059202.

[74] Y. Zhang, P. Li and X. Wang. Intrusion detection for iot based on improved genetic algorithm and deep belief network. *In IEEE Access*, 7: 31711–31722, 2019, doi: 10.1109/ACCESS.2019.2903723.

[75] S. Elsayed, R. Sarker and J. Slay. Evaluating the performance of a differential evolution algorithm in anomaly detection. *2015 IEEE Congress on Evolutionary Computation (CEC)*, pp. 2490–2497, 2015, doi: 10.1109/CEC.2015.7257194.

[76] A. Qureshi, H. Larijani, A. Javed, N. Mtetwa and J. Ahmad. Intrusion detection using swarm intelligence. *2019 UK/China Emerging Technologies* (UCET), pp. 1–5, 2019, doi: 10.1109/UCET.2019.8881840.

[77] A. Cui, C. Li and X. Wang. Real-time early warning of network security threats based on improved ant colony algorithm. *2019 12th International Conference on Intelligent Computation Technology and Automation (ICICTA)*, pp. 309–316, 2019, doi: 10.1109/ICICTA49267.2019.00072.

[78] S. Bhattacharya, P.K.R. Maddikunta, R. Kaluri, S. Singh, T.R. Gadekallu, M. Alazab, and U. Tariq. A novel PCA-firefly based XG Boost classification model for intrusion detection in networks using GPU. *Electronics*, 9(2): 219, 2020.

[79] T.R. Gadekallu, N. Khare, S. Bhattacharya, S. Singh, P.K.R. Maddikunta, I.H. Ra, and M. Alazab. Early detection of diabetic retinopathy using PCA-firefly based deep learning model. *Electronics*, 9(2): 274, 2020.

[80] S.P. RM, P.K.R. Maddikunta, M. Parimala, S. Koppu, T.R. Gadekallu, C.L. Chowdhary, and M. Alazab. An effective feature engineering for DNN using hybrid PCA-GWO for intrusion detection in IoMT architecture. *Computer Communications*, 160: 139–149, 2020.

[81] M. Alazab, S. Khan, S.S.R. Krishnan, Q.V. Pham, M.P.K. Reddy, and T.R. Gadekallu. A multidirectional LSTM model for predicting the stability of a smart grid. *IEEE Access*, 8: 85454–85463, 2020.

[82] T.R. Gadekallu, D.S. Rajput, M.P.K. Reddy, K. Lakshmanna, S. Bhattacharya, S. Singh, and M. Alazab. A novel PCA–whale optimization-based deep neural network model for classification of tomato plant diseases using GPU. *Journal of Real-Time Image Processing*, 1–14, 2020.

[83] M. Alazab, K. Lakshmanna, T. Reddy, Q.V. Pham, and P.K.R. Maddikunta. Multi-objective cluster head selection using fitness averaged rider optimization algorithm for IoT networks in smart cities. *Sustainable Energy Technologies and Assessments*, 43: 100973, 2021.

[84] M.H. Abidi, H. Alkhalefah, K. Moiduddin, M. Alazab, M.K. Mohammed, W. Ameen, and T.R. Gadekallu. Optimal 5G network slicing using machine learning and deep learning concepts. *Computer Standards & Interfaces*, 76: 103518, 2021.

[85] T.R. Gadekallu, M. Alazab, R. Kaluri, P.K.R. Maddikunta, S. Bhattacharya, K. Lakshmanna, and M. Parimala. Hand gesture classification using a novel CNN-crow search algorithm. *Complex & Intelligent Systems*, 1–14, 2021.

[86] J.C. Kimmell, M. Abdelsalam, and M. Gupta. Analyzing machine learning approaches for online malware detection in cloud. *In Proceedings of IEEE SMARTCOMP* 2021.

[87] J.C. Kimmel, A.D. Mcdole, M. Abdelsalam, M. Gupta, and R. Sandhu. Recurrent neural networks based online behavioural malware detection techniques for cloud infrastructure. *IEEE Access* 9 (2021): 68066–68080.

[88] M. Abdelsalam, M. Gupta, and S. Mittal. Artificial intelligence assisted malware analysis. *In Proceedings of the 2021 ACM Workshop on Secure and Trustworthy Cyber-Physical Systems*, pp. 75–77, 2021.

[89] A. McDole, M. Gupta, M. Abdelsalam, S. Mittal, and M. Alazab. Deep learning techniques for behavioral malware analysis in cloud IAAS. *In Malware Analysis using Artificial Intelligence and Deep Learning*, pp. 269–285. Springer, Cham, 2021.

[90] S. Sontowski, M. Gupta, S.S.L. Chukkapalli, M. Abdelsalam, S. Mittal, A. Joshi, and R. Sandhu. Cyber attacks on smart farming infrastructure. *In 2020 IEEE 6th International Conference on Collaboration and Internet Computing (CIC)*, pp. 135–143. IEEE, 2020.

[91] M. Gupta, M. Abdelsalam, S. Khorsandroo, and S. Mittal. Security and privacy in smart farming: Challenges and opportunities. *IEEE Access* 8 (2020): 34564–34584, 2020.

[92] D. Gupta, M. Gupta, S. Bhatt, and A.S. Tosun. Detecting anomalous user behavior in remote patient monitoring. *In Proceedings of IEEE IRI*, 2021.

8

A Big Data Framework
for Dynamic Consent

Wei Yap and *Muhammad Rizwan Asghar**

ABSTRACT

Privacy is a vast and vital area of law with possibly diverse interpretations, legislation
and standards worldwide with the aim to protect data. Consent plays a vital role
in preserving privacy as it ensures that all involved parties understand the reason
for the use and collection of data. Many organisations still have lengthy guidelines
that cause legibility and usability issues. This makes it difficult for a data subject
to understand what they are consenting to and creates a restrictive environment for
consent. Unfortunately, existing works do not provide any solution for implementing
a dynamic privacy consent framework. In this book chapter, we aim at presenting a
dynamic consent framework for big data to ensure that each privacy consent policy
is legible, understandable, usable, and customisable. We propose a new method to
communicate, analyse, and request consent from a data subject in a way that is simple
and understandable. We also aim to ensure that this framework does not increase the
burden on data subjects to provide consent while implementing an ability to simplify
and audit the consent process.

1. Introduction

In today's data-intensive environment, data is considered to be one of the most valuable assets. Whether it is accessing digital news online, watching streaming videos,
or going for a medical examination, privacy protection laws along with consent,
govern the ability for organisations to use and collect data about individuals. Privacy
protection laws such as the Privacy Act 1993 in New Zealand [1] not only regulate
what can be collected but also restrict data disclosure and data usage without express and informed consent. Due to the requirement of consent from a data subject
being "informed", a data subject needs to fully understand the rationale behind the
decisions of data collection in addition to having some idea of the risks and benefits of disclosing data. Having data subjects informed about the consent they have
been requested to decide on limits their ability to add or modify sections of an organisation's privacy policy. This is because it is too cumbersome and not viable to
incorporate each change with a separate privacy policy. One way this complexity can
be simplified is through the use of dynamic consent.

School of Computer Science, The University of Auckland, New Zealand.
* Corresponding author: r.asghar@auckland.ac.nz

Dynamic consent allows for a personalised and ongoing engagement between data subjects and data requesters [2]. Along with ongoing informed engagement, data subjects can provide various types of consent and conditions on data. Having these options allows for additional transparency and control of what is collected. With each option a data subject chooses, such a system should give an up-to-date outlook on the outcomes of decisions they make and also show the benefits and risks associated with the circumstances. A framework that incorporates dynamic consent gives data subjects more opportunities to understand the rationale for data collection with options to personalise the levels of consent they agree to. Such a framework enables data subjects to make better-informed choices on what type of consent they give.

State-of-the-art lacks a privacy framework necessary for dynamic consent. Although some frameworks do attempt to address and provide solutions for different parts of the problem, such as communicating, storing, generating, and auditing privacy consents [3–6]. Unfortunately, existing solutions are far from providing a framework that simultaneously solves all issues related to implementing a truly dynamic consent in a holistic manner. Current framework implementations fail to address the problem of explainable consent with complex conditions imposed by data subjects. Further, they do not provide any standard templates that could be used for capturing consent. Consequently, the current state-of-art is still missing a degree of flexibility and accountability to be truly considered as dynamic consent.

In this chapter, we propose a dynamic consent framework for big data, which allows a data subject to interact, modify, and view a simplified privacy policy at each step of the consent decision process. We also enable attributes to be pre-filled and communicated in conjunction with a privacy policy to simplify how a data subject interacts with a data requester while providing them with a clear view and idea of what data is being shared. Our framework aims at addressing all issues that currently exist for the implementation of a dynamic consent framework so that this framework can begin to replace the current model of consent.

2. Background of Privacy and Consent

In case of informed consent, a data subject knows the reason for data collection and how the data will be used along with the risks and benefits of sharing data. In order to achieve this standard of consent, the New Zealand privacy commission has set out minimum standards so that the consent obtained is more likely to be informed consent [7]. One way this is demonstrated is by ensuring check boxes that involve privacy consent options are not pre-checked before a data subject agrees to the terms. This ensures that a data subject has been given a chance to read through the implications of what they are agreeing to and understand how and why the data collected will be used [7].

A study found if a reasonable person who thoroughly reads privacy policies along with terms and conditions for every website they visited, it would take 201 hours annually [8]. This highlights the fact that without concise and easy to understand language to represent privacy policies, it is almost impractical for a reasonable person to read and understand the purpose and consequences of every privacy policy. Over the years, more and more organisations have been implementing a privacy by design approach to boost transparency and safeguard data subjects from oversharing their personal information. This approach uses a proactive method that defaults all privacy settings to the least intrusive and most restrictive option.

2.1 Privacy Legislation

Most countries around the world have some requirement of consent before collecting data from a data subject. Generally, in New Zealand, most privacy legislation is from the Privacy Act with supplementary privacy codes that are modifications or additions for certain sectors. In regards to New Zealand legislation, "Section 6" of the Privacy Act stipulates several "information privacy principals" every agency in New Zealand is obliged to follow when using or collecting data. In Table 1, we provide a list of the twelve information privacy principals that are grouped within three main themes.

Table 1: A brief description of different themes from the Privacy Act 1993.

Theme	Principal	Description
Data Collection	1	Data is collected for a lawful purpose, which is connected to an agency and collection is necessary.
	2	Collecting data directly from individuals with some exceptions.
	3	Rules that govern the reason for data collection and awareness of collection.
	4	The manor of how data is collected.
Data Storage	5	Rules that govern the reasonable protection of data in storage.
	8	Data must be accurate or checked before use.
	9	Data can only be stored for a reasonable amount of time and must not be kept for longer than necessary.
	12	Organisations should not use the same unique identifier as another organisation.
Data Access	6,7	Allows for individuals to request and correct their own information stored by an agency.
	10	Data should not be used for another purpose unless stated in Principal 1 with some exceptions.
	11	Data must not be disclosed unless there are reasonable grounds.

The Privacy Bill 2020, which amended the Privacy Act 1993, had slight changes to how organisations should operate. Key changes include mandatory data breach reporting and restrictions of data exporting to ensure that there is a level of privacy protection even when data is not within the jurisdiction of the government. The additional privacy principal in the new privacy bill is listed in Table 2.

Table 2: A brief description of the new theme from the Privacy Bill 2020.

Theme	Principal	Description
Data Access	13	Data can not be disclosed to a foreign person or entity unless with express consent or there is reasonable protection similar to the Privacy Act.

While New Zealand's privacy legislation provides protection and standards with personal information, other countries such as the USA, Australia and the UK also share similar concepts. One notable example is the European Union's General Data Protection Regulation (GDPR). While GDPR is extremely similar to New Zealand's Privacy Act, there are additional constraints that provide additional privacy protection [9]. These similarities and differences are highlighted in Table 3.

Table 3: Similarities and differences between the New Zealand Privacy Act principals and articles from the GDPR.

NZ Privacy Principal	GDPR	Similarities and Differences
Principal 3	Article 12-14	GDPR has a similar constraint on data collection but has an increased duty on agencies with enhanced rules on concise and transparent consent.
Principal 5	Article 32	GDPR requires more comprehensive safeguards and risk management ensuring confidentiality, integrity, and availability of stored data.
Principal 6,7,8	Article 15,16,5	GDPR contains equivalent legalisation.
Principal 9	Article 5	In addition to the requirement that agencies need not to hold on to information longer than necessary, GDPR allows for a right to be forgotten.

2.2 Social Licences

Although legislation encompasses the legal obligations of organisations, other emerging codes of practice have also been developed, such as social licenses [10]. As organisations are not bound by these codes of practices nor are they legally required, privacy is still a key focus as it possesses traits that are in line with the ethical ways organisations conduct business [11]. There is no agreed definition of social licenses; however, some key qualities and factors that encompass social licenses are trust, integrity, legitimacy, transparency, and respect [12].

Social licences are helpful as they aim at bridging the gap between legislation and consumers' expectations. While it is entirely possible to follow legal constraints, it is still possible for some users to agree to give a broader range of consent than expected. One current example of this is Clearview AI. Clearview AI harvests public photos over the internet for facial recognition using artificial intelligence [13]. While Clearview AI is operating legally due to the data being publicly available online, there are still expectations from social network users who expect photos that are uploaded and shared publicly online not to be used for these purposes [14]. This is possible due to an exception in Principal 2 in the Privacy Act, which allows for collection if the data is publicly available. As more of our lives revolve around digital information, organisations interacting with data should also consider social licences to be an important component of their ethical obligations [15].

3. Use Case Scenarios and System Requirements

In this section, we describe some general industries where a dynamic consent framework could be used along with a potential scenario for each industry. Next, we list down possible user requirements arising from the given scenarios.

3.1 Use Case Scenarios

Open Banking

Since privacy is such a hot topic in today's digital era, there has been a very close eye on privacy in recent emerging technologies. One such technology is a subset of data sharing called *open banking*. Open banking allows for the integrated sharing of data between banks and potential users using Application Programming Interfaces (API). An API is an intelligent conduit that enables the flow of data between systems in a controlled yet seamless fashion [16].

Having a more integrated approach of data sharing promotes deeper cooperation between different financial institutions, improved customer engagement, more options for customers, and a competitive market for financial products [17]. In open banking, data that is shared between different financial services generally contains highly sensitive information, such as transaction data. Typically, transaction data includes account details, records of deposits, withdrawals, balances, fees, and other information [18]. This raises privacy concerns for data subjects as there is ongoing data sharing and data exchange from multiple organisations, thus bringing up the possibility of fraud and misuse [17]. However, on the other hand, having an open environment gives financial providers more choices and ways to use a client's data to provide meaningful, personalised insights, and analytics.

Open banking is a highly controversial topic for privacy consent since data could be shared with third parties that data subjects might not be fully aware of. Unfortunately, most privacy policy options request an overarching blanket of consent that could be viewed as too broad under privacy legislation. In contrast, having a privacy policy that is too meticulous could hinder the simplicity and ease of access due to the vast numbers of different consents required to be able to process each request.

Use Case 1: Data subject sharing transactional banking data for personalised insights. We consider an application that allows a data subject to view information about costs associated with travelling to a given location. These costs could be for hotels, restaurants, and activities. This application enables data subjects to share data from their vacations to a third party and aggregate spending data to provide accurate recommendations to other users.

One potential scenario could be when a data subject consents to sharing all transactional banking data during their holiday and allowing for aggregate data to be shared with the public. In addition to this, the data subject only allows demographic data such as age and gender to be shared with others who are also sharing theirs. Finally, they want to have categorical data associated with transactions to be deleted after two months but general anonymised aggregated data to be kept online.

Another scenario that could stem from this use case scenario could be when a data subject generally denies data sharing with some notable exceptions. One exception is that they grant consent for some aggregate data to be shared from specific categories such as food and drink only during a particular area and time of the day.

In both scenarios, the application would return aggregated data of those who have also consented to share data based on conditions that they have set. Having these specific restraints on consent gives an additional level of control of how data is used, shared, and presented. The consent conditions and data usage are dependent on the individual user's setting. These specific conditions on data would not be possible in a single privacy policy case without having broad overarching consent and requesting all permissions from a data subject.

Healthcare

Healthcare is a primary sector where privacy plays a key role in each activity and interaction. The healthcare sector creates, accesses, and stores incredibly large amounts of data daily. Such examples could be the creation of information when patients undergo tests such as x-rays for a sprained ankle along with accessing a patient's healthcare information to identify any pre-existing conditions. Another example could be to identify any allergic reactions that could hinder the way a physician prescribes treatments. Once each transaction has been completed, it can be linked and appended to the record of a patient [19].

Use Case 2: Sharing data within the healthcare sector. One scenario for dynamic informed consent in the healthcare sector could be when patients give consent for the use of their medical data for medical healthcare research under certain conditions. Such a condition could be that data can be used for any purpose except, for instance, where the use of medical data is considered unethical, such as genetic modification. Furthermore, the patients would also like to see the outcomes of the reports generated from the use of their medical data along with the purpose.

Another scenario stemming from a healthcare setting could be when a General Practitioner (GP) gets testing results for an infectious virus or disease, say COVID-19. In this situation, after a GP has received information that a patient has received a positive result, immediate action should be taken. In this specific situation, the patient has been requested to give consent for access to location and transactional data for at least 14 days of travel with some restrictions. As for the restrictions, the patient requests all data that is shared to be only used for the purposes relating to anything considered as social good (i.e., a service to the public) and notifying specific individuals over the potential exposure.

Social Networks

Social networks can be considered as an online complex network with entities such as individuals, groups, or organisations that are connected by some inter-dependency say friendships, shared interest or hobbies [20]. With social media on the rise and more content being shared by users every day [21], privacy and consent are considered as areas of focus for these social media networks. This has been demonstrated by research from 2012, showing that over 14 million Americans have not changed their privacy settings [22]. This highlights an important issue as there have been many issues with privacy and consent, such as the Cambridge Analytica scandal or Clearview AI [14,23]. Both organisations tend to obtain overarching consent and use the data collected inappropriately. These situations highlight the need for a way for social media network users not only be able to understand what they are consenting to but also what their decision means and the potential consequences and outcomes of what they choose to share.

Use Case 3: Sharing items on social media with selected individuals. One case study situation that can be drawn from social networks is when a user shares personal information, such as photographs on social media with friends. However, later the user would like to change how this information is shared and might express conditions on who can see the information. This can be only allowing people to view the user's photographs as long as each entity that has a friendship inter-dependency also has a profile photograph. This ideally means that only friends with a profile photograph are authorised to view all photographs from the user. The user would like to make this change for all past and future photographs on the social media network and use this as a template for all future social media requests.

E-commerce

The emergence of e-commerce has revolutionised how firms could conduct business with customers by eliminating spatial and temporal barriers [24]. With this industry experiencing significant growth due to lockdown and social distancing requirements as a result of the COVID-19 pandemic, privacy is one important issue that should be discussed. E-commerce organisations are quite empowered when it comes to the collection of data from individuals. One of these issues comes from the fact that individuals must disclose personal information to be able to complete e-commerce transactions. When an individual exposes personal information to e-commerce websites, this increases the risk of a potential data breach. Over the past few years, there have been many high profile data breaches compromising personal information of, e.g., Uber, Yahoo, and Facebook users. These breaches highlight the need for a robust system to ensure that individuals understand what happens to their data when they make a transaction. Clearly, there must be ways to mitigate potential data breaches in the future, e.g., by introducing retention restraints on personal information.

Use Case 4: Placing a new purchase order on an e-commerce website. One scenario that stems from e-commerce could be when an individual signs up to an e-commerce website to purchase goods. In this scenario, individuals can sign up to the e-commerce website with their personal information and add specific restraints on the retention of data. One such restraint imposed by an individual could be adding an explicit requirement to ensure that information retained by the e-commerce website is to be removed after a certain time, say 1 year after the goods have been delivered. Such restraint on the collection and use of personal information ensures that the data held by an organisation is only stored for a specific time.

3.2 System Requirements

From these use case scenarios discussed above, we can extract potential system requirements for a dynamic informed consent framework for big data. In this section, we will identify and discuss potential system requirements.

Consent Viewing. This means the ability for a data subject to view information on what consent being requested. This requirement is a quintessential part of a proposed system and is present in all of the use case scenarios presented in the previous section. Such a system communicates to data subjects the rationale, purpose of data collection while also allowing the data subjects to explore possible combinations and settings of different privacy consent levels.

Consent Amendment. This requirement sets forth the idea that many different parts of a privacy policy should be able to be amended to suit a data subject's needs. This customised approach allows for a data subject to be able to modify, restrict or revoke consent given based on a consent level at any time. Once again, just like the previous requirement, this requirement can be drawn from all of the use case scenarios presented.

Consent Conditions. This requirement allows for data subjects to create arbitrary conditions and restraints on the consent they give to a data requester. This means data that has been obtained from a data subject can only be used when access conforms to restraints or exceptions imposed by a data subject. The restraints or restrictions may contain many different complex restraints in conjunction with each other. Some examples can be time and location restraints as seen in the open banking or research only constraints in the healthcare scenario.

Informed Consent. This requirement ensures that in every case where a data subject has made amendments to the level of consent, they will still be able to understand the outcome of each amendment. Such a framework should be able to determine the settings that a data subject has granted, show the outcomes of the desired settings, and also be able to inform the data subject on the differences between the modifications and the default settings.

Consent Classing. This requirement is important for a dynamic consent framework as it ensures that the consent obtained can be categorised into distinct classes. These classes can be both in terms of classes of data requesters who access information such as medical staff, teachers, or financial advisors or, it can be classed in terms of data access. Examples of data access classes can be general rejection, full rejection, or general acceptance. The classification allows for the user to have different general limitations of consent depending on the organisation and or the data requested.

Non-Intrusive. This requirement ensures that data subject preferences are saved. This is so that data subjects will not be consistently barraged with privacy consent requests every time they engage with organisations. Unfortunately, having too many privacy consent requests may make it difficult for data subjects to be able to effectively view the terms and make an informed choice [25]. This requirement can be extracted from the social media use case scenario where a user has the ability to reuse the previous privacy settings and also apply them in different ways.

Auditing and Transparency. Auditing and transparency allow data subjects to be able to audit data access from data requesters. That is, data subjects would be able to make adjustments if they feel that the access does not align with the original purpose of collection. This requirement is a direct consequence of the open banking and healthcare case studies, which enables data subjects to audit the usage of their information and verify that each access meets the terms outlined in the consent.

4. Literature Review

A Generic Information and Consent Framework for the IoT. Morel et al. [3] have proposed a high-level framework for a generic information and consent framework that is specific to the Internet of Things (IoT) devices. The framework developed a way for data requesters to transmit a privacy policy to a data subject and also for a data subject to receive and modify a privacy policy before communicating a decision back ensuring a form of informed consent. One issue with this approach is that the application is narrow as it targets devices with some form of wireless communication technology with no clear indication of how to deal with transparency for the data subjects. Another drawback with this framework is that a data requester must format a privacy policy with each specific setting and outcome beforehand. This leads to the burden of transparency and legibility being put on the data requester. Finally, while this does provide a way to use levels and tiers of consent, the consent that is communicated does not necessarily mean it is informed consent as required by legislation.

A Formal Framework for Consent Management. Tokas and Owe [4] propose a framework for a general mathematical solution for consent management. The framework they propose offers modifications and restrictions within a privacy policy and provides run time restriction checking before the data is used. The framework they have formally defined uses policy compliance and an inheritance hierarchy, which increases flexibility for specific specialised consent restraints that override the default policies users have initially consented to. Unfortunately, this framework does not elaborate how to obtain consent in an informed and transparent manner. This framework merely appends a restriction on each consent request.

Analysis of Privacy Policies to Enhance Informed Consent. Pardo and Le Métayer [5] have proposed an interesting formal privacy consent framework that has privacy policies to be autonomously processed to make them easier for a data subject to understand the rationale behind decisions for data collection. This framework uses data items and purposes that describe each privacy policy and the data associated with them, along with conditions and restrictions that can be vague and generic. One shortcoming with this framework is that the restrictions the framework uses can not be overly complex. Further, the framework does not attempt to address explainability of terms within a privacy policy and does not address how a privacy policy can be formatted in a way to show data subjects possible modifications for each term. Finally, in this framework, there are limitations in the detection of privacy violations.

Automating the Generation of Privacy Policies for Context-sharing Applications. Apolinarski et al. [6] have proposed a framework that generates privacy policies automatically through analysis of previous data subject decisions. This framework consists of multiple inputs such as the resource, sharing settings, and a context type. These are used to extend generic privacy policies to a more suitable setting for a specific data subject. While this framework gives insight to an automated privacy policy that aids the data subject in making a consent decision, it does not address the different data categories. As there is no data categories or sensitivity, it would be detrimental if future requests come from consents based on categories or organisations that are not relevant.

Table 4 summarises the different strengths, approaches, and limitations of each related work.

Table 4: A comparison between the different strengths, approaches and limitations of related work.

Name	Year	Strength	Approach	Limitations
A Generic Information and Consent Framework for the IoT	2018	Allows for pre-defined templates to be used in order to provide a data subject with customisable conditions.	This framework uses a high-level approach for consent collection without a large burden of intrusiveness to users.	Customised constraints do not have the ability for further restrictions.
A Formal Framework for Consent Management	2020	Increases the complexity of restrictions and how consent is granted by adding in classes of access.	Uses a mathematical approach to build a consent framework and introduces algorithms to check if access conforms to the purpose of collection.	This implementation does not address informed consent as modifications to restrictions cannot be described.
Analysis of Privacy Policies to Enhance Informed Consent	2019	Allows for additional restrictions to consent, risk analysis checks and detection of privacy violations.	Uses a privacy policy language to create and analyse privacy policies to increase awareness and identify data misuse.	Does not automatically identify data misuse as it requires expressions to be added first.
Automating the Generation of Privacy Policies for Context-sharing Applications	2015	Generates privacy polices using analysis of a user's previous decisions for a user to reuse in a non-intrusive manner.	A high-level framework that incorporates context recognisers on previously used privacy terms to interpret permissions.	Does not consider specific data types and how some might be more sensitive than others.

Current research has shed light on the complications of implementing such a comprehensive framework. Table 5 summarises each of our system requirements and provides a comparative analysis of existing approaches under the light of those requirements.

Table 5: Comparisons between related work and system requirements from Section 3.

System Requirement	[3]	[4]	[5]	[6]
Consent viewing	Yes	Yes	Yes	Yes
Consent amendment	Yes	Yes	Yes	Yes
Adding advanced restraints	No	Yes	No	Yes
Restriction creation	No	No	No	No
Consent classing	No	Yes	No	No
Non-intrusive	Yes	No	No	Yes
Auditing and transparency	No	Yes	Yes	No

Table 5 suggests that current research shows that there is no single framework that fulfils all of our previously defined requirements. Notable gaps in requirements stem from the fact that not many consent frameworks support dynamic consent. This is because they focus on the current binary model of consent to amend default consent options and create complex restraints.

In summary, a dynamic consent framework is an emerging topic with limited prior art. This makes it difficult to implement ideas from the prior art, as most of the issues related works address are only slightly relevant to our system requirements. While current research has been able to solve some system requirements from our case studies, some important issues and barriers still remain.

5. Our Proposed Framework

In this section, we aim to give a high-level overview of how we intend to implement a dynamic privacy consent framework for big data. We also show how our framework can address the use case scenarios we already discussed.

5.1 System Entities

Our proposed solution consists of three distinct entities. In this section, we will describe each of the entities, along with their functions and roles.

Data Subject. This component represents an entity that has been requested to give informed consent and attributes to a Data Requester. This entity also provides attributes and consent decisions from requests they may receive from a Data Requester.

Data Requester. This represents an entity that is requesting a Data Subject to give consent for using and collecting their personal information. A Data Requester can also be an entity that requests attributes from a Data Subject. This entity must ensure that the usage of data collected from a Data Subject conforms to the purposes that have been outlined in a privacy policy.

Privacy Consent Service. This entity provides a service that is responsible for all actions involving privacy consent and the transmission of attributes between a Data Subject and Data Requester. Most notably, it is used to store, verify, and process privacy policy requests from a Data Requester and provide requested attributes to a Data Requester when consent is granted. This service also has the ability to provide additional functionality, such as auditing a Data Requester's usage of their data. This can be both an online service or an offline service.

5.2 Threat Model

Our framework modelled in Figure 1 outlines a generic dynamic consent framework that can be used in a general-purpose environment. Our framework attempts only to provide a solution for a Data Subject to provide consent and communicate requested attributes to a Data Requester to obtain consent using a Privacy Consent Service. Our framework assumes the use of an API service in which data is communicated between the Data Subject and a Data Requester through the Privacy Consent Service. Due to the nature of an API service, it is susceptible to attacks on the availability of service. One example of this can be when the API service of the Privacy Consent Service gets flooded with many rogue requests from one or more adversaries.

We aim to secure our framework using authentication methods at the Privacy Consent Service level. This ensures that only an authenticated and authorised Data Subject can interact with a Privacy Consent Service. Due to the need for authentication, there are varying degrees of coherent risks depending on the authentication method we have selected. Some could be general attacks on security through password attacks; however, this could also be more sophisticated with attacks on biometrics.

Finally, another threat is the possibility of a rouge Data Requester. In the event that a rouge Data Requester misuses the Privacy Consent Service, they have the ability to slow down the processing of a privacy policy. This can occur in a situation where the privacy policy is formatted in a very confusing, unusual or contradictory manner.

5.3 Proposed System Overview

In this section, we provide an overview of our proposed solution and how each system entity interacts with each other. Figure 1 gives an overview of our proposed framework.

5.4 Creating an Account on an E-commerce Website

In this scenario, we have a Data Subject who would like to register for an e-commerce website so that they can make purchases using the platform. However, before a Data Subject can use the platform, consent is required before any personal information can be collected and used by a Data Requester. We make the assumption that the Data Subject does not have any prior dealing with the e-commerce website and that the Data Subject does not have any preexisting templates or previous history that can be drawn to simplify the process. We also assume that this Privacy Consent Service

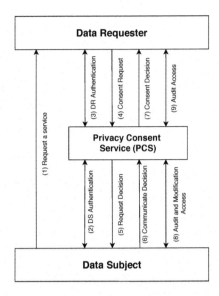

Figure 1: Overview of our proposed dyanmic consent framework for big data.

is a cloud-based service and that a Data Subject is already authenticated. Finally, a Data Subject would like to add a restriction to the usage of their date of birth data.

With the assumptions outlined above, we first consider that they request a service, Step (1), could be the process where a Data Subject submits a request to sign up for an account. In this step, a Data Subject is required to send some additional information, such as the location of the Privacy Consent Service in order for communication to begin. Next, once a Data Requester receives this request, they can initiate an authentication stage in Step (3) using the information obtained in Step (2). This step allows for a Data Requester to transmit a privacy policy along with information to a Privacy Consent Service to provide verification using current cryptography methods. After the Privacy Consent Service has verified the Data Requester, the service will identify any prior history of consents that are relevant to the current scenario. Since we are assuming that there is no prior history, we request a decision from a Data Subject in Step (4). At this stage, we will communicate a simplified version of a privacy policy to a Data Subject to view.

After a Data Subject has the chance to view all necessary terms along with implications of sharing their information, the Data Subject will have the ability to accept, decline, or make modifications to the consent request. As our scenario states that the Data Subject wants to make a modification to the privacy policy, an additional step will occur. The modification is to limit the date of birth information shared only to use this information to receive birthday specials. Once this modification step is complete, and the Data Subject accepts the modified terms, the next is to communicate the decision in Step (5). Once the Privacy Consent Service has received the outcome of the request, it will start to process the request. Processing is done by first saving information about the consent request for future references before communicating the decision back in Step (6). In Step (6), the terms of consent, along with identifying information and requested attributes, are transmitted back to a Data Requester. Finally, once received by the Data Requester, the sign up process can proceed with the attributes requested.

Checking Data Usage on an E-commerce Website

In this scenario, we have a Data Subject who would like to audit instances of data usage from the e-commerce website. Auditing allows a Data Subject to verify data accesses to ensure that the purposes of use align with the purposes of collection. We can assume that the scenario is a continuation of the previous scenario.

Once a Data Subject has authenticated, they can view all previously consented privacy policies that are stored using access from Step (8). From here, a Data Subject have the ability to view information relating to the consent that they have provided to the e-commerce website. Since the Data Subject has provided a general restriction on the use of the date of birth attribute and would like to audit the access of this, Step (9) is initiated. In this step, the Privacy Consent Service requests information from a Data Requester regarding information usage from the date of birth information.

It is expected that information returned from this step back to the Privacy Consent Service contains all previous usage. One example of what it returns could be the use of date of birth information to generate a special coupon based on the Data Subjects age. Finally, the Data Subject has the ability to view this information using the same channel as Step (8).

Managing Data Access on an E-commerce Website

In this scenario, we have a Data Subject who would like to manage data usage from the e-commerce website. The specific example could be when a Data Subject would like to revoke data access from a Data Subject. Using the scenario that has been previously defined with the same assumptions as to the previous scenarios.

Once the Data Subject has access to the Privacy Consent Service with verified credentials, they can make modifications to previously consented policies using the communication channel outlined in Step (8). One example of a modification of a privacy policy from the scenario could be when a Data Subject revokes access of their date of birth for all purposes.

Once a Data Subject has located the consent they would like to change, a request decision is sent to the Data Subject in Step (5). Once the Data Subject made the modification and changed the consent for the date of birth attribute, the outcome is communicated in Step (6) to the Privacy Consent Service. The Privacy Consent Service processes the modification and updates similar consents and templates if required. Once this is complete, the modified policy is sent to the data requester in Step (7) for them to store it and act on the update.

6. Solution Details

Figure 2 provides a technical overview of our proposed framework including additional components within the Privacy Consent Service that was first described in Section 5.

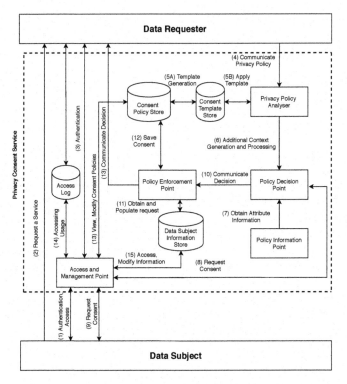

Figure 2: Technical overview of our proposed framework for big data.

6.1 System Components

In this section, we define the components of the Privacy Consent Service in detail, along with their roles and how they interact with other parts of the framework.

Access and Management Point.   A type of software that empowers a Data Subject to view, manage and access all aspects of the consent of a privacy policy. Further, this should have the ability to allow a Data Subject to audit previously consented policies by showing any access that could be considered a deviation from the exact purpose of collection or specific access from a data requester.

Privacy Policy Analyser.   It is an entity that initiates the privacy consent process through privacy policy processing and template lookup. This engine uses information from a Data Requester such as data sensitivity, category, attributes, and a purpose to identify preexisting templates from the consent template store.

Policy Decision Point.   It takes contextual information from the Privacy Policy Analyser and if required, performs simplification. The simplification can be used to aid the Data Subject to make adjustments to the standard privacy policy if necessary and obtain consent. It also tries to identify data leaks or conflicts after consent is obtained.

Policy Information Point. This component allows for a Policy Decision Point to obtain additional contextual information and attributes from a third party. Attributes can include location data, which can aid the decision or populate attributes of a privacy policy.

Privacy Enforcement Point. It identifies the decisions that have been made from a Policy Decision Point and applies the decisions to a consent request. Further, it can populate requested attributes from the Data Subject Information Store if consent has been granted.

Data Subject Information Store. It is a data store that contains attributes or personal information of a Data Subject. Attributes or personal information listed in this data store can be extracted and communicated to a Data Requester using a Privacy Enforcement Point if consent is granted.

Consent Policy Store. It is a data store that stores all the previous privacy policies that a Data Subject has decided on. Such a data store would also show modifications that a Data Subject has made to the original privacy policy along with the attributes requested.

Consent Template Store. It is data store that saves settings generated by a Data Subject to speed up and automate consent decisions with approval. The template store has the ability to add, modify, or delete templates along with inferring potential templates from historical consent decisions.

Access Log. It records the access activity of a Data Subject's data by a Data Requester. It contains information about access and usage and is used when a Data Subject audits data access. This is extremely helpful when consent is granted in a general acceptance or denial with restrictions situation.

6.2 Component Details

Data Requester

The role of the Data Requester is to obtain consent and or attributes from Data Subject before using their personal information. We expand on this idea by including the situations where Data Requester also can be included in a hierarchy structure. Such a structure facilitates the idea of classing and also supports permissions requested by one Data Requester to one or more Data Requesters who have a similar interest and or are within the same realm. This could be an e-commerce and logistics organisation where both organisations are required to fulfil a transaction.

The Data Requester first communicates to the Access and Management Point by authenticating themselves and submitting a consent request. After a Data Subject has made a consent decision, the Data Requester must store the modified terms of usage alongside the unique identification number and user credentials to uniquely link up each of the consent terms with the user.

Access and Management Point

As the role of this component is to be the primary interaction point between the Data Subject and the Privacy Consent Service, this component also serves as a gateway for messages to be communicated between other components of the service. The next section discusses the different roles of this component.

Authentication

Data Subject. One role of this component is the authentication of a Data Subject or Data Requester. In the situation of a cloud-based Privacy Consent Service, this requires authentication to ensure that only the Data Subject can view and make adjustments to the system. After a Data Subject is successfully authenticated, the Privacy Consent Service generates a random user identification number or token that they can use to request services with.

Data Requester. When a Data Subject accesses a service that may require a consent decision, the Data Subject sends additional information such as the address of the Access and Management Point along with identifiable information such as a user identification number. This is so that the Data Requester can submit an authentication request to the correct Access and Management Point when multiple exist on the same address to uniquely identify the Data Subject. The Data Subject uses the user identification number along with its own information such as a digital signature when forwarding information to the Access and Management Point for verification.

Once this step is complete, the Access and Management Point can compare the unique identification number to the current session to see if it is active and valid. Next, the digital signature is verified using public key infrastructure. Once the verification is complete and is proven to be authentic, the Access and Management Point approves the request by communicating a key in which the Data Requester can use to send its privacy policy and other information to the Privacy Policy Analyser. In this step, the Data Requester also transmits additional information such as data sensitivity, data categories, requested attributes, and the pre-allocated settings if they have been set up. This key can be used for future attribute requests if required.

Consent Decision and Modification. The Access and Management Point should provide a simple yet effective way in which a Data Subject is able to make modifications and view decisions related to consent. To achieve this, once a consent request has been received from the Policy Decision Point, information relating to the privacy consent is presented in a simple and understandable manner with options to modify any of the settings within a policy. If consent is granted or rejected, a simple accept code is sent back to the decision point with no more additional information or action required by the Data Subject. In the situation where a more complex restriction needs to be imposed, the linguistic representation is sent to the Policy Decision Point for additional processing.

Another important situation is when a Data Subject wants to view or modify a previously decided policy consent request or template. If the Data Subject queries the consent data stores using the organisation name, we should expect to see all policies and templates stored related to the company to be returned. The information stored also includes previous consent history along with a breakdown of the attributes that have been shared and the rationale behind the consent. The Data Subject also has the ability to query for the templates that have been generated by the Consent Template Data Store.

In the case of a modification of a stored policy or template, the details of the modification and restriction are communicated back to the Access Log and saved. Additional attributes such as the ability to save the decisions made as a template for future decisions can also be requested.

Audit Access. The situation for Audit Access is similar to the previous situation; however, we are focusing on the Audit Access component. For this component, the Access and Management Point can query the Audit Access using credentials to all relevant extract information.

Information Store Access. In the event where the Data Subject would like to add or modify information stored in the Data Subject Information Store, they need to query the Data Subject Information Store to extract existing attributes. They only need to change the returned attribute before submitting the change request. Once this is complete, the Data Subject Information Store processes and updates the request accordingly.

Privacy Policy Analyser

The Privacy Policy Analyser is used to process a privacy policy from a Data Requester and identify similar preexisting consent templates. The Privacy Policy Analyser takes a privacy policy from the Data Requester along with the data sensitivity level, data attributes, purpose, and any configured settings as input. Table 6 provides insight into how the requested attributes and sensitivity levels can be represented. Each data attribute and data sensitivity level depends on the organisation category and can also change depending on the Data Subject. A higher sensitivity ID level can indicate that the attribute requested should be treated with more care as it is more detrimental if the information gets leaked.

With this information, the Privacy Policy Analyser can query for matching templates from the Consent Template Store by sending a query request using the organisation category with the information sensitivity categories related to the specific organisation category. This is to ensure that only related templates from similar organisations or data sensitivity are used as amount of trust between organisations can differ within the same organisation category. The information returned by the Consent Template Store in Step (5A and 5B) allows for the Privacy Policy Analyser to pre-populate consent settings for each requested attribute or data usage term.

In the event where a privacy policy received from a Data Requester does not show any information relating to an information sensitivity or is not configured correctly, the Privacy Policy Analyser needs to run context analysis on it. The analysis is run so that attributes can be matched to corresponding sensitivity levels from a privacy policy. As organisations need to state the purposes of collection and usage clearly, this can be used to identify important segments in the using text and linguistic analysis.

Table 6: Examples of data attributes along with a data sensitivity level.

Attribute	Sensitivity	ID
Email	Low	0
Age	Low	1
Country	Medium	2
Phone Number	Medium	2
Photos	Medium	2
Date of Birth	Medium	3
Payment Information	High	3
Address	High	4
Location	Very High	4
Medical	Extreme	5

Table 7: Examples of organisation categories of a Data Requester with a corresponding ID.

Organisation Category	ID
E-commerce	EC
Financial	FN
News	NE
Entertainment	EN
Government	GV
Social Media	SM
Healthcare	MD

Finally, in a situation where consent has been previously granted, a Data Requester can reuse the key generated by the Access and Management point to authenticate themselves into the system and request attributes. After this stage is complete, the requested attributes, privacy policy and restrictions are sent to the Privacy Decision Point.

Privacy Decision Point

Recall that informed consent is an essential component of obtaining consent. The purpose of this component is to ensure that each component of a privacy policy is understandable to a general user. Further, we expect that the Privacy Decision Point analyses the consent decisions along with the privacy policy to find anomalies after consent has been received.

The Privacy Decision Point obtains information from the Privacy Policy Analyser as the input. This could contain the privacy policy, context, purpose, list of attributes requested, template settings, and restrictions. If all attributes requested have already been allocated a full denial from a template match by the Privacy Policy Analyser, this phase is completely skipped as the decision has already been made.

Before consent can be requested from a Data Subject, there are situations where additional third party attributes such as time, location and other sensory information from a third party provider is required. Therefore, the Policy Decision Point must

Table 8: Examples of data access labels for attributes with a corresponding ID.

Data Access Label	ID
Full Acceptance	A00
Acceptance with notification of change	A01
Acceptance for this week	A02
Acceptance for this session	A03
Acceptance with Restrictions	AR05
Denial unless for Research Only	D01
Full Denial	D00

gather this information from a Policy Information Point and analyse it jointly with a privacy policy. This is useful in situations where a Data Subject would like to add general restrictions such as only allowing data collection during selected hours of the day or when the Data Subject is a European citizen and would like to notify the Data Requester that additional legislation restrictions apply, such as the GDPR.

In the event where all necessary third party attribute information is obtained, a context engine would need to be used to identify what parts of the privacy policy are important. Next, important segments of the policy need to be simplified and converted to an understandable format for a Data Subject using an explainable component. We can expect this explainable component to be able to process natural or legalise language in a way that simplifies the complex linguistics of a privacy policy without withholding any important information. This is to guarantee that the consent framework still meets the legislative requirements of consent.

Next, the Privacy Decision Point can make a general decision based on the consent template from the Privacy Policy Analyser. In the situation where the consent request is completely novel or where templates do not provide full coverage, the simplified privacy policy in its explainable form along with potential modifications, needs to be communicated to the Access and Management Point. The situation also occurs in the event where a Data Subject has set a "ask me each time" condition. From here, once the Access and Management Point has received the information, it prompts the user to make a decision. Table 8 demonstrates potential Data Consent Access Labels with a corresponding ID when a Data Subject returns consent requests for attributes.

The final role of this component is its data leakage abilities. As privacy policies tend to be complete, lengthy and challenging to understand [26]. Moreover, due to conflicts and contradictory parts within a privacy policy or consent that has been granted, there could be ways in which data leakage could occur. We rely on some methods and algorithms developed to decrease the risks of potential data leakage. If any issues occur, such as conflicts with settings or privacy policy, the Data Subject is promoted to address these issues, and the processing step is rerun. Finally, after all processing and consent decisions have been made, the Policy Decision Point communicates the Privacy Policy, list of attributes, modifications and restrictions to the Policy Enforcement Point.

Policy Information Point

This component takes information from any relevant third party source, which is required in a Privacy Policy and communicates these to a Privacy Decision Point when requested. Examples of these can include time zone, geo-location, and device information. Once this information is collected, it can be sent to the Policy Decision Point using key, value pair that designates each attribute and value.

Privacy Enforcement Point

This component takes the input from the Privacy Decision Point and enforces the decisions that have been made by a Data Subject or templates from the Privacy Decision Point. This component also populates attributes that have been consented with a Data Subject's personal information.

In order for the Privacy Enforcement Point to populate the attributes, it queries the Data Subject Information Store for each consent granted in order to populate each attribute request with personal information from the Data Subject. The Privacy Enforcement point can query the Data Subject Information Store using a simple query request such as $query(FullName, Age)$. This is used to populate the name and age fields. Next, the Privacy Enforcement Point communicates the decisions, attributes, Data Subject's unique identification number along with any output from the Privacy Decision Point in terms of the level of access for each specific term to the Data Requester. One example can be seen in Table 8. In the case where there is an additional restriction that is not listed or is too complex, the simplified restriction is sent along with the levels. Finally, the Privacy Enforcement Point transmits a list of the attribute names, Data Subject ID, decisions, and modifications along with the privacy policy to the Consent Policy Store so it can be stored in a log.

Data Subject Information Store

This component is in charge of storing personal information so that a Privacy Enforcement Point can securely query this Data Store to extract the necessary attributes. As some attributes can have multiple values, we have split out each address into many different components. Splitting out attributes into smaller components ensures that we do not overshare information where only a small portion of an attribute is required. One example of how this data store can be formatted is shown in Table 9. In addition, we have appended a numeric value after some attributes names as Data Subject's can have multiple attributes with the same name.

Table 9: Examples of data representation in a Data Subject Information Store.

ID	Attribute Name	Value
01	Age	22
02	Address01_Road	Piha Road
03	Address01_Number	12
05	Address01_PostCode	0772

Consent Policy Store

The role of this component is to store requested attributes, privacy policies, consent decisions, and modifications from a Data Subject. This key component allows for a Data Subject to view what they have consented to in the future and modify any of the previous decisions to suit their needs. The Consent Policy Store component first takes input from the Privacy Enforcement Point. This message contains the simplified and explainable version of a privacy policy along with any identifying information, restrictions, and settings.

As a privacy policy can have the potential to be broken up into many different components using tools such as Explainable AI (XAI) [27] or lexicon analysis [28], we can store each important element of what is being requested by a Data Requester. This can be seen in Table 10. This example shows an expanded view of attributes and a simplified view of how the Data Requester uses each attribute.

In the situation where there are two requests from the same data requester but for a different purpose, another row is generated as seen in Rows 1 and 2 along with Rows 3 and 4 in Table 11. This demonstrates the idea of a hierarchy of consent. The hierarchy structure occurs where a Data Subject has agreed to collection from one party but, allows parties who are related and have an established relationship to access their data. We also note that in this table, the values for the data sensitivity are extracted from the data attributes for each specific data organisation category. This can be seen in the first line as the data sensitivity for transactional data and email data is given a rating of three and zero, respectively. Finally, one additional attribute that is listed is the "Similar Request" attribute. This attribute allows the reuse of the settings to be automatically used in situations where there are similar consent requests which can be used for template generation.

Table 10: Examples of simplified explanations of each requested attribute for one consent request.

UniqueID	Data Requestor	Data Attribute	Simplified Usage
GWN72064Jr	MINHEALTHA	Height	Calculate BMI
GWN72064Jr	MINHEALTHA	Weight	Calculate BMI
GWN72064Jr	MINHEALTHA	Age	Group similar age ranges
GWN72064Jr	MINHEALTHA	Location	Contact Tracing

Table 11: Example of the representation of elements of a privacy policy and how each one is stored.

UniqueID	Data Requestor ID	Data Requester Category	Data Attribute	Data Sensitivity	Modifications	Similar Request	Decision
a5ZqQeGnve	BANK01A	FN	Transactions, Email	3,0	None	Yes	A01
hi3zl0dNZA	BANK01B	FN	Email, Phone	1,2	None	No	A00
GWN72064Jr	MINHEALTHA	GV	Age, Height, Weight Location	3	Restrict Purpose, Research Only	Yes	D01
GWN72064Jr	GPDR058A	MD	Location	3	Restrict Purpose, Research Only	Yes	D01
JK8hfn7Ybd	GPDR058B	MD	Medical	5	Ethical Research	No	AR05
BLtk0N1unm	FBPRIVA	SM	Photos, Phone Number	2,2	Access to friends only	No	AR05
UUTonkovwg	EBAY01A	EC	Address	2	None	Yes	D00
S8t7Fhf6Fk	BANK02C	FN	Age, Gender	1,1	None	Yes	AR01
S8t7Fhf6Fk	BANK02C	FN	Tranactional, Location	4,4	20200125, All	Yes	AR02 & AR03

Consent Template Store

As seen in the previous subsection, we have developed a comprehensive way to store each privacy policy and its modifications. Due to a large amount of potential privacy consent decisions, it is impractical for our framework to be able to store each and every decision and provide suggestions to each new request. This is because, with an increasing amount of stored consents, this decreases the performance of the Consent Storage Data Store. We rectify this by implementing a Consent Template Store, which generates skeleton templates using the previous decisions that can be multipurpose and can be used for one or more organisation categories or attributes.

This is done by periodically scanning the Consent Policy Storage by organisation categories with the "Similar Request" field. As the Consent Policy Storage gradually fills up with consent decisions over time, we can try to make predictions on the generation of settings similar to Apolinarski et al.'s approach [6]. Table 12 gives an example of how this is represented.

Table 12: Examples of the representation of templates in the Consent Template Store.

Data Requester Category	Data Attribute	Data Sensitivity	Modifications	Decision
FN	Transactions, Email	3,0	None	A01
GV	Location	3	Restrict Purpose, Research Only	D01
MD	Location	3	Restrict Purpose, Research Only	D01
EC	Address	2	None	D00
FN	Age, Gender	1,1	None	AR01
FN	Tranactional, Location	4,4	20200125, All	AR02 & AR03

Access Log

This component allows for a Data Subject to audit data usage from a Data Requester. One important idea that highlights the need for this component is when a Data Subject provides data for the purposes of research only. In this situation, a Data Requester should provide transparency in its data usage by allowing the Data Subject to audit all instances of data access. This is to ensure that data is only accessed in an appropriate manner and allows for Data Requesters to be held accountable if there is any misuse. To solve this issue, an Access Log allows for a Data Requester to communicate each usage situation and stores it in a data store. This not only allows for the communication of usage from a Data Requester but, also allows for communication of other events such as a Data Breach. In the situation where information is requested by a Data Subject for a particular organisation, the Data Subject can send the query the data store using the organisation unique ID. This will return timestamp and information relating to its usage. Table 13 shows one potential layout of the data representation within the Access Log.

Table 13: Example of a potential method of representing data within the Access Log Data Store.

UniqueID	Time Stamp	General Reason	Detailed Reason
hi3zl0dNZA	2020-07-14T22:12:20	Security	Fraud Alert Message
UUTonkovwg	2020-08-16T19:17:40	Shopping	Estimate Shipping
GWN72064Jr	2020-10-12T14:48:31	Medical	Contact Tracing
JK8hfn7Ybd	2020-11-23T13:17:31	Research	Longitude Study 2020

From the Data Requester point of view, if they would like to add a record to the Access Log store, they would need to use the unique ID along with authentication similar to what is required in the Access and Management Point to be able to communicate each instance of usage.

6.3 Implementation Details

In this section, we aim to discuss how each of the components can be implemented using some examples based on current tools and technologies.

Access and Management Point. As discussed in the previous sections, this is the main component that a Data Subject uses in order to be able to interact with the other components. The intended implementation of such a component can be through a cloud-based where there is a portal where a user accesses through logging in similar to current identification providers such as RealMe in New Zealand. In contrast to this, we also have the option to represent such a portal in other formats that are not cloud-based. These can be through browser plugins or programs installed on a device through an app. We expect that all methods of implementation include all system requirements and feature such as access management using one or more types of authentication, token generators and the ability to verify digital certificate for the basic requirements.

For the purposes of token generation, one way that this can occur can be through any token-based generation framework, which has the ability to perform authorisation and authentication. One example of this is the OAuth framework [29]. With this framework, we can consider a Data Requester generating a token and communicating this token to the Access and Management Point. Suppose the verification step is successful and the Data Requester is genuine, the Access and Management Point sends the Data Requester an authentication token, which can be used to authenticate themselves to the Privacy Policy Analyser. One important advantage to this keyed approach is that we allow for a Data Requester to request information from the Data Subject in the future, this allows for a Data Requester to update their copy of the attributes at any time if required without the need for the full consent process.

Access Log, Consent Policy Storage, Consent Template Store, Data Subject Information Store. These quintessential components are represented as Data Stores within our framework. As these components are Data Storage devices that are used to access, manipulate and store data, we can use any of the common relational database languages such as MySQL. The way we set up the tables within our databases needs to conform to the data representations. In this way, all other components can make simple queries to extract the necessary information required. One difference for the Access Log is that this log must only be write-only to prevent Data Subjects or Data Requesters from hiding any previous data accesses.

As for the Consent Template Store, a method that we can generate templates can be based on prior research by Apolinarski et al. [6]. While they have considered a method to generate a privacy policy, we aim to generate templates that can be used to pre-populate required requests. This information can be gathered from the Consent Policy Store and fed into an engine. Similar consents can be grouped together based on data similarity and organisation types. Once enough consent requests can be gathered, we can predict and generate a skeleton template.

Privacy Policy Analyser. When a Data Subject initiates a request to this component, it communicates through an API with a token that has been provided from the Access and Management Point. This to ensure that the Data Subject has already been authenticated and verified.

As for the extraction and analysis of the security levels within a Privacy Policy, we can use current methods [30] that provide some degree of text classification for sensitivity identification. Although we can not directly implement the exact idea, we can modify and build on the work done to identify data security labels within a privacy policy. From here, we can use this information to extract the potential use cases of data, as seen in Sarne et al.'s research [31].

Privacy Decision Point. To implement the Privacy Decision Point, we aim to rely on current research and tools that can be used to develop an explainable component. Examples of this could be using a new Artificial Intelligence (AI) approach called XAI. Explainable AI is a form of AI, where actions and decision of the algorithm can be portrayed in a human explainable form. If this form of explainable component were to be applied, we could rely on similar and implementations that have been seen in research on legal document review using XAI [27].

We can use XAI to feed important information from a privacy policy, such as the data being used, the rationale of why it is being collected and how it is being used to build a picture of the whole life cycle for a particular attribute. Since the actions of XAI can be explainable in an understandable format, we can pass on the outcomes of each attributes life cycle to the Access and Management Point with minimal processing required to generate a high degree of understandably. This can also be tuned to fit a data subject's requirements in terms of granularity by increasing or decreasing how the XAI engine works.

After the explainable component has been completed, the next step of this component is to conduct tests to identify any possible misuse or data leakage. Prior research from Pardo and Le Métayer [5] have identified a way to use integrated risk analysis to check entities and identify potential violations. We can potentially apply similar analytical tools to identify data leakage or misuse. This can be done by analysing the explainable privacy policy in line with pre-defined templates as proposed in Pardo and Le Métayer's paper [5]. However, additional research may be required to conduct this in an automated and effective manner to identify every instance.

Policy Information Point. As this component can be extremely complex and flexible, there are many different implementations of this specific component. Since this component's role is to provide additional attribute information from other sources, we can assume that this component can be one or multiple different providers of information. We do not specifically limit how this component is implemented as this constrains the potential ways our framework can access additional attribute information. In this way, this method is very flexible and also allows queries from any third party.

Policy Enforcement Point. This component is also difficult to implement as it has many possible ways it can be implemented. First, we must consider that this component needs to operate in a secure environment. This is because it deals with sensitive information from the Data Subject Information Store. In order to meet this requirement, we will use a secure API. This secure API ensures that communication can only be done through a strict format and must follow all relevant protocols and security measures.

Since communication to the data requester done through an API service and contains sensitive information, we do not want to transmit this information through clear text. One way to secure this communication channel is by using the digital certificate, which was provided in the authentication step. The Policy Enforcement Point can use the keys from the digital certificate to encrypt all communication between itself and the Data Requester and ensures that there is no data leakage between the Privacy Consent System and the Data Requester.

7. Conclusions and Future Work

Consent is an integral part of privacy that dictates what and how we can use information. Current consent obtaining methods involve complex privacy policies that are rigid and do not provide a way to have customisable levels of consent. In this book chapter, we presented a novel dynamic consent for big data.

7.1 Limitations

While our proposed framework can be used to address dynamic consent, there are still some limitations that exist. The following section will discuss some limitations that arise from our implementation. First, the most important limitation is the ability to process privacy policies accurately. As we discussed in our framework, we have an assumption where privacy policies communicated from a data requester are prepared and communicated in a way that makes it easy to identify or change different levels or settings within them. While we consider this to be the gold standard approach, this may not be practical in a real-life setting. With this in mind, while there are fallbacks in place to process privacy policies using tools such as lexicon analysis or artificial intelligence. However, these tools may not be completely accurate and provide limited customisability to a privacy policy. Hence, this could cause our framework not to be able to provide its full potential to each and every case of consent. While it is true that current research and methods do provide some ability to recognise text and class them, the ability to have true free input complex restrictions is a tough problem to solve. With such freedom to enter whatever a data subject sees as a way to restrict data, one main challenge to this is an ability to effectively balance such restrictions so that the conversion of these restrictions are still understandable to data requesters.

Another limitation with our framework comes from legal issues. Due to the current framework of consent not being based on a dynamic consent approach, there could be additional legislative hurdles that must be met before our framework can be applied. While we aim to follow the current legislative guidelines of consent by communicating a modified privacy policy and using this policy for all interactions between a data subject and a data requester similar to a counteroffer in contract law. We expect to see that our framework should not have any negative legal implications as we are making a modification to the privacy policy itself instead of creating a contract for access of data that is used in conjunction with a privacy policy.

Finally, the ability to enforce such restrictions that a data subject has made also comes into question. As we have said that the primary purpose of our framework is to develop a dynamic consent framework, the issue that still raises concerns is the ability to enforce such restrictions from a data requester's point of view. Even though a data subject has done all steps necessary by adding restrictions to prevent usage, a rouge data requester may still be able to bypass our frameworks access control mechanisms.

7.2 Future Work

One of the main tools that enable this framework to work effectively is with the processing of privacy policies. Current research provides methods for text analysis to extract classes or identify and group similar clauses within a policy. However, further research needs to be done to ensure that the methods or algorithms that are used can deal with increasingly complex legal semantics with a low computational cost.

We hope to see the field of Explainable AI to continue to grow and be able to support a higher degree of explainability to provide better reasoning to a data subject. While current work does show some promise into the future of these tools as seen in the current application of scanning legal documents [27], improvements can be certainly made to create algorithms that are tailor-made for this application specifically.

We also would like to see advancements and changes to current privacy legalisation, which are geared towards dynamic consent. This would make it easier to verify and test our framework in line with guidelines to ensure that our framework is operating in a way that can be considered as consent.

Another aspect of our framework is the efficiency in which we are able to process privacy policies. As the processing of text can take a considerable amount of time, we need to ensure that any potential bottlenecks arising from the processing steps can be effectively managed.

With our framework being a novel and intriguing approach to solve the problem of privacy and consent, it is necessary to discuss how such a framework can be evaluated using metrics to ensure that it is a suitable replacement for current privacy consent methods. To this end, there are evaluation factors to guarantee that our framework is appropriate. Some of the key evaluation factors include usability, simplicity along with comprehensibility. These factors ensure that our framework is understood and easy to use. Without these key factors, users may not fully understand the need for advanced restrictions. Next, we need to ensure that our framework can be evaluated by the ability to enforce applicable restrictions on the data. As this is one of the main benefits of our framework, robust testing of complex restrictions should ensure that our framework is capable of providing a method for possible restrictions one can imagine. Finally, we must consider auditing and transparency to be another important evaluation factor. This factor ties in with the factors mentioned above as it encompasses usability with restrictions to ensure that our framework has the intended effect.

Acknowledgments

This research is supported by *'Our Generation, Our Voices, All Our Futures'*, a research programme funded by the New Zealand Ministry of Business, Innovation and Employment (MBIE).

References

[1] New Zealand Legislation. Privacy Act 1993. https://legislation.govt.nz/act/public/1993/0028/latest/DLM296639.html, 1993.

[2] J. Kaye, E.A. Whitley, D. Lund, M. Morrison, H. Teare, and K. Melham. Dynamic consent: A patient interface for twenty-first century research networks. *European Journal of Human Genetics*, 23(2): 141–146, 2015.

[3] V. Morel, M. Cunche, and D. Le Métayer. A generic information and consent framework for the IoT. *In 2019 18th IEEE International Conference on Trust, Security and Privacy in Computing and Communications/13th IEEE International Conference on Big Data Science and Engineering (TrustCom/BigDataSE)*. IEEE, pp. 366–373, 2019.

[4] S. Tokas, and O. Owe. A formal framework for consent management. *In International Conference on Formal Techniques for Distributed Objects, Components, and Systems*. Springer, pp. 169–186, 2020.

[5] R. Pardo, and D. Le Métayer. Analysis of privacy policies to enhance informed consent. *In IFIP Annual Conference on Data and Applications Security and Privacy*. Springer, pp. 177–198, 2019.

[6] W. Apolinarski, M. Handte, and P.J. Marron. Automating the generation of privacy policies for context-sharing applications. *In 2015 International Conference on Intelligent Environments*. IEEE, pp. 73–80, 2015.

[7] J. Edwards. Click to consent? not good enough anymore. https://www.privacy.org.nz/blog/click-to-consent-not-good-enough-anymore/, Sep 2019.

[8] A.M. McDonald, and L.F. Cranor. The cost of reading privacy policies. *Isjlp*, 4: 543, 2008.

[9] W. Fussey, and N. Hermansson. https://iapp.org/news/a/gdpr-matchup-newzealands-privacy-act-1993/, May 2020.

[10] K. Jenkins. Can i see your social license please? *Policy Quarterly*, 14(4): 2018. [Online]. Available: https://ojs.victoria.ac.nz/pq/article/view/5146.

[11] P. Edwards, and S. Trafford. Social licence in New Zealand what is it? *Journal of the Royal Society of New Zealand*, 46(3-4): 165–180, 2016. [Online]. Available: https://doi.org/10.1080/03036758.2016.1186702.

[12] J.C. Penelope. How to earn a social licence to operate. https://ruralleaders.co.nz/wp-content/uploads/2018/08/Penny-Clark-Hall-Howto-earn-your-Social-Licence-to-Operate.pdf, 2018.

[13] B. Sobel. HiQ v. LinkedIn, Clearview AI, and a new common law of web scraping, 2020.

[14] M. Betkier. Clearview AI exposes our regulatory shortcomings, 2020. [Online]. Available: https://www.privacyfoundation.nz/wp-content/uploads/2020/02/Commentary-on-Clearview-AI.pdf.

[15] T. Stewart. We have the data, now how can we use it? How social licence applies to data use, 2020. [Online]. Available: http://www2.cio.co.nz/article/645370/we-data-now-how-can-we-useit-how-social-licence-applies-data-use/.

[16] L. Brodsky, and L. Oakes. Data sharing and open banking. *McKinsey & Company*, 2017.

[17] H. Wang, S. Ma, H.-N. Dai, M. Imran, and T. Wang. Blockchain-based data privacy management with nudge theory in open banking. *Future Generation Computer Systems*, 110: 812–823, 2020.

[18] S. Farrell. Open for better-applying open banking to small business banking: The Australasian journal of applied finance. *AJAF*, (2): 18–23, 2019. [Online]. Available: http://ezproxy.auckland.ac.nz/login?url=https://wwwproquest-com.ezproxy.auckland.ac.nz/docview/2255554030?accountid=8424.

[19] C. Esposito, A. De Santis, G. Tortora, H. Chang, and K.-K. R. Choo. Blockchain: A panacea for healthcare cloud-based data security and privacy? *IEEE Cloud Computing*, 5(1): 31–37, 2018.

[20] P. Campisi, E. Maiorana, and A. Neri. Privacy protection in social media networks a dream that can come true? *In 2009 16th International Conference on Digital Signal Processing*, pp. 1–5, 2009.

[21] A. Perrin. Social media usage. *Pew Research Center*, pp. 52–68, 2015.

[22] 13 million U.S. facebook users don't use privacy controls, risk sharing updates beyond their "friends", 2012.

[23] J. Isaak, and M.J. Hanna. User data privacy: Facebook, cambridge analytica, and privacy protection. *Computer*, 51(8): 56–59, 2018.

[24] Z.A. Mohammed and G.P. Tejay. Examining privacy concerns and e-commerce adoption in developing countries: The impact of culture in shaping individuals' perceptions toward technology. *Computers & Security*, 67: 254–265, 2017. [Online]. Available: https://www.sciencedirect.com/science/article/pii/S0167404817300548.

[25] J.A. Obar, and A. Oeldorf-Hirsch. The biggest lie on the Internet: Ignoring the privacy policies and terms of service policies of social networking services. *Information, Communication & Society*, 23(1): 128–147, 2020.

[26] B. Fabian, T. Ermakova, and T. Lentz. Large-scale readability analysis of privacy policies. *In Proceedings of the International Conference on Web Intelligence*, ser. WI '17. New York, NY, USA: Association for Computing Machinery, pp. 18–25, 2017. [Online]. Available: https://doi.org/10.1145/3106426.3106427.

[27] R. Chhatwal, P. Gronvall, N. Huber-Fliflet, R. Keeling, J. Zhang, and H. Zhao. Explainable text classification in legal document review a case study of explainable predictive coding. *In 2018 IEEE International Conference on Big Data (Big Data)*, pp. 1905–1911, 2018.

[28] J. Bhatia, and T.D. Breaux. Towards an information type lexicon for privacy policies. *In 2015 IEEE eighth international workshop on requirements engineering and law (RELAW)*. IEEE, pp. 19–24, 2015.

[29] D. Hardt. The OAuth 2.0 authorization framework. RFC 6749, October, Tech. Rep., 2012. Source: https://datatracker.ietf.org/doc/html/rfc6749.

[30] G. Berardi, A. Esuli, C. Macdonald, I. Ounis, and F. Sebastiani. Semiautomated text classification for sensitivity identification. *In Proceedings of the 24th ACM International on Conference on Information and Knowledge Management*, ser. CIKM '15. New York, NY, USA: Association for Computing Machinery, pp. 1711–1714, 2015. [Online]. Available: https://doi.org/10.1145/2806416.2806597.

[31] D. Sarne, J. Schler, A. Singer, A. Sela, and I. Bar Siman Tov. Unsupervised topic extraction from privacy policies. *In Companion Proceedings of the 2019 World Wide Web Conference*, pp. 563–568 2019.

9

A Low-Level Hybrid Intrusion Detection System Based on Hardware Performance Counters

Ansam Khraisat,* Iqbal Gondal, Peter Vamplew and
Joarder Kamruzzaman

ABSTRACT

Traditionally, Intrusion Detection Systems (IDSs) rely on computer program behaviors at the operating systems' level to detect malware. Most of these techniques use high semantic features such as functions and system calls. These highly semantic features are susceptible to malicious attacks at higher privilege levels. In particular, a malicious malware rootkit may bypass intrusion detection by manipulating system data or operating system code. In this paper, a framework for profiling normal and malicious activities is proposed. This framework is based on Hardware Performance Counters (HPCs) and hybrid IDS to detect malware. Extensive experiments have been conducted to study the effectiveness of the HPCs that could distinguish between malware and normal applications. The performance of the proposed approach has been tested on Windows-based malware families and demonstrated a detection rate of 99%.

1. Introduction

The sheer amount of malware has been increasing and causing severe damage to Internet applications over the past few years [1, 32]. McAfee threats report have revealed that during the first quarter of 2017 more than 40 million different malware were identified in the wild [2]. Furthermore, malware authors are gaining complete control over a computer's system by shifting their efforts to the lower layers by

School of Engineering, Information Technology and Physical Sciences, Federation University Australia VIC, Australia.
Emails: iqbal.gondal@federation.edu.au; p.vamplew@federation.edu.au; joarder.kamruzzaman@federation.edu.au
* Corresponding author: a.khraisat@federation.edu.au

designing more sophisticated malware. These malware pose a great threat by disabling the installed anti-malware system [3]. Recently, there have been research efforts to identify intrusion by examining the utilization of Hardware Performance Counters (HPCs). The aim of these works is to distinguish a malware on the basis of its profile that characterizes the manner in which it impacts execution counters that are incorporated into the processor of the machine. Existing research has concentrated on running malware pairs while gathering HPC data and utilizing that information to create Intrusion Detection System (IDS) based on different machine learning techniques [34–36]. Initial outcomes have been promising, showing detection rates of over 91% [4]. However, rootkits intrusion identification is not promising. Rootkits are an uncommon kind of malware that modifies parts of the running operating system bit so as to conceal the existence of malicious activity on a computer. Modern rootkits are extremely obfuscated to evade detection and analysis, feature encrypted files, encrypted connections, and a flexible design that permits various kinds of malware to collaborate in order to exploit a computer system. Advanced rootkits perform malicious activities, such as concealing malware activity, payload functionality, sending spam emails, stealing user information and easy installation. Rootkit detection is difficult as a rootkit might subvert the IDS. Though Demme et al. achieved some success in detecting rootkits with some initial experiments, the detection accuracy was low [5].

Conventional malware analysis employs virtualization [6, 7, 32] and emulation [8, 9] methodologies to explore malware behavior at runtime. These methods execute the malware in a Virtual Machine (VM) or use emulators to analyze the software to examine the presence of malware. Unfortunately, the malware author can simply evade this analysis technique by applying different anti-debugging, anti-virtualization, and anti-emulation techniques [10, 11]. Malware can simply detect the presence of a VM or emulator and can change their behaviors. In addition to this, malware authors regularly use advanced techniques such as obfuscation to avoid detection. This can lead to zero-day attacks being undetected by the existing intrusion detection systems [12, 33]. Polymorphism and metamorphism are two common obfuscation methods used by malware authors. For example, to evade detection, malware can hide their persistence by encrypting malicious payload and decrypting it during runtime. A polymorphic malware obfuscates using several transformations, such as adding some extra instructions to malware to change its appearance, but keeps its functionality intact, or changing the sequence of instructions and adding jump instructions to keep the original malware functionality [12]. It is quite simple for malware authors to write different malware variants that are functionally the same but can evade signature methods [3].

It has been argued that hardware-level detection is more suitable than other kinds of detections [5, 13–15]. This is because it is harder for a malicious program to defeat an intrusion system that uses hardware events, due to the difficulties faced by the malware author to control low-level hardware events [5, 15]. For instance, an attacker can more easily change high semantic information than low semantic information. Therefore, building IDS directly on the top of hardware gives significant advantages, such as a reduction in the overhead introduced, as only the virtual machine needs to be changed. Furthermore, hardware-based IDSs are easy to deploy as they are not tied to any specific operating system and implementation can happen transparently underneath various operating systems [5].

This paper proposes a Hybrid IDS to improve the performance of hardware-based malware detectors utilizing a few very low features of micro architectural events HPCs that are extracted at run-time by current HPCs. In this chapter, an analysis of the effectiveness of HPCs to distinguish between malware and normal applications is conducted. HPCs are counters built in the modern computers to store the counts of hardware-related activities within computer systems such as cache hits, clock cycles, and integer instructions. We experimentally show how several types of intrusion and attack techniques that affect the HPCs and reveal which significant HPCs can be used in distinguishing malware. Our results show that the HPCs are impacted severely by system call hooking attacks.

The main contributions of this chapter are as follows:

- We investigate which malware and attack techniques impact HPCs and how these HPCs can be used for successful malware detection.
- Apply information gain principle to select the top HPC features which show maximum improvement in detection.
- Design of a low-level intrusion detection system (IDS) based on HPCs. We adopt a hybrid approach that exploits the strength of signature and anomaly-based methods utilizing features extracted from HPC events. The proposed IDS demonstrates promising performance.

2. Background

For the development of the HPC based IDS extensive literature review on IDSs, HPCs and threat models are presented to develop the motivation of our work.

2.1 Intrusion Detection System

IDSs are typically classified into Signature-based Intrusion Detection System (SIDS) and Anomaly-based Intrusion Detection System (AIDS). SIDS relies on pattern matching techniques to decide whether a given pattern is a known attack. SIDS usually attains high accuracy in detecting known malware [16], however, it has difficulty in detecting zero-day attacks as the zero-day pattern does not exist in the training databases.

On the other hand, AIDS relies on events related to normal system behaviors [16, 17], so abnormal behavior can be taken as attacks. In general, IDSs can be used to monitor the system activities at different system levels. Table 1, shows such IDSs at different levels along with their capabilities [16].

Application-level IDSs have more abilities to detect and classify attacks as compared to IDSs at lowers level. Many features may have an extra overhead during feature extraction. IDSs at OS level function by monitoring the system calls being executed by the programs. VMM IDS only needs features that are obtained from the VMM layer, and this helps to reduce the overhead. The VMM-level IDS have a great ability not to be affected by malicious attacks, whereas application-level and operating system semantics are still susceptible to malicious attacks due to higher

Table 1: Intrusion detection systems level.

Level characteristics	IDS levels			
	Application	**Operating System(OS)**	**Virtual Machine Monitor (VMM)**	**Network Level**
Description	IDSs rely on the information that is available from software applications	The Operating System IDS observe resource usage of the OS and the network resource	VMM-level architectural events	An IDS is placed at points in a network so that it can monitor the traffic between various devices
Example of Features	Files, Downloads, File Systems, API calls	System Calls, Memory, Dynamic Instructions, System Calls, Registry Entries	uArch Events	Packet size, Source port, Destination port, Time stamp
Semantics	High	Medium	Low	Medium
Robustness	Low	Medium	High	Medium
Ease of deployment	Low	Medium	High	High
Applicability	High	High	Medium	High

privilege levels exploitation. For instance, a rootkit may bypass both the application level and OS level security check but may be detected at VM level. Network intrusion detection systems are implemented at dedicated devices within the network, where it can inspect inbound and outbound network packets.

2.2 Hardware Performance Counters (HPCs)

HPCs are a collection of special-purpose registers in modern microprocessors to collect the counts of hardware-related activities, such as cache misses and cache hits for various cache levels, pipeline stalls, processor cycles, instruction issues, and branch misprediction [13]. Initially developed by computer hardware engineers for debugging CPUs, HPCs can also be programmed to calculate CPU events such as instruction types and executed code paths.

However, the performance of the CPU is significantly affected by how a program uses its resources, e.g., memory access patterns effecting cache performance, instruction control flow effecting cache performance and branch prediction, the amount of inherent parallelism in the instructions affecting the utilization of functional units, data cache misses indicating important signs about slow/fast program code. Therefore, there are a lot of events happening inside a CPU which indicate performance.

Cyber security researchers have proposed HPCs based techniques for identifying intrusions. An intrusion detection system based on HPCs creates a profile of software by examining the counter values standard regularly. Next, machine learning could be used to differentiate malware behaviors among normal applications. There are many advantages to building an intrusion detection system based on HPCS. (1) Reduction in performance overhead in detecting malware. (2) It is very hard for the attackers to bypass intrusion detection based on HPCs as the HPCs features are reliable in showing the nature of the application whether it is Consequently or malware.

2.3 Threat Model

In this chapter, we focus on malware attacks that have a high level of privilege within the guest VM. These malware can pose dangerous threats to the guest VM's kernel space on both hypervisor and operating system level, as it has sufficient privileges so that they may successively change the boot process to run their malicious code, e.g., rootkit. Rootkits are used by malware authors to avoid detection and maximize their probability of a successful attack on the target computer systems.

The rootkit normally hides their attack activity, by changing the configuration of the operating system to obscure specific processes, network ports, and directories; and installs Kernel Hooks in an attempt to remain stealthy. Once the rootkit is set up, it controls the victim operating system and is able to hide its persistence from traditional IDSs [14]. Detection systems attempt to identify these malicious activities by deploying IDS at higher privilege levels, resulting in competition between security vendors an attacker to control the lower levels of the system. Therefore, traditional detection mechanisms operate at the operating system levels, such as memory-based integrity scanners or heuristic-based analysis, which are not adequate to identify rootkits on lower system levels [17].

2.4 Motivation

Before we present our IDS, we will give an intuitive explanation of the underlying ideas. Figure 1 shows the results of execution of both pieces of code while capturing four HPCs related to the L1 cache. We execute those examples on Intel processors, running 64-bit Windows 7 operating system (OS).

Before we present our IDS, we will again give an intuitive explanation of the underlying ideas. For example, consider the two matrix operation code samples in

Example 1	Example 2
int main (void)	int main (void)
{	{
int i, j;	int i, j;
for (i = 0; i < 1000; i++)	for (i = 0; i < 1000; i++)
for (j = 0; j < 1000; j++)	for (j = 0; j < 1000; j++)
array[j][i]++;	array[i][j]++;
return 0;	return 0;
}	}

Figure 1: Two Examples of matrix manipulation.

Table 2: Values of two examples measured by HPCs.

Name	Instruction Executed	L1-I cache load misses	Li-d cache load-misses	L1-dcache store-Misses	L1-dcache pre-fetch misses
Example 1	21,270,318	1,991,540	999,121	1,092,899	993,746
Example 2	21,265,465	20,412	24,976	20,485	3,761

Figure 1. The only difference between the two is the order of the array indices on the inner loop. However, their performance varies significantly because of cache performance.

Table 2 shows the results of execution of both pieces of code while capturing four HPCs related to the L1 cache. We execute those examples on Intel processors, running 64-bit Windows 7 operating system (OS).

The difference in profiles between the two examples listed above raises a question,can an Intrusion detection system based on HPCs distinguish between malware and normal applications? In this chapter, we assess the effectiveness of HPCs in capturing the behavioral semantics of a program. To this end, we profile normal applications and malicious applications using HPCs and report the performance of building an intelligent intrusion detection system.

3. Related Work

Current IDSs can be categorized based on two main characteristics: the detection approach and the malware features used for their detection.

Various features are used to build IDSs, e.g., memory, dynamic instructions, system calls, registry entries, and others [18, 19]. The usage of low-level hardware events for building intrusion detection system is a recent research direction. Consequetly, there have been very few related works focusing on how to use HPCs as features for building IDS, but recently the feasibility of designing malware detection with performance counters has been studied. Demme et al. found that existing performance counters can be used to identify malware [5]. They investigated a small set of program behavior within a family of malware on Android and Intel Linux platforms. The work demonstrated that offline machine learning techniques could be used to classify malware based on performance counters. They achieved prediction accuracies ranging from 30% to 98% across different Android malicious software. However, their methodology lacks any information about which HPC events could be used for detection purpose [20].

The work of de Melo et al. [21] used unsupervised machine learning to build profiles of the HPC patterns of benign wares and then identify abnormalities. de Melo et al. have applied F-Score as their feature selection and have provided a comparison of performance while using different sampling frequencies for the HPCs. They used only two applications namely, Internet Explorer and Adobe Acrobat, in their proof of concept and Metasploit to create the exploits for the applications. We avoid using the F1-score feature selection as it does not reflect any mutual dependence between the collected events. F-score discloses the discriminative power of each feature individually as one score is calculated for the first feature, and another score is calculated for the second feature. But it does not consider the utility of everything on the combination of both features.

In [22], Ousoy et al. proposed a Malware-Aware Processor (MAP) which is a sub-semantic hardware malware detector. This work investigated several sub-semantic feature vectors, and built an online hardware-supported malware detector while using various architectural features in distinguishing malware from normal programs online.

4. Experimental Setup

To investigate if HPC deviation could be used as features to identify malware, we conducted numerous feasibility experiments by building IDS using existing machine learning techniques and validating their detection effectiveness based on the standard performance measures. In the following sections, we describe our experimental setup and explain how we collect normal and malware applications and extract their HPC features.

4.1 Measurement Infrastructure

All the experiments and measurements were executed on the VM Ware Virtual Machine environment, installed with Windows 7, 64-bit and running a single-core with 512 MB of RAM. VTune Performance Analyzer [23] was used to collect Hardware Performance Counters (HPCs) from both malware and benign ware. Anti-security was disabled and connected to the network while HPC features were extracted from malware. Every time a programmed event occurred, the count register was incremented. The quantity of hardware events that can be gathered simultaneously is limited by CPU abilities [24].

4.2 Collection of Clean and Infected Measurements

In order to collect clean normal HPCs for Windows, normal Window's command was executed, such as nslookup, ping, tasklist, netstat, and ipconfig command.

Each command was executed individually and HPCs were extracted. For HPC data collection from malware, different variants of malware were used such as ZeroAcces, ZeusBoot, and Turla. Malware was chosen that had the following capabilities: hide processes, hidden services, hide listening TCP/UDP ports, hide kernel modules, hidden drivers, hide files and hide registry entirely. After execution of a single command, VM is restored to the normal state. This guarantees the HPC events are collected independently across normal and exploit execution. The dataset used in this experiment contains 1,185 executable applications in total, as shown in Figure 2. Among them, 496 malicious software have been collected from the honey net project, VX Heavens [25], Virus Total [26] and other sources. Three different attack techniques were included. Table 3 shows a summary of the three-malware functionalities used in this study.

In our study, 237 HPC features were extracted into vectors as presented in Table 4. An additional column of "class" has been added to each row in which extracted data is labeled as "Malware" or "Normal" depending on the application type.

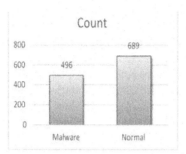 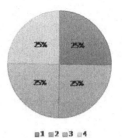

Figure 2: Distribution of malware and normal.

Table 3: Malware attack techniques used in this study.

Attack techniques	Functionality
Direct kernel object manipulation (DKOM)	DKOM is a common malware method to hide possibly harmful processes, drivers, files, and intermediate connections from the task manager and event scheduler. Malware escalates the privileges of processes to gain control.
I/O Request Packet (IRP) hooking	Malware make specific files or processes disappears by avoiding them from showing in any file entries or task managers e.g. hiding file using IRP hooking or hiding process using IRP hooking
Process Hiding using System Service Dispatch Table (SSDT) hooking	Malware can change the original pointer value of an entry by the address of a function with the same prototype in kernel mode. For example, process Hiding SSDT hooking or file hiding using SSDT Hooking

Table 4: HPC features were extracted into vectors Sample.

ICACHE.IFETCH_STALL	ICACHE.MISSES	IDQ.ALL_DSB_CYCLES_4_UOPS	IDQ.ALL_DSB_CYCLES_ANY_UOPS	....	Class
4995	4652	3985	6725	......	Malware
5249	4554	4215	6474	......	Malware
. . .	. . .	. . .	. . .	.	. . .
4846	4662	4251	6547	......	Malware
4149	3055	1641	2633	......	Normal
4150	2772	2075	2698	......	Normal
4177	2474	1831	2602	......	Normal

5. Proposed Hybrid Model for IDS

We rely on machine learning techniques and use HPC features to build an intrusion detection system. Hybrid IDS is created to overcome the drawback of SIDS and AIDS as it coordinates SIDS and AIDS to identify both zero-day and known attacks. In our approach, AIDS is utilized to distinguish zero-day attacks, while SIDS is utilized to recognize known attacks. The key idea of our approach is to consolidate the benefits of both SIDS and AIDS to create a robust IDS. Our model contains the following components as shown in Figure 3.

- Hardware Feature Extraction—Extracting the HPC events from both malware and benign ware.

- Feature selection—Selecting suitable features from 237 HPC features, which can efficiently decrease the redundant and inappropriate features in the original large HPC features. Feature selection often leads to increased detection accuracy and reduced false alarm rate.

- SIDS: Normal Model Creation—Model is created using the HPC features selected by the previous stage. Once the suitable subset of HPC features is nominated, this subset is then used in the classifier training phase where machine learning techniques are applied.

- AIDS: Anomaly Detection—Identifying abnormal behavior that differentiates from normal behavior shown in Figure 3.

Figure 3 shows a Hybrid IDS that could overcome the disadvantage of SIDS and AIDS. Our system integrates SIDS and AIDS to create an efficient hybrid IDS to detect both unknown and known attacks. In our approach, AIDS is used to identify zero-day attacks, while SIDS is used to identify well-known attacks. The central idea of the novel approach is to combine the strengths and advantages of SIDS and AIDS to build further efficient IDS.

AIDS aims to profile the normal applications activity that would be accepted and would raise a malicious alarm when the difference between a given observation at an instant and the normal request exceeds a predefined feature selection threshold.

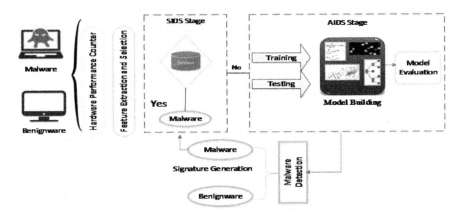

Figure 3: High-level design of the HPC-based on intrusion detection system.

Applications profile is created by employing records that are recognised as benign actions. Next, it observes the behaviour of the traffic and matches the new records with the built profiles and attempts to identify abnormalities. If malicious request is identified, the system will save it in the signature database. The primary purpose of storing the malicious pattern in the database is towards achieving protection against a similar attack in the future.

5.1 Feature Extraction

Feature extraction should result in a set of non-redundant and low-dimensional features from the HPCs. The HPC features applied in this study describe the typical behavior of an application. They include various metrics, such as CPU Cycle, branch-instruction, and branch_misses. Table 5 shows a sample of HPC features which are extracted at the program execution stage. A kernel driver that configures the Hardware Performance Counters was developed and written for collecting the micro architectural events and storing them in a database, which contains an execution of a million instructions to form the selected feature.

Figure 4 shows a comparison of the distribution of events from normal runs versus different malware. Variations are cleared from baseline features because of the changing phases of malicious execution. In a box plot, we draw a box from the first quartile to the third quartile. In malicious activities, it has two malicious activities,namely, the application that hid the process and the application that used TCP hooking to hide the TCP ports from netstat.exe. In normal applications, normal applications were executed without any malicious activity.

A lot of extracted features can cause many problems, for example, misleading the classification algorithm, over-fitting, decreasing generality, rising model complexity

Table 5: HPC Features.

Event Name	Description
ALL_BRANCHES	All (macro) branch instructions retired.
CONDITIONAL	Conditional branch instructions retired.
CONDITIONAL_PS	Conditional branch instructions retired.
NEAR_CALL	Direct and indirect near call instructions retired.
NEAR_CALL_PS	Direct and indirect near call instructions retired.
NEAR_CALL_R3	Direct and indirect macro near call instructions retired (captured in ring 3).
NEAR_CALL_R3_PS	Direct and indirect macro near call instructions retired.
ALL_BRANCHES_PEBS	All (macro) branch instructions retired.
NEAR_RETURN	Return instructions retired.
NEAR_RETURN_PS	Return instructions retired.
NOT_TAKEN	Not taken branch instructions retired.
NEAR_TAKEN	Taken branch instructions retired.
NEAR_TAKEN_PS	Taken branch instructions retired.
FAR_BRANCH	Far branch instructions retired.

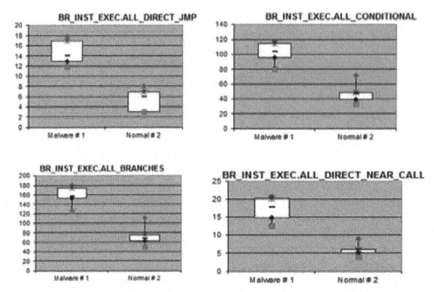

Figure 4: Comparison of the distribution of events from normal runs versus different malware.

and the execution time. These aspects can have a negative impact when applying machine learning techniques on IDSs. Every time the guest operating system needs to interact with the hardware, the Virtual Machine Monitor (VMM) must intervene. Therefore, HPC features are extracted from this intervention. Hence, any abnormality in performance traces can be used as signs of potential attacks. With the extracted labeled collection, the relevance features are analyzed for both normal and attack and to determine the most relevant feature.

HPC features are extracted from both applications and malicious application by using VTune, a tool primarily designed to help programmers in optimizing their applications [19]. For malicious activities, Zeus as malware is executed. In normal applications, normal applications are executed without any malicious activity.

5.2 Feature Selection

One of the main issues with IDSs is dealing with many irrelevant features, which can cause overhead on the system. Therefore, most IDS apply feature selection. As some of the features might be unimportant, which lead to the false detecting of malware. Therefore, the purpose of the feature selection is to identify significant features which can be used in the IDS to detect various malware efficiently.

We applied an information gain method for feature selection, due to its fast execution time to select the best performing feature set for that particular type of model. Information gain is regularly used to reveal how well each distinct attribute separates the given data set. The overall entropy "I" of a given dataset "S" is described as [27].

$$I(S) = -\sum_{i=1}^{C} p_i log_2 p_i$$

Where C is the total number of classes and p_i is the portion of instances that belong to class i. The decrease in entropy or the information gain is calculated for each feature:

$$IG(S, A) = I(S) - \sum_{v \in A} \frac{|S_{A,v}|}{|S|} I(S_v)$$

For both normal and attack classes, information gain is calculated, and we remove the feature set whose information gain was less than predetermined thresholds of 0.5. This calculation involved the estimation of the conditional probabilities of a class for a given term and entropy computations. The feature with good information gain is considered the most discriminative feature. Table 6 presents the information gain of HPC features. In total, 237 features are examined. Among them, 22 HPCs are the most significant concerning malware detection. A higher rank points out that the feature distinguishes well between normal and malware applications. The features in Table 6 are presented in the descending order of their contribution in identifying a malware.

Table 6: Information gain for different HPC features.

Ranked	Features
0.7814	BR_INST_RETIRED.ALL_BRANCHES_PS
0.6482	ITLB_MISSES.WALK_DURATION
0.6187	BR_INST_RETIRED.NEAR_CALL_R3_PS
0.6168	L2_RQSTS.DEMAND_DATA_RD_HIT
0.6083	BR_INST_EXEC.TAKEN_CONDITIONAL
0.6008	BR_INST_RETIRED.NEAR_RETURN_PS
0.5977	L2_RQSTS.REFERENCES
0.5965	BR_INST_RETIRED.ALL_BRANCHES
0.5902	L2_RQSTS.CODE_RD_HIT
0.583	BR_INST_EXEC.TAKEN_DIRECT_JUMP
0.5821	L2_LINES_IN.S
0.5794	BR_INST_RETIRED.NOT_TAKEN
0.5639	L2_RQSTS.CODE_RD_MISS
0.5612	L2_LINES_IN.E
0.5504	BR_MISP_EXEC.ALL_BRANCHES
0.5457	L2_RQSTS.ALL_DEMAND_REFERENCES
0.5327	L2_RQSTS.MISS
0.53	BR_INST_RETIRED.NEAR_CALL_R3
0.5252	OFFCORE_REQUESTS_OUTSTANDING.DEMAND_RFO
0.5183	MEM_LOAD_UOPS_L3_HIT_RETIRED.XSNP_NONE
0.5169	BR_INST_EXEC.TAKEN_DIRECT_NEAR_CALL
0.5098	BR_INST_RETIRED.NEAR_CALL

5.3 Building Classification Models

Once HPC features are selected, we ran experiments using Hybrid IDS to evaluate their capability to distinguish between malicious and normal execution. In order to achieve high accuracy and low false alarm rates, we combined two different classifiers execution [28]. The proposed model involves two phases: the SIDS phase uses C5 classifier [28], and AIDS stage one-class SVM is used [29]. Each phase has two stages, training and testing. In the training stage, the normal activities profile is labeled by using standard programs that are accepted as normal behaviour; but at the testing stage new data set is used. The hybrid model can classify activities of new applications either normal profile (no attack) or deviation from the normal profile (attack).

6. Performance Evaluation of the Proposed IDS

In this section, we provide the detailed results of the experiments achieved using the proposed framework with the selected HPC features.

6.1 Evaluation Metrics for Models

In this experiment, we have evaluated the effectiveness of our IDS using the Confusion Matrix as shown in Table 7. Various elements are:

- True positive (TP): Number of correctly identified malicious code.
- True negative (TN): Number of correctly identified benign code.
- False positive (FP): Number of wrongly identified benign code, when a detector identifies the benign file as a Malware.
- False negative (FN): Number of wrongly identified malicious code, when a detector fails to detect the Malware because the virus is new and no signature is yet available.
- Total Accuracy: Proportion of completely accurately classified instances, either positive or negative.
- The Detection Rate (DR) is calculated according to the following equation:

$$DR = (i) = \frac{Xii}{\sum_{i=1}^{6} Xij}$$ False alarm rate of IDSs can be computed by

$$F(i) = 1 - \frac{Xii}{\sum_{i=1}^{6} Xij}$$

Table 7 shows the confusion matrix, the element $X(1 <= i <= 6; 1 <= j <= 6)$ denotes the number of records that belong to class and were classified as class j by IDSs. Therefore, based on the confusion matrix, we can easily compute other performance criteria.

Table 7: Confusion matrix of our proposed IDSS.

classified as	a	b	c	d	e	f
a=DKOM	X11	X12	X13	X14	X15	X16
b=File Hiding IRP hooking	X21	X22	X23	X24	X25	X26
c=File Hiding using SSDT Hooking	X31	X32	X33	X34	X35	X36
d=port filtering using IRP Hooking	X41	X42	X43	X44	X45	X46
e=Process Hiding using SSDT hooking	X51	X52	X53	X54	X55	X56
f=Normal	X61	X61	X63	X64	X65	X66

6.2 Experiment Results

As discussed in the feature selection section, we determine the specific feature for each rootkit functionality, as well as the normal characteristics.

Stage one: SIDS Results

Confusion matrix results for C5 classifier in stage one are shown in Table 8 Malware signature generation samples. For malware signature, we applied C5 , a rule learning program, to our training data [30]. C5 is fast and creates accurate rule sets. Presents generation c5 rules from the SIDS stage for classifying all diversity of malware.

The detailed analysis of the accuracy of C5 decision tree classification is shown in Table 10.

Table 8: Malware signature generation samples.

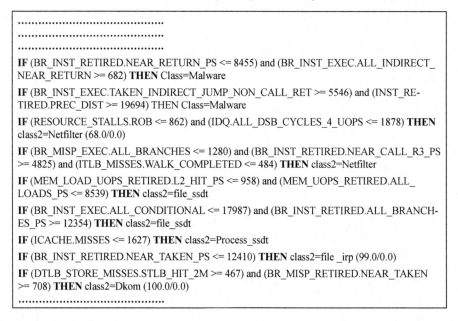

```
...........................................
...........................................
...........................................

IF (BR_INST_RETIRED.NEAR_RETURN_PS <= 8455) and (BR_INST_EXEC.ALL_INDIRECT_
NEAR_RETURN >= 682) THEN Class=Malware

IF (BR_INST_EXEC.TAKEN_INDIRECT_JUMP_NON_CALL_RET >= 5546) and (INST_RE-
TIRED.PREC_DIST >= 19694) THEN Class=Malware

IF (RESOURCE_STALLS.ROB <= 862) and (IDQ.ALL_DSB_CYCLES_4_UOPS <= 1878) THEN
class2=Netfilter (68.0/0.0)

IF (BR_MISP_EXEC.ALL_BRANCHES <= 1280) and (BR_INST_RETIRED.NEAR_CALL_R3_PS
>= 4825) and (ITLB_MISSES.WALK_COMPLETED <= 484) THEN class2=Netfilter

IF (MEM_LOAD_UOPS_RETIRED.L2_HIT_PS <= 958) and (MEM_UOPS_RETIRED.ALL_
LOADS_PS <= 8539) THEN class2=file_ssdt

IF (BR_INST_EXEC.ALL_CONDITIONAL <= 17987) and (BR_INST_RETIRED.ALL_BRANCH-
ES_PS >= 12354) THEN class2=file_ssdt

IF (ICACHE.MISSES <= 1627) THEN class2=Process_ssdt

IF (BR_INST_RETIRED.NEAR_TAKEN_PS <= 12410) THEN class2=file _irp (99.0/0.0)

IF (DTLB_STORE_MISSES.STLB_HIT_2M >= 467) and (BR_MISP_RETIRED.NEAR_TAKEN
>= 708) THEN class2=Dkom (100.0/0.0)
...........................................
```

Table 9: Confusion Matrix results of using C5.

classified as	a	b	c	d	e	f
a=DKOM	99	0	0	0	0	1
b=File Hiding IRP hooking	7	93	0	0	0	0
c=File Hiding using SSDT Hooking	1	0	91	5	2	0
d=port filtering using IRP Hooking	3	0	0	93	0	2
e=Process Hiding using SSDT hooking	2	0	5	0	92	0
f=Normal	4	0	0	0	0	685

Table 10: Detailed analysis of accuracy by applying C5.

classified as	TP Rate	FP Rate	F-Measure
a=DKOM	0.49	0	0.658
b=File Hiding IRP hooking	1	0	1
c=File Hiding using SSDT Hooking	1	0.006	0.971
d=port filtering using IRP Hooking	1	0	1
e=Process Hiding using SSDT hooking	0.939	0	0.969
f=Normal	1	0.103	0.964
Weighted Avg.	0.952	0.06	0.945

Stage two: AIDs Results

One-class SVM with RBF kernel was implemented using LIBSVM. Results in the form of a confusion matrix of stage two are shown in Table 11. The detailed analysis of the accuracy of One-Class SVM classifier are shown in Table 12.

Table 11: Confusion Matrix results of using one class support vector machine.

classified as	a	b	c	d	e	f
a = Dkom	100	0	0	0	0	0
b=File Hiding IRP hooking	0	100	0	0	0	0
c=File Hiding using SSDT Hooking	0	0	99	0	0	0
d=port filtering using IRP Hooking	0	0	0	98	0	0
e=Process Hiding using SSDT hooking	0	0	0	0	99	0
f = Normal	100	0	0	0	0	589

Table 12: Detailed analysis of accuracy by applying one class support vector machine.

Class	TP Rate	FP Rate	F-Measure
a=DKOM	1	0.092	0.667
b=File Hiding IRP hooking	1	0	1
c=File Hiding using SSDT Hooking	1	0	1
d=port filtering using IRP Hooking	1	0	1
e=Process Hiding using SSDT hooking	1	0	1
f=Normal	0.855	0	0.922
Weighted Avg.	0.916	0.008	0.926

Stage Three: the Combination of the two stages

In Hybrid IDS, the C5 classifier is applied as a first stage, and one class SVM is employed as the second stage to create hybrid IDS. Stacking ensemble methods is used to combine those two stages. K-fold cross-validation is applied for assessing the results of a statistical analysis generating an independent dataset using 10 folds. For k = 10 folds, 90% of full data is used for training and 10% for testing. Training and testing were performed using 10-fold cross-validation on all malware and benign ware dataset. Confusion matrix of combination of the classifiers in stage three is shown in Table 13.

Table 13: Confusion matrix by using Hybrid classification.

classified as	a	b	c	d	e	f
a=DKOM	100	0	0	0	0	0
b=File Hiding IRP hooking	0	100	0	0	0	0
c=File Hiding using SSDT Hooking	0	0	95	1	2	1
d=port filtering using IRP Hooking	0	0	0	98	0	0
e=Process Hiding using SSDT hooking	0	0	3	0	96	0
f=Normal	3	0	0	0	0	686

The accuracy of stage 3 is shown in Table 14.

Table 14: Detailed analysis of accuracy by applying the Hybrid classifier.

Class	TP Rate	FP Rate	F-Measure	ROC Area
DKOM	1	0.003	0.985	0.998
File Hiding IRP hooking	1	0	1	1
File Hiding using SSDT Hooking	0.96	0.003	0.964	0.978
port filtering using IRP Hooking	1	0.001	0.995	1
Process Hiding using SSDT hooking	0.97	0.002	0.975	0.984
Normal	0.996	0.002	0.997	0.997
Weighted Avg.	0.992	0.002	0.992	0.995

As shown in Figure 5, the accuracy of detection of malware is 94.6% in stage one. While the accuracy of detection of malware is 91.56% in stage two. In stage 3, the

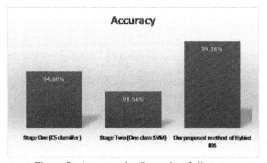

Figure 5: Accuracy details results of all stages.

accuracy result is 99.16%, which has improved significantly as compared to stage 1 and stage 2. Therefore, the general performance of the suggested framework is enhanced in terms of the detection rate and low false alarms rate in contrast to the current methods.

7. Conclusion

HPCs feature to differentiate between normal and abnormal activity. Our results show that our hybrid IDS improved intrusion detection as it is capable of detecting known as well as unknown attacks. The use of these features to build hybrid IDS are more reliable because it is difficult for a malware author to change hardware information. Our proposed method has been evaluated with the use of recent Windows rootkit. Experimental results indicate that our approach could detect malware with a high detection accuracy of 99%. This demonstrates the value of using HPC and hybrid IDSs to detect malware attacks successfully.

References

[1]   F. Zhang, K. Leach, A. Stavrou, H. Wang, and K. Sun. Using hardware features for increased debugging transparency. *In 2015 IEEE Symposium on Security and Privacy*, pp. 55–69: IEEE, 2015.

[2]   McAfee. (2016, August). *McAfee Labs Threats Report: March 2016.* Available: http://www.mcafee.com/au/resources/reports/rp-quarterly-threats-mar-2016.pdf.

[3]   A. Alazab, J. Abawajy, M. Hobbs, and A. Khraisat. Crime toolkits: The current threats to web applications. *Journal of Information Privacy and Security*, 9(2): 21–39, 2013.

[4]   H. Sayadi, N. Patel, P. D. S. M. A. Sasan, S. Rafatirad, and H. Homayoun. Ensemble learning for effective run-time hardware-based malware detection: A comprehensive analysis and classification. *In 2018 55th ACM/ESDA/IEEE Design Automation Conference (DAC)*, pp. 1–6, 2018.

[5]   J. Demme, M. Maycock, J. Schmitz, A. Tang, A. Waksman, S. Sethumadhavan and S. Stolfo. On the feasibility of online malware detection with performance counters. *ACM SIGARCH Computer Architecture News*, 41(3): 559–570, 2013.

[6]   A. Dinaburg, P. Royal, M. Sharif, and W. Lee. Ether: malware analysis via hardware virtualization extensions. *In Proceedings of the 15th ACM conference on Computer and Communications Security*, pp. 51–62: ACM, 2008.

[7]   Z. Deng, X. Zhang, and D. Xu. Spider: Stealthy binary program instrumentation and debugging via hardware virtualization. *In Proceedings of the 29th Annual Computer Security Applications Conference*, pp. 289–298: ACM, 2013.

[8]   L.-K. Yan, M. Jayachandra, M. Zhang, and H. Yin. V2E: combining hardware virtualization and software emulation for transparent and extensible malware analysis. *ACM Sigplan Notices*, 47(7): pp. 227–238, 2012.

[9]   M. Egele, T. Scholte, E. Kirda, and C. Kruegel. A survey on automated dynamic malware-analysis techniques and tools. *ACM Computing Surveys (CSUR)*, 44(2): 6, 2012.

[10] R. R. Branco, G. N. Barbosa, and P. D. Neto. Scientific but not academical overview of malware anti-debugging, anti-disassembly and anti-vm technologies. *Black Hat*, 2012.

[11] M. A. Pavlyushchik. System and method for detecting malicious code executed by virtual machine, ed: Google Patents, 2014.

[12] M. Alazab, S. Venkatraman, P. Watters, M. Alazab, and A. Alazab. Cybercrime: the case of obfuscated malware. *In Global Security, Safety and Sustainability & e-Democracy*: Springer, pp. 204–211, 2012.

[13] A. Tang, S. Sethumadhavan, and S. J. Stolfo. Unsupervised anomaly-based malware detection using hardware features. *In International Workshop on Recent Advances in Intrusion Detection*, pp. 109–129: Springer, 2014.

[14] X. Wang and R. Karri. Reusing hardware performance counters to detect and identify kernel control-flow modifying rootkits. *IEEE Transactions on Computer-Aided Design of Integrated Circuits and Systems*, 35(3): 485–498, 2016.

[15] B. Singh, D. Evtyushkin, J. Elwell, R. Riley, and I. Cervesato. On the detection of kernel-level rootkits using hardware performance counters. *In Proceedings of the 2017 ACM on Asia Conference on Computer and Communications Security*, pp. 483–493: ACM, 2017.

[16] M. Alazab. Profiling and classifying the behavior of malicious codes. *Journal of Systems and Software*, 100: 91–102, 2015/02/01/ 2015.

[17] R. Vinayakumar, M. Alazab, K. P. Soman, P. Poornachandran, A. Al-Nemrat, and S. Venkatraman, Deep learning approach for intelligent intrusion detection system. *IEEE Access*, 7: 41525–41550, 2019.

[18] E. M. Shakshuki, N. Kang, and T. R. Sheltami. EAACK—a secure intrusion-detection system for MANETs. *IEEE Transactions on Industrial Electronics*, 60(3): 1089–1098, 2013.

[19] H.-J. Liao, C.-H. R. Lin, Y.-C. Lin, and K.-Y. Tung. Intrusion detection system: A comprehensive review. *Journal of Network and Computer Applications*, 36(1): 16–24, 2013.

[20] S. Huda, J. Abawajy, M. Alazab, M. Abdollalihian, R. Islam, and J. Yearwood. Hybrids of support vector machine wrapper and filter based framework for malware detection. *Future Generation Computer Systems*, 55: 376–390, 2016/02/01/ 2016.

[21] A. C. de Melo. Performance counters on Linux. *In Linux Plumbers Conference*, 2009.

[22] M. Ozsoy, C. Donovick, I. Gorelik, N. Abu-Ghazaleh, and D. Ponomarev. Malware-aware processors: A framework for efficient online malware detection. *In 2015 IEEE 21st International Symposium on High Performance Computer Architecture (HPCA)*, pp. 651–661, 2015: IEEE.

[23] VirusTotal. *Analyze suspicious files and URLs to detect types of malware* Available: https://www.virustotal.com/#/home/upload.

[24] R. K. Malladi. Using Intel® VTune™ Performance Analyzer Events/Ratios & Optimizing Applications. *http:/software. intel. com*, 2009.

[25] V.X. Heavens. 2011, 2/3. *VX Heavens Site*. Available: http://vx.netlux.org/.

[26] V. Total. VirusTotal-Free online virus, malware and URL scanner. *Online: https://www. virustotal. com/en*, 2012.

[27] R. M. Gray. *Entropy and information theory*. Springer Verlag, 2010.

[28] J. R. Quinlan. Learning decision tree classifiers. *ACM Comput. Surv.*, 28(1): 71–72, 1996.

[29] I. Sumaiya Thaseen and C. Aswani Kumar. Intrusion detection model using fusion of chi-square feature selection and multi class SVM. *Journal of King Saud University - Computer and Information Sciences*, 29(4): 462–472, 2017/10/01/ 2017.

[30] W. W. Cohen. Fast effective rule induction. *In Machine Learning Proceedings 1995*: Elsevier, pp. 115–123, 1995.

[31] N. Etaher, GRS Weir, and M. Alazab. From zeus to zitmo: Trends in banking malware. IEEE Trustcom/BigDataSE/ISPA, pp. 1386–1391, 2015, doi: 10.1109/Trustcom.2015.535.

[32] S. Venkatraman, and M. Alazab. Use of data visualisation for zero-day malware detection. *Security and Communication Networks*, 2018. https://doi.org/10.1155/2018/1728303.

[33] D. Vasan, M. Alazab, S. Wassan, H. Naeem, B. Safaei, and Q. Zheng. IMCFN: Image-based malware classification using fine-tuned convolutional neural network architecture. *Computer Networks*, Vol. 171, 2020, https://doi.org/10.1016/j.comnet.2020.107138.

[34] D. Vasan, M. Alazab, S. Wassan, B. Safaei, and Q. Zheng. Image-Based malware classification using ensemble of CNN architectures (IMCEC). *Computers & Security*, 92: 101748, 2020.

[35] M. Alazab and R. Broadhurst. Spam and criminal activity. Trends and Issues in Crime and Criminal Justice, 1–20, 2016.

[36] D. Vasan, M. Alazab, S. Venkatraman, J. Akram and Z. Qin. MTHAEL: Cross-Architecture IoT malware detection based on neural network advanced ensemble learning. *In IEEE Transactions on Computers*, 69(11): 1654–1667, 1 Nov. 2020, doi: 10.1109/TC.2020.3015584.

[37] Gupta, Maanak, Feras M. Awaysheh, James Benson, Mamoun Al Azab, Farhan Patwa, and Ravi Sandhu. An attribute-based access control for cloud-enabled industrial smart vehicles. *IEEE Transactions on Industrial Informatics* (2020).

[38] Gupta, Maanak, James Benson, Farhan Patwa, and Ravi Sandhu. Secure V2V and V2I communication in intelligent transportation using cloudlets. *IEEE Transactions on Services Computing* (2020).

[39] McDole, Andrew, Mahmoud Abdelsalam, Maanak Gupta, and Sudip Mittal. Analyzing CNN based behavioural malware detection techniques on cloud IAAS. *In International Conference on Cloud Computing*, pp. 64–79. Springer, Cham, 2020.

[40] Awaysheh, Feras M., Mamoun Alazab, Maanak Gupta, Tomás F. Pena, and José C. Cabaleiro. Next-generation big data federation access control: A reference model. *Future Generation Computer Systems*, 108 (2020): 726–741.

[41] A. Yadav, Ritika, and, M.L. Garg. Monitoring based security approach for cloud computing. *Ingénierie des Systèmes d'Information*, 24(6): 611–617, 2019. https://doi.org/10.18280/isi.240608.

10

Comparative Study on Machine Learning Methods to Detect Metamorphic Threats

Sean Park,[1] Iqbal Gondal,[2,]* Joarder Kamruzzaman[3] and Jon Oliver[1]

ABSTRACT

As the sheer volume of incoming samples exponentially increases every year, one of the critical tasks in the defense pipeline is to identify probabilistically suspicious samples that require further investigation. The task essentially involves filtering out a large volume of unknown samples and producing a manageable set of potentially malicious samples with sufficiently high confidence. Today the majority of malware samples possess metamorphic properties where various mutations over the original set of code blocks occur before they are released. This arbitrary custom-designed mutation algorithm applied at each outbreak constitutes the crux of the constant battle between the attackers and the defenders. Therefore it is crucial to capture this non-linear metamorphic pattern unique to the mutation in order to detect the variants. This paper compares the performance of various clustering methods against metamorphic malware samples to identify the model that best suits in practical threat hunting. Results have shown that Adversarial autoencoder performs better than well-known techniques such as HDBSCAN, KNN, and SDHASH.

1. Introduction

Modern threats are created using a script that automatically generates an arbitrarily large number of diverse samples that share similar characteristics in program logic, which is a very cost effective way to evade detection with minimum effort. For

---

[1] Trend Micro, 15/1 Pacific Highway, North Sydney NSW 2060 Australia.
  Emails: spark@trendmicro.com; jon_oliver@trendmicro.com
[2] School of Computing Technologies, RMIT University, 124 La Trobe St, Melbourne VIC 3000.
[3] ICSL-Federation University, University Dr, Mount Helen VIC 3350 Australia.
  Email: joarder.kamruzzaman@federation.edu.au
* Corresponding author: iqbal.gondal@federation.edu.au

instance, a series of malware outbreaks originating from the same automated script constitutes a malware campaign that distributes seemingly diverse but identically rooted variants. This diversity comes from metamorphism that forms the basis of modern threats [1].

As the scale of incoming samples rises, many machine learning methods have been attempted to detect those threats, for example predicting spam emails [25]. Class imbalance problems become the greatest issue in data mining [26]. The survey by Ye et al. [2] essentially shows that it is very difficult to accurately classify malware samples. With the lack of machine learning models with the desired accuracy over real world samples, triaging unknown samples has been increasingly important. In particular, it is required to produce a smaller number of potentially malicious samples which human analysts can manually inspect or other tools with finer-grained detection capability can analyse.

Although several triaging methods have been previously published with respectable results [9, 10], it has always been challenging to gain a certain degree of confidence in the correctness of triage. The triage result is more reliable when it is interpretable. Particularly the extensive use of *blackbox* dataset with unknown characteristics used in most studies makes it difficult to validate the triage result for unlabelled samples. Considering this limitation, given that the vast majority of modern malware samples exhibit similar patterns in the automatically generated instruction sequences, we argue that triage result is less likely to be incorrect if instruction-wise characteristics are similar. For instance, let us consider Figure 1 that shows the variants of a *Cerber* malware family captured in the wild that spanned across several weeks. Similar instruction-wise characteristics are present in basic block (BBL) level, function level, or somewhere in between. A reasonable degree of newly introduced or removed code fragments are observed, which can be considered as a minor noise. Despite various metamorphic techniques in place, the instruction patterns for this malware campaign are clearly similar to each other to humans. Even though a significant portion of the code is related to unpacking the hidden code, these surface level instructions still carry the semantics of the metamorphic code combined with the original unpacking code.

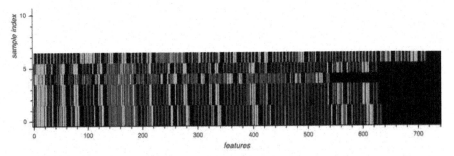

Figure 1: Visualisation of 7 Ransomware Cerber variants. Each row represents a per-sample feature, which is a sequence of instructions of a malware sample. Each instruction is rendered as horizontal stripes with a unique colour assigned to different instructions. X axis is the feature. Y axis is the sample number.

This paper focuses on static instructions as a base feature, which possesses semantic representation of potentially metamorphic samples. Statistical features are not considered in this paper due to its inherent vulnerability demonstrated by the evasion method based on reinforcement learning [3]. In this paper, the instruction IDs are used as a base feature instead of raw binary instructions [4] in order to avoid instruction differences caused by register transposition metamorphism [1] and language compiler differences.

To the best of our knowledge, no comparative study has been conducted on the efficacy of semi-supervised learning methods against metamorphic samples. The main contribution of this paper is the comparison of various machine learning methods that best detects malware variants with similar campaign-wise metamorphic similarity. Our study shows that Adversarial Autoencoder has shown better performance as compared with other techniques.

2. Related Works

Sebastián et al. [5] devised a malware labelling method over a large scale malware dataset. Primarily using Anti-virus vendor detection labels as a feature, the approach did not show a promising way of gaining confidence on unlabelled samples. Shalaginov et al. [6] provided a good introduction on applying machine learning to classification problems using n-gram as a feature.

Li et al. [7] described the fundamental risk of blindly clustering using labels obtained from Anti-virus voting, which describes the problems of biased or misconfigured clusters. Their research points out the significance of choosing the right ground truth cluster samples based on their underlying features for the clusters to build.

Rieck et al. [8] established an embedding method in vector space using instruction q-gram from arbitrary malware features, which has become a fundamental building block for many machine learning research studies later on. Hu et al. [9] created the *MutantX-S* system using prototype-based clustering algorithms over opcode n-gram features. Although the time complexity of the clustering method is close to linear, the confidence for unlabelled samples has not been discussed in detail. Pai et al. [10] studied the efficacy of K-means and Expectation Maximization (EM) clustering over opcode sequence. They created a separate Hidden Markov Model (HMM) instance for each family in an attempt to produce similar representations for intra-cluster samples. However, the experiment did not show the resiliency of the model since the number of benign samples used in testing was significantly low to prove its accuracy on false positives. Dilokthanakul et al. [11] demonstrated the use of variational autoencoder (VAE) over image clustering. Although deep learning has recently proven to be effective in many fields, discrete symbol data as input has remained challenging.

This paper will consider several machine learning methods to find their efficacy in detecting similar variants of a family that shares core instruction-wise characteristics.

3. Methods

There are a plethora of machine learning methods that can be used for malware triage. We selected four different methods for comparison that meet the following requirements.

- The model must be widely deployed in similarity detection field.
- The model must provide a method to find the closest training sample for a given test sample since the similarity of a test sample is evaluated by checking if its closest training sample and itself belong to the same cluster.
- The model must be able to predict in the absence of total cluster count information. Since most threats evolve over time with minor changes, no explicit decision boundary between adjacent clusters exists in practice. In fact, many clusters exhibit similar metamorphism with variations. Therefore the evaluation based on strict cluster matching can interfere with correct detection of the threats.

Below we briefly describe the four methods in the light of the above selection requirements.

3.1 KNN

K-Nearest Neighbour (KNN) [12] is one of the most widely used machine learning methods in similarity search. Despite its long history, it still shows reasonably competitive results in many research papers and provides a non-parametric interface for ease of use. The hyper parameters include search algorithm and distance metric. The implementation can leverage either *KDTree* [13] or *BallTree* [14] for efficient pairwise distance computation. Since KNN requires fixed length inputs, it uses n-gram of instruction feature as input, as discussed in the next section. We use *BallTree* to cope with high dimensional n-gram variables with '*minkowski*' having the parameter equal to 2 for distance metric [15].

3.2 HDBSCAN

Hierarchical Density-Based Spatial Clustering of Applications with Noise (HDBSCAN) [16] is widely used unsupervised clustering method that creates clusters with varying densities. As with KNN, n-gram is used as input due to fixed input restriction of the model '*euclidean*', which is identical to '*minkowski*' with parameter 2, is used as the distance metric of HDBSCAN. The primary hyper parameters include the following.

min_cluster_size=5, min_samples=None, metric='euclidean', alpha=1.0

Different ranges of these hyper parameters have been experimented during the evaluation and the best result is compared against the rest of the models.

3.3 SDHASH

Fuzzy hashing has been widely used when determining the similarities of documents by maximising the probability of local hash collision. Popular algorithms include

SDHASH [17], SSDEEP [18], and TLSH [19]. SSDEEP calculates edit distance to recognise identical blocks, TLSH uses n-gram frequency distribution for similarity measure, and SDHASH uses normalized entropy measure to find statistically improbable features. Studies show SDHASH and TLSH outperforms SSDEEP [20, 21]. In this paper, we show the results for SDHASH because TLSH shows similar results. Since fuzzy hashing can deal with variable length input, raw instruction feature is used as input to the model. The distance is calculated by normalising the inverse of the similarity score returned by SDHASH.

3.4 AAE

Adversarial Auto-Encoder (AAE) is a dimensionality reduction method based on deep learning that compresses an arbitrary length input to a fixed length latent representation. The model implemented by Park et al. [4] is used for the evaluation, which combines the power of generative adversarial network [22] and location-resilient convolutional neural network [23]. Raw instruction feature is fed to the model as input. The distance is computed by taking the mean squared error of the difference of z values, which are the latent representations at the bottleneck.

4. Evaluation

4.1 Dataset

In this paper, we use interpretable family-wise metamorphic malware samples that possess similar instruction-wise characteristics instead of arbitrarily chosen malware dataset from the *blackbox*. To deal with the biased ground truth cluster problem [7], we carefully created the dataset for the experiment in such a way that each cluster holds the core semantics of the campaign's metamorphism. A commercial vendor provided 3,390 unique malware samples from multiple isolated in-the-wild campaigns, which is a representative dataset from a larger sample pool. The 3,390 samples are further reduced to 1,012 samples after removing duplicate samples with identical instruction sequences are removed. Using various machine learning methods combined with manual analysis, these 1,012 instruction-unique samples have been identified to form 211 clusters. We used half of each cluster for training and used the rest for testing. In addition, we reduced a large pool of benign testing samples to 5,854 by taking representative samples with similar TLSH digest values. The dataset for the experiment is summarised in Table 1.

The malicious samples contain major ransomware, backdoor, and banking Trojans in Windows operating system. The colour-coded instructions of randomly chosen families are depicted in Figure 2.

Table 1: Train/Test dataset split.

	malicious	benign
Train	485	0
Test	527	5854

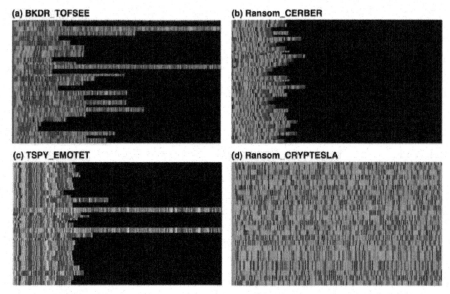

Figure 2: Horizontal lines represent samples showing each family can contain variable length malware variants exhibiting different instances of metamorphism.

4.2 Instruction Feature

As described in [4], instruction sequences are extracted from each binary sample from which instruction IDs are calculated using capstone [24]. Input feature is essentially a sequence of variable length integers representing instruction characteristics. Models can choose different types of random variables for the input. KNN and HDBSCAN require fixed length inputs whereas SDHASH and AAE accept variable length inputs. To utilise the maximum potential of the model, SDHASH and AAE use the original instruction feature with minimum pre-processing. For KNN and HDBSCAN, we deploy n-gram, which is one of the most widely used tools that generate fixed length inputs. We use n = 2, which generates 7,302 features for the instruction feature.

4.3 Evaluation Criteria

Let *ground_truth* be a mapping where is the input feature prepared for each model as explained in the previous section and is a label obtained through the process described above. Let *is_similar* be a function defined by each model that calculates the distance between the first argument and the second argument and returns the closest sample within the second argument, and *threshold* be the hyper parameter for each model. The process for strict evaluation is described by the algorithm in Figure 3. The algorithm sets the decision metrics (*tp, tn, fp, fn*) if the predicted cluster number strictly matches the true cluster number. In addition to this strict matching criteria, relaxed evaluation is also performed to see if models are capable of separating malicious samples from benign samples given that our ultimate goal is malware detection. In relaxed evaluation, an exception is made to line 16 of the

	Algorithm: Process for strict evaluation
1:	$train\_xs = x$ for all x $train\_malicious$
2:	$test\_xs = x$ for all x $\{test\_malicious, test\_clean\}$
3:	$tp = 0, tn = 0, fp = 0, fn = 0$
4:	**for** $test\_x$ **in** $test\_xs$**:**
5:	$ytrue = ground\_truth[test\_x]$
6:	$Distance, similar\_train\_x = is\_similar(test\_x, train\_xs)$
7:	**if** $distance < threshold$**:**
8:	$ypred = ground\_truth[similar\_train\_x]$
9:	**else:**
10:	$ypred = 0$
11:	**if** $ytrue == ypred$**:**
12:	**if** $ytrue == 0$: $tn += 1$
13:	**else:** $tp += 1$
14:	**else:**
15:	**if** $ytrue == 0$: $fp += 1$
16	**else:** $fn += 1$

Figure 3: The algorithm used to compute the performance metrics of the models tp, tn, fp, fn describe the count of True Positive, True Negative, False Positive, and False Negative respectively.

algorithm in which *tp* is incremented if both *ytrue* and *ypred* have a valid malicious cluster number.

4.4 Results

The model performances are depicted as ROC curves in Figure 4. The top performing model is AAE, followed by KNN with a decent gap. SDHASH finds the correct malware clusters approximately for 50% of the test samples. On the contrary, HDBSCAN performed extremely poorly in strict settings while its accuracy remained around 50% in a relaxed setting.

First of all, the AAE model that utilises convolutional autoencoder performs *global* max pooling at the last encoder layer, which captures translation invariant features insensitive to locational variations of the instructions. Furthermore, generative adversarial network finetunes the latent representation in a non-cooperative minmax game, making it more resilient to artificially generated similar samples. The result also shows locality sensitive hashing does not adapt well in identifying the similarities between metamorphic malware samples in the same cluster. Above all the fact that metamorphism involves frequent code transpositions renders location-dependent SDHASH simply ineffective in clustering similar malware samples. In the meantime, KNN performs reasonably well although insufficient to compete with AAE. A straightforward Euclidean distance comparison over location-independent histogram of n-gram appears to support KNN's decent performance. Finally,

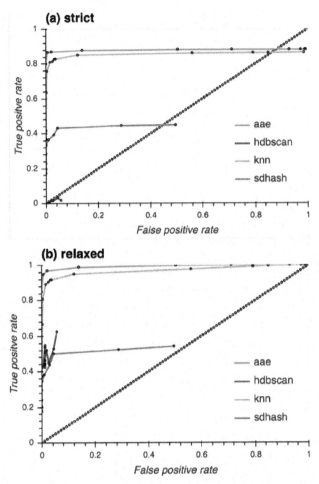

Figure 4: ROC of model performances. (a) shows the performance for a strict match while (b) shows for a relaxed match.

HDBSCAN shows poor performance with the result unpredictable both in strict and relaxed settings. Especially HDBSCAN in strict settings shows worse results than random decisions.

5. Conclusion

In this work, we presented a comprehensive comparison of various machine learning methods on their capabilities in identifying the variants of malware families that show similar characteristics in their core instructions. The result shows adversarial network combined with convolutional network with global max pooling outperforms the rest of the machine learning techniques in this task. Since it is critical to generalise the distribution under metamorphic threats, this result suggests that models with translation invariant property are more resilient to metamorphic threats than the ones that leverage traditional distance metrics.

Acknowledgements

Internet Commerce Security Lab was established in collaboration with Westpac bank, IBM Federation University.

References

[1] You Ilsun, and Kangbin Yim. Malware obfuscation techniques: A brief survey. *2010 International Conference on Broadband, Wireless Computing, Communication and Applications.* IEEE, 2010.

[2] Ye Yanfang et al. A survey on malware detection using data mining techniques. *ACM Computing Surveys (CSUR)* 50.3: 41, 2017.

[3] Anderson, Hyrum S., Anant Kharkar, Bobby Filar, David Evans, and Phil Roth. Learning to Evade Static PE Machine Learning Malware Models via Reinforcement Learning. *Web*, 2018.

[4] S. Park, I. Gondal, J. Kamruzzaman, and J. Oliver. Generative Malware Outbreak Detection. *IEEE ICIT*, 2019.

[5] Sebastián Marcos et al. Avclass: A tool for massive malware labeling. *International Symposium on Research in Attacks, Intrusions, and Defenses.* Springer, Cham, 2016.

[6] Shalaginov Andrii et al. Machine learning aided static malware analysis: A survey and tutorial. *Cyber Threat Intelligence.* Springer, Cham, pp. 7–45, 2018.

[7] Li Peng et al. On challenges in evaluating malware clustering. *International Workshop on Recent Advances in Intrusion Detection.* Springer, Berlin, Heidelberg, 2010.

[8] Rieck Konrad et al. Automatic analysis of malware behavior using machine learning. *Journal of Computer Security* 19.4: 639–668, 2011.

[9] Hu Xin et al. Mutantx-s: Scalable malware clustering based on static features. *Presented as part of the 2013 {USENIX} Annual Technical Conference ({USENIX}{ATC} 13).* 2013.

[10] Pai Swathi et al. Clustering for malware classification. *Journal of Computer Virology and Hacking Techniques* 13.2: 95–107, 2017.

[11] Dilokthanakul Nat et al. Deep unsupervised clustering with gaussian mixture variational autoencoders. *arXiv preprint arXiv:1611.02648*, 2016.

[12] Altman, Naomi S. An introduction to kernel and nearest-neighbor nonparametric regression. *The American Statistician* 46.3: 175–185, 1992.

[13] Bentley Jon Louis. Multidimensional binary search trees used for associative searching. *Communications of the ACM* 18.9: 509–517, 1975.

[14] Omohundro, Stephen M. *Five Balltree Construction Algorithms.* Berkeley: International Computer Science Institute, 1989.

[15] https://en.wikipedia.org/wiki/Minkowski_distance.

[16] McInnes Leland, John Healy, and Steve Astels. hdbscan: Hierarchical density based clustering. *J. Open Source Software* 2.11: 205, 2017.

[17] Roussev Vassil. Data fingerprinting with similarity digests. *IFIP International Conference on Digital Forensics.* Springer, Berlin, Heidelberg, 2010.

[18] Kornblum Jesse. Identifying almost identical files using context triggered piecewise hashing. *Digital Investigation* 3: 91–97, 2006.

[19] Oliver Jonathan, Chun Cheng, and Yanggui Chen. TLSH—a locality sensitive hash. *2013 Fourth Cybercrime and Trustworthy Computing Workshop.* IEEE, 2013.

[20] Roussev Vassil. An evaluation of forensic similarity hashes. *Digital Investigation* 8: S34–S41, 2011.

[21] Pagani Fabio, Matteo Dell'Amico, and Davide Balzarotti. Beyond precision and recall: Understanding uses (and misuses) of similarity hashes in binary analysis. *Proceedings of the Eighth ACM Conference on Data and Application Security and Privacy.* ACM, 2018.

[22] Makhzani Alireza et al. Adversarial autoencoders. *arXiv preprint arXiv:1511.05644*, 2015.

[23] Radford Alec, Luke Metz, and Soumith Chintala. Unsupervised representation learning with deep convolutional generative adversarial networks. *arXiv preprint arXiv:1511.06434*, 2015.

[24] Quynh Nguyen Anh. Capstone: Next-gen disassembly framework. *Black Hat USA*, 2014.

[25] K. N. Tran, M. Alazab, and R. Broadhurst. Towards a feature rich model for predicting spam emails containing malicious attachments and URLs. pp. 161–172. *In*: P. Christen, P. Kennedy, L. Liu, K. -L. Ong, A. Stranieri, and Y. Zhao (eds.). *Data Mining and Analytics 2013—Proceedings of the 11th Australasian Data Mining Conference, AusDM 2013* (Vol. 146). Australian Computer Society, 2013.

[26] S. H. Ebenuwa, M. S. Sharif, M. Alazab and A. Al-Nemrat. Variance ranking attributes selection techniques for binary classification problem in imbalance data. *In IEEE Access*, 7: 24649–24666, 2019, Doi: 10.1109/ACCESS.2019.2899578.

Index